Conscious Communication

CONSCIOUS COMMUNICATION

How to Establish Healthy Relationships
and Resolve Conflict Peacefully
while Maintaining Independence

A Language of Connection

Miles Sherts

LANGDON STREET PRESS

Cover and interior illustration by Rod Thomas

Langdon Street Press
212 3rd Avenue North, Suite 290
Minneapolis, MN 55401
612.455.2293
www.langdonstreetpress.com

ISBN - 978-1-934938-60-7
ISBN - 1-934938-60-2
LCCN - 2009937907

www.SkyMeadow.org
www.LanguageOfConnection.com
www.MilesSherts.com

Printed in the United States of America

LANGDON
STREET
PRESS

Dedicated to:

The Peace that Passeth Understanding

Acknowledgements

I am deeply grateful to Michelle Demers, Julia Shipley, Matthew Remski, Cella Sherts, and all the other people who supported and encouraged me in writing this book.

Contents

Author's Note:

In order to be gender neutral, I have chosen to use plural pronouns such as: they, their, them, and themselves, when referring to individual people. I understand the awkwardness of this usage and hope those of you who find this style uncomfortable will be able to hear the message despite this flaw. I simply have not found a better way to refer to women and men with equal emphasis.

Introduction

Why Consciously Communicate?

There are few things more important now than learning to communicate with each other in a way that supports our individuality while also recognizing our interdependence. Most of our familiar social rules are changing so rapidly that it is difficult to pinpoint what is essential in our relationships with other people. We are experiencing an unprecedented degree of personal independence, yet the price we are paying is an increased sense of isolation from each other. This leaves many of us feeling confused about where we belong, and with whom we feel genuinely connected.

The old formulas for relationships are failing because they do not allow for each of us to be our own person. And, our new emphasis on personal growth and individual freedom has left us without a good way to connect with each other.

> We think we cannot be ourselves
> *and* maintain close relationships with other people.
> Yet this is not so;
> *we simply have not yet learned how.*

The aim of *Conscious Communication* is to provide a clear way for us to invest in our relationships with other people, while also investing in ourselves.

The Dilemma of Relating to Other People

All of us are in relationships of some kind. We each have family, and most of us have neighbors, friends, and people with whom we work or socialize. Nations relate to other nations, and communities relate to other communities. In spite of being surrounded by people, however, many of us have a nagging sense of being alone.

No matter how close we are to others, it seems they frequently do not understand us. At the same time, *they* often baffle *us* with their annoying complexities and contradictions. It is easy to become disillusioned with other people when they fail to provide the kind of support we want, or when we just don't understand them. We may then find ourselves wishing that everyone would just go away.

But, when everyone does go away, we get scared. Few of us are comfortable in isolation, and while we may condemn the failings of our neighbors, friends, or family, *we need them*. It seems that we can't live with other people, yet we also can't live without them. We often cope with this dilemma by trying to keep a safe distance from others, only to end up hopelessly trapped in relationships that do not work.

> Caught between our need for connection,
> and our desire for freedom,
> we are not able to fully realize either.

Many of us today are perplexed about relationships and confused as to why they can be so difficult. From couples to corporations, and neighbors to nations, we are experiencing more conflict, and few of us want to look at it directly because we don't know how to respond. We tend to avoid these tense situations with other people, or charge into them aggressively, hoping to make them go away as quickly as possible. But these tactics only make matters worse, and we find ourselves with a closet full of broken and discarded relationships that ultimately undermine our sense of peace and security in the world.

A Fatal Habit

While our society has made impressive advances in technology that enable a level of material comfort unthinkable to our ancestors,

> our way of relating to each other
> has not changed much since the Stone Age.

Most of us rely on our instincts of fight or flight when we feel threatened, and still believe that attacking or withdrawing will resolve our conflicts with other people. Yet withdrawing from other people or forcefully trying to get them to change doesn't work. And, we can see the tragic result of our lack of relationship skills all around us today, from the epidemic of divorce to the frequent outbreaks of war throughout the world.

With more than six billion of us now sharing the resources of our small planet, tensions between people can only increase, and our inability to cooperate with each other may be the largest threat we face to our survival as a species. In an age of nuclear weapons, global climate change, massive environmental pollution, and a worldwide economy, it is clear that the actions of each one of us affect everyone else here on earth. Given the condition of our world and the consequences of perpetuating conflict, our reliance on primitive survival instincts to manage our relationships makes no sense. If we continue to choose competition over cooperation, we insure our own eventual demise.

Analysis Is Not Enough

Relationships are so basic to our existence that it is surprising how little training we have in how to make them work. Our efforts to resolve conflict are often focused on diagnosing a problem from a rational perspective. While psychology can help us understand how relationships work and why people do the things they do, this kind of theoretical understanding does not actually change anything. We may think we have changed because we have a new story that explains what is happening. Yet we are still judging each other, and the only thing different is that we have a more sophisticated basis for our evaluations.

In the end, behavioral analysis does not resolve the problem of feeling separate from each other, because we have not shifted our fundamental orientation. We are still trying to sort everything into categories of right and wrong, thinking this will somehow solve our conflicts. Yet, this approach of dividing the world into good and bad *creates* much of the tension we feel between ourselves and other people. When we try to categorize human behavior, we are using the same mental process that is the *cause* of our conflict.

Adopting a new set of rules or establishing a universal moral code cannot resolve our differences. Knowing that polarized conflict is ultimately destructive has not changed our ways. Something draws us into power struggles with each other even though we know it doesn't work. We may have a firm intention to cooperate, yet when strong emotions are stirred, we end up fighting with each other because we cannot help ourselves.

Getting to the Root of the Problem

Why do we keep trying the same approach even though it causes so much damage? It seems that by now that we should be civilized enough to know how to get along. Yet no amount of knowledge or idealism has changed our basic human nature. This is because the conditions that cause conflict are ingrained in the way we think, and if we want to be free from conflict we have to question the usual way we explain our disagreements.

Notice how children typically respond to conflict between themselves. When asked to explain what is happening, their normal answer is to blame someone else. Each child is convinced that their actions are justified by the wrongs of another child. With children, it is easy to see that this kind of response does not make sense, and doesn't solve anything. However, it is much harder to see this in our own behavior.

When tensions arise between people, we usually describe the situation in terms of a victim and a villain, thinking this will help us resolve the problem. Most of us try to explain opposition in terms of right versus wrong. And since few of us want to see ourselves as wrong, we naturally conclude that the other person is at fault. We each view *ourselves* as the victim, and then become mired in conflict with both sides, trying to prove that we are innocent and the other people are guilty. We blame the other side for causing the problem, which justifies our attacks against them and further escalates the struggle.

This urge to be right is an automatic response to controversy that does not address what we actually want, and instead leads to more conflict. It is a habit so instinctual that we barely notice it, and we often don't see the damage it causes to our relationships. When our goal is winning instead of simply meeting our basic needs, we end up creating more tension between ourselves and other people and then lose sight of our own well-being.

What is Conscious Communication?

In order to be effective in relating to each other, we have to get beyond setting up conflicts as right against wrong, and recognize that winning is not the same as having our needs met. Life is not a competition, and we do not find peace or satisfaction by getting our way over other people. Yet, we cannot change such a fundamental habit by merely adopting new ideals of peaceful cooperation. It is only when we see for ourselves that being right does not make us happy that we naturally let go of competing, and focus instead on finding what we really want.

Being more conscious in communication begins with simply paying attention to how you relate to other people, especially when strong emotions are stirred up, and noticing if your current approach is working. The first chapters in this book highlight our most common responses to other people and help us assess how well these old communication habits work. The next chapters introduce an entirely new way to think about relationships. Simple practices are clearly laid out that unlock you from your current perspective so that you can see things from a new angle.

This approach is *not* a new set of rules for good communication. These are specific tools that interrupt the normal way we view other people. This new language merely disrupts your familiar patterns long enough for you to become conscious of them, and enables you to see the destructive effect that competition has on your relationships. This allows you to shift your attention away from your imagined fears, and focus instead on your immediate needs.

Once you have made this shift in perspective, you realize that your sense of belonging with other people is a fundamental requirement for your security and well-being, and cooperating becomes far more interesting than competing. These skills then offer a new way of relating that enables you to get your basic needs met, while also allowing other people to meet their needs.

The Skills

Conscious Communication will teach you how to address your differences directly, while maintaining your sense of connection. These tools enable you to listen to other people without becoming defensive or trying to fix their problem, and to be honest about your feelings and needs without blaming someone else or making them responsible.

At the heart of this approach are guidelines for listening with empathy, speaking responsibly, and staying connected through conflict until everyone's basic needs are addressed. These three skill sets are presented in the main body of the book as Supportive Listening, Assertion Messages, and Collaborative Negotiation, and they follow a natural progression, with each set building on the others. The book culminates in a section on how to apply the skills in a primary intimate relationship, and concludes with an exploration of how this new language can help us achieve a more democratic and just society.

The skills and theories you will learn here apply to any type of relationship, from interactions within families and communities to those between corporations or nations. They work in any situation where two or more people have contact, because they address the basic beliefs and attitudes that govern the primary ways we interact with each other.

This approach offers a way to resolve peacefully the struggles that have plagued humanity and continue to make destructive conflicts such a tragic part of our history. It differs from many other paths to peace, however, in that it actively addresses our personal attitudes and beliefs and offers a means to grow and expand *individually* through our relationships with other people. It teaches us how to relate to each other in ways that nourish and support each of us as individuals *and* as a whole.

Making Room for a New Perspective

Consciously communicating involves questioning your own judgments and opinions and being willing to see things from a new perspective. Consider the possibility that the source of much of the conflict and struggle in your life is not the people who seem to be opposing you. Rather,

> you may be stuck
> in a primal, patterned way of thinking
> that causes you to approach other people defensively,
> assuming you are the victim
> of a world that is out to get you.

Questioning your basic assumptions can be difficult, and may seem like more work than you want to take on. Yet it is far easier and more realistic than trying to change other people, live up to some ideal of harmony, or pretend that conflict does not exist at all. In the end, the only thing you actually *can* do effectively is to face the situation in front of you honestly and allow your own attitudes and beliefs to be tested by reality.

Instead of simply challenging or avoiding people who seem to be opposing you, there is a way to learn from these struggles. If you redirect your attention to yourself when you are upset, it is possible to reveal patterns of thinking that are not working for you. In this way, you can avoid repeating the same behaviors and landing in the same place of frustration, anxiety, and despair in your life.

When we feel threatened, we often become consumed by imaginary fears that have little to do with what is really happening. You may notice that you are building a conflict up in your mind without having much solid information. Or you might recognize that you have drawn a conclusion about other people's behavior without really understanding *why* they are acting the way they are.

Most of us are viewing the world through an outdated set of conceptual filters that have programmed us for opposition. Our survival mentality interferes with our ability to see what is actually going on around us, especially when we become emotional. And, this unfortunate habit undermines our capacity for cooperation, friendship, and intimacy.

We can build new societies based on the ideals of peace and cooperation, yet if we do not learn to alter our individual responses, we will inevitably find ourselves mired in conflict again. Changing the way institutions, governments, or nations relate to each other, therefore, has to begin with transforming our own personal patterns. To bring about real change, each one of us has to let go of our habit of dividing the world into opposing sides, and be willing to question our comfortable conclusions of what is right and wrong. Once we see for ourselves how we unconsciously create or feed conflict, it becomes easier to stop these instinctive reactions that undermine our happiness and peace, and learn a new way.

Communication Habits

Chapter 1

The Roots of Conflict

Most of us think that someone else is the cause of the conflict in our lives. This seems obvious because we get upset only when *that* person does *that* particular thing. It is natural to blame other people for hurting us and think that they are the problem. We usually focus our attention on them and what they are doing to interfere with our happiness. However,

> when we react to other people
> as if they are responsible for our feelings,
> we enter conflict from a direction
> that makes it more difficult to resolve.

When we label other people as wrong or bad, it becomes difficult to maintain a connection with them and deal with our emotional response at the same time. From this viewpoint our only options seem to be withdrawing from them, or getting them to change. Either way, our real feelings and needs are not addressed, and our relationships become further strained.

Many of us could agree that conflict is a problem in our personal lives and threatens the security of our world. If you are reading this book, you may have come to this conclusion and want to do something about it. The problem with most approaches to conflict, however, is that they do not question the fundamental way that we *think* about opposition.

Changing Our Approach

In most of our conflicts we assume that other people are *trying* to hurt us. Our survival instincts teach us to see opposition, and then respond to protect ourselves. Once we have labeled other people as a threat, we tend to separate from them and focus on how they are different from us. We become afraid and imagine all the ways they might harm us, and these thoughts justify our usual responses of withdrawal or attack.

When we suspect a threat, we tend to harden ourselves, bracing for the other's attack or preempting it with an attack of our own. Our animal brains are programmed to expect the worst so we can be prepared. Seeing threats everywhere and not letting down our guard is a necessary security measure in a hostile wilderness, where defense and attack are required for survival. Yet this approach does not work well in human relationships, especially if we are trying to establish trust or safety with another person, or another nation of people.

If we cannot tell when our safety is genuinely at risk, we respond to *any* suggestion of danger with *all* of our defenses. This way of trying to protect ourselves keeps everyone at a distance and actually increases our fear and insecurity because we feel so alone. If we see other people as enemies when they do something that hurts us, we shut down the possibility of a deeper relationship. We sacrifice our connection with them for what looks like safety. And, we usually end up feeling more isolated and less safe than if we worked through the conflict while staying connected.

Developing close relationships does not mean that you simply ignore your own safety. It means being intelligent about where your safety lies.

> While there may be real threats that require us
> either to fight or to run for our lives,
> *in most of our conflicts, the danger we face is imagined.*

To protect against a real threat to your safety, it is wise to know more about those who appear to be against you and what is behind their actions. At least then you will have some idea of what to expect from them, and you can more easily avoid getting hurt. If you set aside your normal defenses for a moment when you feel threatened by other people, you can try to understand *why* they are doing what they are doing.

Listening to other people who appear threatening with the aim of understanding their motivation can also help to replace your fear with understanding. You often realize they are not out to destroy you, but are merely trying to achieve safety for themselves in the only way they know how. You can then see the conflict from a bigger perspective that includes the other person as someone with feelings and needs like your own. This is a necessary step if you want to resolve the tension, instead of avoiding it or forcing your way through it.

A New Perspective

Some of us recognize that fighting does not work, and have concluded that it is not right. We often then take a religious or moral perspective and focus on forgiving the other person for hurting us. We try to rise above the conflict and use surrender as a means to establish harmony. Yet, this approach assumes the same premise, that the other person is the cause of our discomfort. And, while forgiveness may feel better than retaliation, it does not resolve the problem, because we still believe the other person is trying to hurt us.

Changing the way you approach conflict is not a simple matter of adopting a new belief or attitude. This is why religion, morality, and psychology, unless they are accompanied by a genuine shift in perspective, do not result in lasting change. If you try to understand and resolve a problem through analysis, or by applying a set of rules, you merely override your emotions and needs with rational thought. Nothing really different happens because the situation that caused the conflict has not been fully recognized, and your frame of reference remains the same.

Real change does not happen by focusing on other people. You may get the other person to be different through force, persuasion, or submission, or you may leave that relationship and find a new one. Yet after a while, you will notice that the same frustrations and conflicts begin to appear again. This is because you are not effectively addressing their root cause.

You cannot get out of conflict by fighting harder, by being more submissive, or by trying to be good.

> A way through conflict opens
> when you see that the cause
> is *not* the other people who seem to be opposing you
> – it is the way you *perceive* those people
> and the *assumptions* you make about them
> that create the problem.

True and lasting peace comes only when you allow your perceptions to be challenged and see what is happening from a different point of view. The problem with changing your point of view, however, is that you cannot *make* this happen, either by force or by rote. You cannot learn a new perspective by copying, remembering, or believing in it. A new perspective is an *experience*, not an idea, and you have to realize its validity by feeling it for yourself. Your patterns of thought have to rearrange themselves in order for a real shift to occur. So the theories and skills presented in *Conscious Communication* are designed to produce new perspectives simply by interrupting your habitual responses, and making space for you to experience the same situation from a new angle.

The practices suggested in this book are intended to challenge your *story* about what is going on so that you can see what is *actually* happening. They disrupt the tendency to see opposition in other people's words or to interpret their actions as a personal attack, which will allow you to see the situation from *their* point of view for a moment.

> Conflict begins to resolve spontaneously when you understand *why* other people are doing what they are doing.

A slight shift like this can change the whole conflict from a fight for personal survival to an opportunity for a deeper connection. And often this change in point of view reveals a simple solution that you could not see before.

Healing a Broken Relationship

This underlying source of conflict became clear to me in the difficult relationship I had with my father. For much of my adult life, it seemed that my father was trying to direct and control me through his judgments and criticisms. I distanced myself from him and often saw him as an enemy. Family visits were stressful, and I felt more alone in the world because I did not trust my father or feel safe in his presence. Then, one day, all this changed.

I was planning a trip that included traveling for a time with my younger sister to some remote, third-world countries. My sister and I were both in our thirties and had traveled like this before. We had been planning our trip for several months when my father called me one night to tell me he did not want me to go. He spoke in a demanding voice, saying he would not allow me to make this trip or to take my sister with me.

I had been through conversations like this with my father before and had been able to ignore him. This time, however, I was consumed with rage. Furious, I screamed at him, my body shaking all over as I told him he had no right to talk to me like that. The conversation ended quickly with my father speechless.

After the phone call, I could not sleep. I felt terrible about the way I had treated my father. I was still angry with him and did not want him telling me how to live my life, yet I did not feel good about the level of force I had used to establish this boundary. I called him early the next morning, not knowing what to expect and fearing that he would never want to talk with me again.

I apologized to him and said I did not feel good about my response the night before. I was expecting him to be cold, angry, or defensive. Yet, much to my surprise, my father *apologized to me.* He told me he had thought about the situation after our phone call and realized that he *was* interfering in my life and had no right to do that. He went on to explain that he felt very uneasy when I went off on these adventures to remote countries, because if something bad should happen to me he could not protect or help me.

When I heard this from my father, tears welled up from a deep place within me, and soon I was sobbing uncontrollably. It had never occurred to me that my father's authoritarian behavior was coming from his love for me, and from a desire to protect me from harm. I had only seen him as trying to control me. Suddenly, my father appeared very different, and I saw him in a whole new light.

A sense of deep compassion and caring for my father arose spontaneously and filled me with love. I told him that I loved him, and he said that he loved me. This was the first time in my life I could remember him apologizing or expressing this kind of parental affection. A long-sealed door opened in my heart and allowed him in, and suddenly my life felt more whole and complete. We were able to talk about things in a new and lighter way, and I went to visit him without the sense of dread and defensiveness I usually felt.

A Genuine Connection

A year later, my father lay in a hospital bed, dying of cancer. It was late afternoon and my whole family had been by his side most of the day. The nurse came in to say that visiting hours were over and it was time for us to leave. I was suddenly overwhelmed by love for my father and knew that I could not leave him alone that night. I told the nurse I was staying, and she pointed to a couch in the room that I could use.

I napped through the night, waking often to the sound of my father's labored breathing, knowing he was still alive. Around dawn I awoke again. His breath had slowed and become shallower. Sitting up and taking his hand in mine, I began to sing a song that my father had composed a few years earlier about dying and going to heaven. As I sang, I heard him take his last breath and felt the life slip out of his body.

During all those years of struggle with my father, I had tried to be a good son and care about him. Yet deep down I often resented him for being so forceful and controlling. The truth was that I had felt no real connection with my father, and our relationship was mostly a veneer of polite formalities. This pretense of connection could never have motivated me to stay up all night by his bedside as he was dying or to speak passionately about him a few days later at his funeral.

Hearing what my father had been thinking when he tried to stop me from traveling, and understanding later the protective intention behind his words, had instantly changed the way I felt about him. I saw that he did not want to threaten or control me, but rather that he was caring about me in the only way he knew. I was then able to care about him because I was no longer trying to protect myself from him.

> It is difficult to be at odds with your father
> and to be at peace with the world.

For many years, there had been an empty place in my life because I had put my father out of my heart. When I realized what my father's real intentions were, something miraculous happened that I could never have predicted: an emotional dead spot suddenly came alive again because there was no longer a wall between us. It was as if some part of me had returned home.

It had taken years of built-up tension followed by a cathartic explosion to open the way to a deeper understanding with my father. After all that, it was simply a change in perspective that allowed me to feel connected to him again. I finally understood what was behind his harsh-sounding demands and could see him from an entirely different point of view.

Sometimes these clearings between people happen spontaneously and relationships finally heal, as happened in this story. Too often, however, misunderstandings destroy the fabric of a relationship and it never mends. The idea of learning relationship skills is that we can do something about these tragic situations before they are beyond repair. We can find a way to address relationship issues directly and understand each other's intentions, *without* years of emotional distancing or angry explosions.

Setting Aside Our Own Story

A major obstacle to connecting with other people is our constant concern about securing our needs. We are often occupied with our own life drama, and when our minds are focused primarily on ourselves, we cannot experience other people as *they* are. When we listen to others speak, we hear only how their words affect *us* and see them merely as part of *our* story.

This unconscious frame of reference sets up an immediate block to relationship. Our habit is to evaluate someone else's story or behavior by comparing it to ours. Most of us make these judgments and comparisons thinking they are necessary for self-protection, and this way of thinking is so familiar that we rarely notice we are doing it. Yet when we see other people only in terms of how they affect us, instead of for who they really are, we undermine the kind of intimacy and connection that many of us are looking for.

In the previous story, I could not recognize the protective instincts of my father when he criticized me for going traveling. I assumed that he was only trying to prevent me from doing what I wanted to do with my life because he thought it was wrong. My reaction was then to defend myself from him, so that he could not control me. And the result was a misunderstanding that distanced us from each other for many years.

Trying to Be Nice

Another block to connection is our habit of denying our emotions and needs for the sake of harmony. Instead of addressing conflict directly, we frequently try to avoid confrontation by making it look like we have no needs or self-interests and we care only about other people. While this response may work in some situations, it usually fails when strong emotions such as hurt, resentment, or anger are triggered by another person's actions. If we try to appear caring while harboring negative feelings, it merely dilutes our relationships by putting a comfortable distance between us.

Most of us don't like to admit to our negative reactions of anger, resentment, or hatred. We want to be seen as caring and compassionate instead of as defensive and self-absorbed. So we may try to be nice, hiding our own feelings and needs and making an effort to seem interested in the other person. We try not to hurt anyone, yet in the name of being polite or considerate, we often distance ourselves from other people. We do not say how we really feel, and our relationships tend to stay superficial.

When we force ourselves to live up to an ideal like love, we often find the way full of struggle. This is because we are fighting against our own will and trying to make ourselves do something we really don't want to do. When I tried to love my father, despite the anger and resentment I held toward him, I had to work hard to deny my feelings and needs. The outcome was a superficial friendliness between us that lacked intimacy or depth. However, when I understood that behind his demanding words was a deep sense of responsibility for my well-being, I could immediately care about him again.

Self-care versus Self-absorption

There is an important distinction between self-absorption and self-care. When we are absorbed with ourselves, most of our energy goes into worrying about our needs and how to meet them. The underlying belief is that we are *not* going to get what we need, or we *are* going to be hurt in some way. These haunting fears make us anxious and occupy a lot of our time and attention. We tend to be on guard and more focused on what we lack than on what we have, which drains energy from ourselves and the people around us. As a result, we are constantly looking for other people to shore us up because we feel so insecure.

Our standard way of handling this situation is to ignore our needs and pretend that we are all right. We have developed elaborate formalities that disguise our personal insecurities with a mask of self-confidence and concern for other people. Our common rules of etiquette are often attempts to cover over our basic self-centered impulses by *acting* in a caring way toward others. However, despite our polite outward concern, we are still privately worried about our own needs. We have no space within us to truly recognize the feelings and needs of other people, because we are not acknowledging or caring for our own needs.

When we are taking care of ourselves, on the other hand, most of our energy goes into learning what our basic needs are and finding ways to meet them. The underlying belief here is that we *can* care for ourselves and our needs *will* be met. This makes us less needy and gives us more energy and attention to give to other people. By attending to our basic needs, we can then reach out to help others from a place of fullness and contentment.

Learning to Care for Ourselves

Relationship skills teach us how to care for ourselves so we do not spend our lives in fear that we will not get what we want. We learn to address our needs directly and take responsibility for meeting them. As we are able to nourish ourselves, we grow and mature, and our sense of self naturally expands to include other people.

While most of us tend to be self-absorbed more than we would like to admit, we *do* have the capacity for genuine empathy and compassion. We *can* expand beyond our personal concerns and experience deep caring for others that has nothing to do with our own fear and anxiety. As we care for our own needs, we naturally become able and are interested in caring about others, and we no longer have to force ourselves to be kind or considerate.

Communicating consciously is not about *trying* to be more loving or accepting of other people. Neither is it about armoring ourselves so we don't get hurt. It begins with simply interrupting our habit of seeing other people as either threats or opportunities and the automatic responses that follow. In this way we create an opening for our deeper needs to be met.

When we see other people primarily only in terms of how they affect us, we deny our basic need to feel connected with them, and we remain isolated in our own world. We sacrifice relationship for a false sense of security that comes from focusing on our own survival, and our needs for belonging, love, and understanding often go unmet.

Once we make our own inner wellness a priority, we realize that we cannot be truly happy in isolation, and our need to nurture and be connected to other people will naturally surface. We recognize that relationships often meet more of our basic needs than having our own way, and one of our greatest joys is to help and support others. Instead of seeing other people only in terms of our survival, we see healthy relationships as essential to our basic happiness.

> When we take care of our well-being,
> instead of trying to defend ourselves against other people,
> we realize that one of our basic needs
> is to nourish and care for others
> and contribute to something larger than ourselves.

Chapter 2

Our Need for Connection *and* Independence

Many of us are haunted by a fear of being alone in life. We live with a deep anxiety that there is no one who truly understands or cares for us. If you remember a time when you were sad, depressed, or discouraged, you will likely recall that you also felt separate and isolated from the people around you. In our worst moments, we feel abandoned or rejected and have a sinking feeling of being marooned, struggling through life all by ourselves. This creates a natural desire to seek out other people for companionship to relieve us of our burden of loneliness.

All too often, however, our relationships end in conflict or misunderstanding. The person who provided a sense of comfort and belonging suddenly does something that threatens us or hurts our feelings. When we respond by attacking them back or withdrawing from the relationship, things often get worse, until there is little safety or trust left between us. These failed attempts at friendship or intimacy then make us cautious to get too close to others. And this, in turn, can increase our sense of isolation as we become caught between our need for connection and our fear of being hurt.

Our seemingly opposite needs for belonging and personal safety can make relationships quite challenging. We need other people, yet at the same time we easily feel threatened by them. So, we may end up sacrificing our personal safety for the sake of relationship, and let other people trample on us. Or we harden ourselves to block out the pain of relationships, and remain isolated behind our protective walls.

Facing Despair

Most of us have felt the deep emotional pain of having our ideals shattered by reality. Things don't turn out the way we hoped they would, or thought they should, and we take it as a personal defeat. We weather these blows as best as we can, clinging to some shred of hope that keeps us from drowning in our own despair. Yet, in the end, many of us deal with life's traumas by sealing off our hearts, encasing our feelings within the hidden resentment of believing we have been denied what we most want.

Few of us allow our secret desolation to come out in the open. We hide it so we can appear positive and happy, and cope with disappointment by trying to tune out our idealism. When we do take another chance on something we believe in, and our hopes are crushed again, we further insulate our hearts, thinking that will make the pain go away. This tragic pattern leads to "lives of quiet desperation," cut off from our source of inspiration and alienated from our own true desires.

Some approaches to human suffering tell us to ignore and override the pain with a veneer of "everything is just fine" and "have a happy day." These simplistic formulas sound good and may make us feel better momentarily, but they lack substance and offer no real solution. When we realize that putting on a happy face does not solve our problems, we may try the opposite approach of glorifying the tragedy and hopelessness of human existence. We become cynical, believing that the one thing we can count on in life is disappointment.

Either way, we are left feeling stuck. We are unable to erase our dreams of the way things could be, yet we cannot ever seem to get there. This seems like an unhappy ending, yet at this moment, if we can just realize that we are lost, we can focus on finding a way out. In order to find a new way, however, we first have to admit that our current approach is not working.

Things usually have to get worse before we pay enough attention to improve them. Once we recognize that conflict has undermined our sense of security and blocked our capacity to care, from our intimate family connections to relations between nations, we may be motivated to change the way we do things. When we honestly admit that our efforts to find meaning or genuine connection have failed, we may finally be able to see that the problem is not other people, but the *way we are approaching them.*

Familiar Ways

The communication habits most of us have learned come from a time when relationships followed traditional rules imposed by family and society. The emphasis was on fitting in and playing our role in order to maintain an appearance of order. The expectations were clear and uniform, and our choices were simpler because we did not have to pay so much attention to personal feelings or desires.

In traditional Western culture, clear lines of authority created a structure for relationships. Wives deferred to husbands, children to parents, students to teachers, and people to governments. We've had little use for interpersonal skills because the fabric of these relationships was held together by deference to the person in charge, and our focus was on conforming and obeying, not on meeting our emotional needs.

These traditional models focused on what a relationship was supposed to look on the outside, not how it felt on the inside. Relationships were standardized; there was little room for personal variation, and the emphasis was on fitting in instead of personal satisfaction. Communication followed established patterns and there was no real need for us to learn how to handle our emotions or meet our needs. In order to maintain stability, individuality was simply denied and suppressed, and differences between people were minimized.

The problem we face today is that expectations for relationships have changed dramatically in recent years, and these old ways simply do not work anymore. Our familiar patterns of relationship are hopelessly inadequate for dealing with each person as a unique individual. We simply are unprepared for the complexity of issues that arise when the old social structures no longer dictate our behavior.

Our New Ideals

We have seen a progression in the recent centuries of Western civilization from strict monarchies where kings and queens had absolute power over their subjects, to democracies where ordinary people have more control over their lives. Since the United States was founded on the principles of "a government of the people," we have steadily evolved as a society toward greater individual freedom and less submission to authority figures. The social revolutions of the 1960s further accelerated this movement by empowering women, African Americans, and others whose individual rights had been denied. In this time of rapid cultural change, the very idea of one person having authority over another was deeply challenged.

The impact of these changes on ordinary relationships has been revolutionary. We have outgrown an era in which we were content to follow social standards, and most of us now recognize a deeper need than conformity or security in our interactions with other people. Individual creativity and personal expression have become more urgent than the sense of stability we get from following a set of rules or obeying an authority figure. Our sense of well-being no longer comes from receiving approval from others. Most of us now want a higher degree of intimacy and cooperation and expect to have relationships that recognize our individual needs.

Today, women expect to be equal partners in a marriage or domestic partnership, sharing power and making decisions together. Employees expect to be treated as individuals and have their feelings and needs taken into account in decisions made by their employers. Citizens of democratic countries increasingly expect their opinions to be considered and their individual rights to be respected. Children expect their parents and teachers to listen to them and not ignore their personal preferences.

Correspondingly, many men want a domestic partner who can take charge and share responsibility for the family's finances and physical needs. Employers want workers who are independent and self-motivated. Parents want children who are strong individuals and can take care of themselves. And governments expect citizens to be self-reliant, help make decisions, and share leadership.

We've come a long way on this road to independence, and the price of conforming to other people's expectations is now more than most of us are willing to pay. Our primary need today is to be recognized for who we are as individuals. We want autonomy and personal freedom and are not satisfied to ignore our deeper longings for the sake of efficiency or harmony.

Yet, we still have to live and work together, and it seems that getting along with each other in this new era of personal autonomy is only becoming more difficult. Before we exhaust ourselves in conflict, it may be wise to consider that we need a new way to structure our relationships to make them nourishing and supportive instead of limiting and confining.

> Conscious communication skills
> enable us to be true to ourselves
> and connect deeply with other people
> at the same time.

Revealing the Hidden Scripts

The idea of learning skills for relating to other people is surprisingly new for many of us. We have little context for learning *how* to be in relationship, and our habits are so familiar that we rarely think about them. We tend to assume that communication is obvious and natural, and there is nothing to learn about it. This is because our society has had clear rules governing how people relate to each other, and we didn't need to know anything else.

Now that these rules are changing so rapidly, however, things are not so clear. Without being conscious of the way we communicate, we limit ourselves to playing traditional roles and repeating familiar patterns that no longer work. We want a greater sense of equality, intimacy, and collaboration. Yet our way of relating to other people often keeps a formal distance between us and increases our sense of competition and isolation. To help us understand what is happening, it may be useful to take a critical look at how we communicate now.

When children are starting to be verbal, they simply copy what they hear from others. We all learned to speak at such a young age that most of us have no memory of it. Our communication may seem natural and spontaneous, yet most of the time we are merely following patterns we copied from other people. These formulas that govern our unconscious communication are not visible to us anymore because we are so accustomed to them. They seem genuine simply because they are so familiar that we no longer notice the underlying script.

The main problem with these hidden scripts is that they often do *not* reveal what is happening for us in the moment. Usually, they are words and gestures we have rehearsed over and over again to *hide* our true feelings and needs so that we will not expose any weakness or vulnerability. Most of us learned to focus on our thoughts and opinions, rather than on the more immediate experience of how we feel or what we need. So our "natural" way of interacting, which is to express ideas instead of feelings, tends to keep a distance between us and defeats the purpose of relationship.

Many of us now recognize that these scripted ways of relating to each other do not allow for our individual feelings and needs or provide the level of intimacy and independence we want. We have outgrown the formalities that held relationships together in the past because they no longer work for us. Yet we have not developed a new approach. As a result, our culture is marked by a disintegration of the social fabric, which strains ordinary relationships and leaves us with little sense of stability.

In our quest for individuality, it now seems that we have lost our capacity to get along with each other at all. Neighbors often don't know each other, few of us have a sense of living in a cohesive community, and our families are breaking apart at an alarming rate. We may be cautious about adopting any new structures for relationships because we are just breaking free of the traditional roles and don't want to be restricted in this way again. However, in the absence of *any* structure or methods, relationships often become chaotic, confusing, and painful.

Developing Tools Instead of Rules

It is important now for us to be able to distinguish between *rules* and *tools*. Rules tell us how to be so we can be accepted as normal or seen as good. They provide a uniformity, which in turn gives us a feeling of security. Yet, this approach is based on trying to conform to a standard instead of recognizing what is true for us in the moment. Therefore, the sense of stability we achieve often depends on ignoring our deeper longings. It is a fragile foundation that easily comes undone, as we see happening in our society today.

Tools, on the other hand, do not prescribe a certain outcome. They enable us to do a task, but they do *not* determine what that task is. Relationship skills are simply a new kind of tool that enables us to relate to each other in the present moment, without the prescribed formulas that we now use unconsciously. They give us a way to express the emotions and needs we are experiencing directly, and to listen to those of another person. In this way we can stay connected, while at the same time being honest and working through our differences.

> Rules dictate a standard outcome,
> while tools allow us the freedom
> to create any outcome we want.

Our way of containing relationships has been to establish rules for everyone to follow that minimize conflict and create uniformity. This may work to establish a veneer of harmony, yet the price we pay is that our differences have to be concealed or denied.

A new approach is to equip each one of us with a set of tools that enables us to creatively build relationships where we are recognized and accepted as we are, and encouraged to meet our own needs. While the old rules kept a formal distance between us based on social etiquette, these new tools give us a way to be more authentic and genuine with each other and establish relationships based on trust, honesty, and personal integrity.

The next chapter will focus on patterns of response we have learned that keep distance between us instead of fostering a greater sense of connection. Once we learn to recognize how our familiar ways of communicating do not lead to the outcomes we want, we can begin to replace them with new and more effective habits.

Chapter 3

Blocks to Connection

We all learned to communicate initially by copying the people around us. And rarely do people take the time to examine their communication or learn different approaches to relationships. As a result, many of us share the same habits that have been passed along unconsciously for many generations. Our natural ways of responding to other people may sound right and good because we are so used to hearing them. But they often don't work to meet our needs, help the other person, or bring us closer together.

In this chapter, we will look at some of our most common responses to other people and how they affect our relationships. I call these learned responses Disconnects because they tend to distance us from other people, especially when one or both of us are feeling strong emotions. To illustrate Disconnects, each of these responses is given in the context of the following conversation, which begins when a friend calls us up and says:

> *"Things at work are really tough right now. My boss keeps telling me I'm not taking enough initiative, and then he tells me I always do things without asking him first. I just can't seem to please the guy. It's been going on like this for years, and I'm getting sick of it. I'm thinking of quitting, and we are even considering moving. It may be time to start all over in a new place."*

Possible responses to this statement that illustrate each of the Disconnects will be centered in italics following the descriptions below.

Referring to Yourself

This is the tendency to refer back to your own life circumstance as soon as the other person has finished talking. If the other person is talking about job struggles, you immediately talk about *your* own job struggles.

"Yeah, bosses can really do you in. My boss right now is not so bad, but every so often, he gets weird on me and I think about moving on, too."

This habit is quite natural because listening to another person's experience tends to stimulate you to think of your own similar experiences. However, it makes for superficial conversation in which you both simply talk about yourselves, and there is little understanding of what is really going on for each other.

Digging for Facts

If you think it is your responsibility to offer the other person an opinion about the situation, there is a tendency to ask fact-oriented questions in order to establish your perspective.

"How long have you worked there now?" or

"So, where would you move to?"

While these questions are genuine and show interest, they focus on facts and tend to distract the person who is speaking from their immediate experience. Listening supportively does not require that you understand all the facts of the other person's circumstance. Connecting with other people happens when you understand how *they* relate to *their own* circumstance, and how the situation is affecting them.

Being Logical

If you think you have enough facts, you may offer logic, thinking the other person just can't see what is happening and hearing it from you will make everything clear.

"That may not be the best idea. Jobs aren't as easy to find as they once were."

Logical explanations imply that the other person is not capable of seeing their own situation clearly, so you have to point it out to them. Being logical is tempting because you can usually see parts of their dilemma that they may not be able to see yet. This is often because they are too emotional to think clearly. In this case, it is more supportive to help them release their emotions so they can think clearly again.

Analyzing

Once you have heard enough information to form an opinion, you may tend to assume that supporting other people means telling them what you think about their situation:

> *"You just have not tried hard enough to get along with him. You always take things he says personally and then sulk off to lick your wounds!"*

While this perspective may have some truth in it, this kind of communication tends to stop the conversation because it is so final and absolute. It is also more effective when the person speaking is able to come up with this kind of analysis on their own.

Taking Sides or Blaming

You may think that being supportive means siding with the person speaking:

> *"You don't deserve that kind of treatment, and you shouldn't have to put up with that nonsense."*

Or you might try to solve the other person's problem by blaming someone else:

> *"That guy sounds like a real jerk. If he can't be a better manager than that, he deserves to lose his employees!"*

You may think that siding with someone connects the two of you so that you can be together against someone else. Yet, conflict is rarely so black and white, and there are always two sides to a story. By expressing your opinion in this way, you reinforce the struggle and opposition rather than helping other people work through their dilemmas and resolve conflicts constructively.

Using Shame and Guilt

Sometimes we even blame the person we are listening to:

"Sounds like you are really blowing it again. You just can't seem to get along with anyone who tells you what to do."

Or, we may use shame and guilt to try to get the person to shape up:

"Well maybe if you paid attention for once you would understand what your boss is asking you to do and get it right. You never were very good at following instructions."

Using shame and guilt is a common way of trying to change another person. Some people fall into this habit regularly without ever realizing the impact it has. No one likes to be made to feel ashamed or guilty. While this approach sometimes works, it usually undermines the safety and trust in a relationship. In the long run, it rarely motivates people to make real changes.

Imposing Your Own Values

Some people assume that solving another's dilemma is merely a matter of sorting out right from wrong:

"You shouldn't think of quitting just because things are rough. Too many people believe that leaving will solve all their problems. You should think about how it will affect your co-workers, friends, and neighbors."

There may be some truth in these statements, but they tend to polarize a situation and shut down the conversation with their sense of finality. People sometimes assume that discerning right from wrong is very important. Yet most of the time, such distinctions are arbitrary and just a matter of personal opinion with little bearing on what is really happening. In the end, they do little to help the person resolve their situation.

Disguising Judgments as Questions

Some of us express a judgment about another person's behavior in the form of a question:

"Why do you think quitting your job and moving will solve your problems?"

Which really means:

"This move is not going to solve your problems."

Here are some more examples:

Judgmental Question	Real Meaning
"How would you like it if someone did that to you?"	*"You did a bad thing that hurt someone."*
"Why don't you ever ask for help before taking on such big projects?"	*"You take on more than you can handle and mess everything up because you don't ask for help."*
"How come these spoons keep ending up in the knife drawer?"	*"You keep putting the spoons in the wrong place."*
"What were you thinking?"	*"You really screwed up."*

When we ask questions like these, we don't really want to know the other person's response. They aren't real questions, and they tend to confuse the situation because they *sound* like questions. People receiving our disguised judgments know that we are judging them but they cannot see the judgments clearly, and this creates an uneasy feeling in the relationship.

Responses that contain opinions or judgments tend to shut us down because most of us are afraid of being criticized or judged by another person. These disguised judgments often undermine open communication even more than clearly stated judgments because they are indirect.

Advising

Assuming it is your job to fix the other person's problem, you may offer advice:

"You should just tell him how you feel. Talking these things out can make a big difference."

Advising may be a way of showing concern and trying to help out, and the suggestions you make could be effective ideas. Yet this common Disconnect takes the problem solving out of the hands of the person with the problem and can create an unhealthy dependency over time. It also moves the conversation from direct experience to solutions and tends to close rather than open communication.

Reassuring

Sensing that other people feel bad, you may try to cheer them up:

"Your boss was probably just having some bad days and didn't realize he was contradicting himself. Just hang in there; things are bound to get better."

Other examples include:

"Cheer up, everything will work out fine in the end."

"Things can't be as bad as they seem. Just wait a few days and things will look better."

Reassuring is a frequent response when a situation appears serious and you don't know what else to say. You feel compelled to say something that will make everything seem all right. The problem with this approach is that everything is not all right, and the other person knows it. So reassurance can sound as if you are not really interested or don't want to get involved.

Praising

You may sometimes try to make other people feel better by telling them how great you think they are:

"Well, you certainly have not done anything to deserve this kind of treatment. You are a great worker and employee."

Other examples include:

"You are such a good girl."

"You always do the right thing. This mess couldn't be your fault."

Praise is often seen as a positive way to give feedback, especially with children. The problem is that praise is an evaluation. When you give praise, you are judging the other person's behavior. Although praise is a positive judgment, it feeds the habit of relying on other people's evaluations to know how we are doing. When you offer other people approval, you may be setting up a dependent relationship in which they need your praise to feel good about themselves.

Also, praise does not address what is actually happening for the other person. It may sound good, but if people are not feeling good about themselves, they usually don't believe it, and praise can signal that you are not really paying attention to what is going on inside them.

Responses of reassurance and praise are common and are attempts to make a situation better by sugarcoating it. While praise and reassurance may make someone feel better for a moment, they do not address the real situation and may sound hollow or empty. They also have an air of finality and tend to end the conversation. People receiving these responses may conclude that you are not really interested in their situation.

Hinting

Indirect suggestions are often used to get someone else to do what you want:

"If you guys move, we won't get to see you much."

Which means:

"I don't want you to move because if you do I will really miss seeing you."

Other examples include:

Hint	Real Meaning
"Boy, am I tired. I've had one heck of a day!"	*"I need help with the dishes."*
"I can't stand this kitchen! It is such a mess all the time that I can't find anything I need!"	*"I don't like a messy kitchen and I need help keeping things in order."*
"We never go out anymore."	*"I want to go somewhere interesting with you."*

Hinting is a way many of us have learned to assert our feelings and needs. While it can be helpful to let other people know what you want, hinting requires a lot of interpretation. It can create confusion and misunderstanding as they have to guess about your feelings or needs and may miss your message altogether. Hinting can cause other people to pull away because they know we want something from them, but they don't know exactly what it is.

Demanding and Threatening

When we want people to do something, we often command them, especially if we are in a position of power and authority. This is more likely to happen with our children, spouse, parents, employees, or students, because of our familiarity.

"You can't just quit like that. You have to try harder to make this work out."

Such a response may also sound like:

"You have to be at meetings on time!"

"You must eat those vegetables!"

When a demand does not seem strong enough, a consequence may be attached if the other person doesn't do what we want them to do:

"If you quit your job and move away just like that, don't expect me to come visit you!"

Other examples include:

"If you don't come to meetings on time, you will be out of a job!"

"If you don't eat those vegetables, you will be grounded for the rest of the week!"

Demanding and threatening can create power struggles because they invite resistance and rebellion. They put up barriers in relationship because they rely on force to get another person to do what you want or what you think is right. These Disconnects are attempts to change other people's behavior through fear, and they usually create more distance.

Being Sarcastic

Some of us have the habit of criticizing or evaluating another person's situation through witty comments that are biting and judgmental.

"Well that sure is a good way to deal with a conflict at work – just quit and leave town!"

People tend to be sarcastic when they have built up an emotional charge in relation to another person. Sarcasm is often an indirect way of communicating that a feeling or need of your own is not being met and you want the other person to do something about it. Yet because it is indirect, it often creates confusion and distrust in a relationship and rarely results in you getting your needs met or encouraging the other person to change.

The Nature of Disconnects

Some Disconnects are ways we have learned to get other people to meet our needs without making ourselves too vulnerable. They tend to be either indirect or forceful, and they often undermine the trust between people and create a sense of discomfort in the relationship.

We use other Disconnects because we think they are ways to demonstrate that we are good listeners and helpers. The assumption is that being helpful and supportive means fixing other people's problems. We come up with solutions, offer our perspective, or say things we hope will wrap up another person's dilemma in a neat bundle. We often sense that these responses are not working, but we don't know any other way. We *do* want to help, yet we don't know how to do it effectively.

We may think we are being helpful when we try to solve other people's problems, yet we are really signaling that we don't trust them to find their own solutions. Most people's problems are too personal and complex for anyone else to solve. Trying to do so does not work in the long run, and actually tends to undermine other people's own efforts to help themselves.

We use other Disconnects as a way to appear helpful when we don't want to take the time to listen or are afraid of becoming too involved. Our own personal dilemmas may be so pressing that we don't want to devote the effort required to effectively help another. So instead, we reach for instant solutions, offering judgments or conclusions that make the problem seem simple or easy to solve.

Beware of Judging Yourself and Others

Once you understand these ineffective communication habits and how they affect relationships, it is easy to judge yourself and others for being bad communicators. Despite having learned about Disconnects, you will probably find yourself still using them on a regular basis. And when you notice other people using Disconnects, it may be tempting to point it out to them.

However, if you call others on using Disconnects, it will only create more confusion and separation in your relationships. They won't know what you mean and will only hear your judgment and disapproval. If someone close to you has a habit of using Disconnects, the Assertion skills described later in this book will help you to address the situation directly and constructively.

You also may feel guilty or self-critical when you notice yourself using a Disconnect. You may think you should have known better, or that you should no longer fall into old habits like these now that you know how they can undermine the connection you want. Keep in mind that you have spent most of your life learning Disconnects, and they are not likely to disappear overnight. The fact that you are noticing them is a big step forward. Once you become aware of a habit like this, it has already begun to change.

What Do You Really Want?

In order to become more aware of Disconnects, it helps to recognize what you really want out of your interactions. You usually have some intention when you interact with another person. A Disconnect is when your communication does not do what you intended it to do. So the first step is to ask yourself:

"Why am I communicating with this person?"

Once you know why you are communicating with another person, you can ask:

"Is my communication doing what I intended it to do?"

Answering this question will allow you to evaluate how your communication is working so that, if necessary, you can change your approach to make your relationships more fulfilling. Since there are many reasons for communicating, this question obviously does not have one right answer. The important thing is to check in with yourself and recognize what you want so you are more likely to achieve that outcome.

The Need for Connection

I went through a time in my life when I felt a deep discontent with my family, friends, and society in general. I knew that something essential was missing, yet I could not tell what it was. As I explored my frustration, I realized that I was approaching my interactions as an exchange, like a business deal. I entered relationships focusing on what other people could do for me, or what I could get out of the situation. Even when my intention was to help other people, there was an unconscious motivation to benefit myself by being the hero and rescuing them.

This way of viewing other people was so familiar that I did not recognize I was doing it until I began to be more aware of my own internal process. As I began to ask myself why so many exchanges felt empty and unsatisfying, I realized that I was constantly measuring how much I was getting from each interaction. And, the scale I was using seemed to indicate that most of the time I was losing.

I made a choice at this point to focus on my sense of connection with each person rather than on the business or emotional exchange that seemed to be the reason for the interaction. I gave up trying to get people to like me or respond in ways that *I* wanted. I put aside my good intentions to be helpful in emotional situations, or my wish to get a bargain in business deals, and focused on relating for the sake of companionship in the moment.

This shift in focus made all the difference in my relationships. Instead of measuring interactions according to the results and weighing each outcome as a gain or loss, I concentrated on the value of feeling connected to the other person during the conversation. I discovered that this sense of connection was what I really wanted, whether in a personal friendship or a business exchange. Once I recognized this, my relationships worked better and became more satisfying.

My experience suggests that what most of us want out of our interactions with others is a sense of belonging or connection. We communicate primarily so that we do not feel so alone or isolated. Disconnects are communications that fail because they leave us feeling more separate rather than more connected. So, a simple way to tell if you are using Disconnects is to ask yourself:

"Does the way I am communicating
help me feel more connected to this person
or does it put more distance between us?"

In the following chapters, we will explore some of the attitudes that underlie Disconnects and the often damaging results that follow. We will also consider new communication patterns to replace these familiar ways. It is much easier to move away from old habits when we replace them with new and more effective ones.

Disconnects

Referring to Yourself:	Focusing on your own story rather than on the other person's experience.
Digging for Facts:	Asking questions that do not relate directly to the other person's experience.
Being Logical:	Thinking you can solve the other person's dilemma by using logic.
Analyzing:	Trying to solve the other person's problem by sharing your perspective on it.
Taking Sides or Blaming:	Trying to make other people feel better by taking their side or blaming someone else for their situation.
Using Shame or Guilt:	Trying to get other people to change by pointing out their mistakes.
Imposing Your Own Values:	Thinking the solution to another person's dilemma lies in simply pointing out right from wrong.
Disguising Judgments as Questions:	Trying to get other people to see their mistakes by asking leading questions.

Advising:	Thinking you have the solution to another person's dilemma, and that solving the problem is just a matter of them following your suggestion.
Reassuring:	Trying to solve another person's problem by making things look better than they are.
Praising:	Thinking you can help other people by judging them in a positive way.
Hinting:	Trying to get other people to do what you want without asking directly.
Demanding:	Trying to get other people to do what you want by ordering them to do it.
Threatening:	Trying to get other people to do what you want by making them fear your punishment if they do not comply with your demands.
Being Sarcastic:	Using witty or biting comments that indirectly criticize another person in an attempt to get your needs met, or change that person.

Chapter 4

Unconscious Communication

We humans spend a lot of time talking, yet we rarely pay attention to *how* we do it. Having conversations is as familiar as walking or breathing, and as we expand ways to share our thoughts with each other, from cell phones to the internet, the number of verbal interactions we have each day keeps increasing. The amount of time we spend communicating shows us how important it is to feel connected. Yet, for all this talk, it can seem like nothing is happening. We often leave a conversation *without* a deeper sense of understanding or caring for each other.

One reason our interactions can leave us feeling more alone is that when we listen to other people, we tend to evaluate what they say and form our own opinions about it. We assume that it is our responsibility to judge their ideas as right or wrong in order to establish what is true. However, this practice puts up a barrier between us and other people because we are interpreting what they are saying by filtering it through the lens of our own judgments.

When we compare what other people say with our own ideas, we are not really hearing them. We are measuring the other person's thoughts and feelings against our own opinions, and we are not actually hearing what they are expressing about themselves. Instead, we are hearing our *interpretation* of what they are saying. When we respond, we tend to share our interpretations in some form, and in so doing, bring the focus of the conversation unconsciously back to ourselves.

Trading Opinions Instead of Listening

Listen to any ordinary conversation and you will likely hear two or more people trying to be heard at the same time. A kind of chaos and confusion exists in the way we talk and listen to each other that we consider normal because it is so common. We learn some basic etiquette, such as that it is rude to talk when someone else is talking and that it is polite to wait until the other has finished before we respond. Yet this is as far as our usual training goes when it comes to communication.

Many conversations consist of merely trading opinions and judgments back and forth unconsciously. Both people are trying to be heard and validated, but neither is receiving what they want because each is trying to get their need for recognition met *at the same time*. Our habit of comparing and evaluating other people's views, in order to formulate our own ideas, prevents us from simply being present and accepting another person's experience as it is.

A typical conversation between two co-workers on lunch break together might begin like this:

Sue: *"My husband and I are at each other again, and it always seems to be about money."*

Ann: *"Yeah, I know what you mean; we don't even try to talk about it anymore. I just pay the bills and hope there will be enough in the account to cover it all."*

Sue is trying to talk about a problem she is having at home. She probably would like some empathy and understanding so that her dilemma will not seem so overwhelming and she will not feel as if she is carrying her burden alone and unrecognized. Instead, Ann refers back to herself and her own dilemma with a similar issue. Sue does not get the relief of being heard and having her feelings acknowledged, and she is not able to fully respond to Ann's situation, either.

Both people are talking about their own private dilemmas at the same time, and each of them wants to be heard and understood. This is how our communication habits can interfere with a sense of connection between us. Instead of bringing us closer together, talking in this way can actually make us feel more separate and alone. When we fall into these unconscious habits of communication, neither person feels heard, and neither is really listening to the other.

In our normal everyday conversations, most of us are referring what the other person says back to ourselves. We may actually hear the words the other is saying, but we immediately translate these into something that relates to us. This habit of self-referral is one of the primary obstacles to connection, as we saw in the last chapter on Disconnects. It keeps each of us stuck inside the bubble of our own worlds, unable to step out long enough to really understand the other person's point of view.

> The most common block to connection
> is the habit of referring everything
> someone else says or does back to ourselves.

Competition in Communication

When we each refer back to ourselves, conversations usually consist of comparing opinions in a way that is unconsciously competitive. While we are listening, we are evaluating the other person's statements and waiting for a turn to express our own point of view. It is an exchange of concepts that is primarily a mental activity, and tells us little about each other beyond what we think.

Without realizing it, we can make everyday relations with the people around us into a contest where each of us is competing to see who will win. We compare our stories and look for areas where our perceptions either agree or disagree. And when we are measuring other people's experiences in this way, we are not able to simply acknowledge or empathize with them.

Imagine that someone says:

"Wow did I have a tough day! I had to get the car to the garage to fix that oil leak and then make it to a meeting by ten o'clock. I ended up running through town and broke a sweat. I was afraid I would look pretty disheveled by the time I got there, but I didn't have a moment to go to a bathroom, so I just walked in and sat down like all was normal. I guess it went all right because no one made any comments to me. But it took me a while to focus on the business of the meeting."

A typical response to this might be:

"You think you had a rough day?! One of the kids was sick and I had to leave work early to pick her up from school. I spent the rest of the day cleaning up vomit and trying to figure out what was going on with her. Then the toilet backed up on me, and I had a huge mess all over the bathroom floor!"

In a scenario like this, hearing about the other person's difficulties can spark us to think about our own crisis, and we have this overwhelming urge to compare dilemmas. We are both subtly competing with each other to see who has the more difficult problem, and neither of us gets the recognition we wanted.

Or, a conversation might begin like this:

"This government makes me want to scream. I can't believe they're spending billions on defense and war toys and then cut money for school programs that help kids who really need some support! Sometimes I get so disgusted I want to move to another country!"

And a typical response might be:

"Well, you think the answer to everything is helping out the disadvantaged. Why can't they help themselves? No one ever helped me out. I had to do it myself. And what do you want the government to do – point water pistols at people who are threatening us? We need to be able to defend ourselves, and in today's world, that means being prepared for anything!"

In a scenario like this, the response assumes that the other person's perspective is a direct challenge. So we react a bit defensively by asserting our own point of view, as if this were a debate or contest to see who is right and who is wrong. Although the feelings and personal needs are more hidden, both people are trying to be heard and have their perspectives validated. And again, neither person receives such an acknowledgment from the conversation.

Both of these examples illustrate how the habit of self-referral cuts off the connection between people and does not meet our basic need for understanding and acceptance. We tend to think of this self-oriented approach to life as our basic human nature, because it seems so prevalent and impossible to change. However, this is a *learned* response.

Referring to ourselves in conversations is a habit we pick up from copying other people. These responses are *unconscious* because they are so familiar that we don't think about them. Habits like this are appealing because we don't have to pay attention to what we are doing. It is like pushing a button on your computer and having the machine do the rest. With something as ordinary as daily communication, we tend to follow the same patterns without noticing what we are doing or how it impacts our relationships.

Identifying Ourselves by Our Ideas

An assumption underlying many of our unconscious communication patterns is that our *perception* of what is going on is the most important information we can share with another person.

> We assume that what matters most
> is what we *think* about something.

We tend to identify who we are by our opinions. Our judgments and perceptions are often presented as reality and become the dominant focus of conversation. This limits our connections with other people to comparisons of abstract ideas and sets up relationships to be either competitive or codependent. We are either struggling with other people to get them to agree with us, or we are agreeing with them so we can be on the same side.

In the previous example, where someone is complaining about the government, we looked at a response that led to a sense of competition between two different opinions. Another response might have been to agree with the other person:

> *"Boy you sure said it! Those guys are really out of control. They are spending money and starting wars and running this country like a bunch of reckless teenagers. I wish someone would knock some sense into their heads."*

This kind of response can create a bond between people because it seems that both are on the same side of an issue. However, there are negative side effects to basing a connection on sharing the same opinion. In order for you to be right, someone else has to be wrong. This approach often requires a common enemy who both of you are against, which tends to increase conflict rather than resolving it. Also, the connection is fragile and limited to areas where each of you can agree with the other's opinion. As soon as disagreement arises, the relationship is likely to become more distant or fall apart.

In the earlier example, where someone is describing a harried day at work, a different kind of response might have been to try to make the other person feel better:

"I'm sure you did fine at the meeting. You always make a good impression."

While this kind of response may feel better than the competitive one, and does create more sense of support, it also tends to invalidate the other person's experience. The person telling the story was expressing some deep discomfort about what had happened and did not know they did fine. The response of trying to make them feel better simply sugarcoated the traumatic experience with praise and reassurance, without acknowledging what happened or how it was for them.

When communication stays in the realm of ideas and judgments, it often leaves you feeling alone and disconnected from other people because you have little sense of knowing what is really going on for them. When you focus on abstract ideas on which the two of you agree or disagree, the interaction remains relatively superficial. You hear only what other people have concluded about their experience and do not get to share the experience itself.

Even when you ask the simple question, "How are you?" you do not normally expect people to tell you what they are experiencing in that moment or how they really feel. Most people don't know how to express such direct experience, anyway, and don't think you really want to hear it. So they often respond with a simple, "Fine," and proceed to share ideas or information. This is an example of how conversation often maintains a distance between people that most of us have come to consider normal. Looking at it honestly, however, you might recognize that you feel frustrated and alone in these exchanges with others because you really want a deeper connection.

Getting Stuck in Our Heads

While conversations that focus on exchanging opinions may feel safe and familiar, they are not very nourishing. Your thinking mind remains in control of the interaction and keeps you distant from what is really going on in your heart. The problem for many of us is that we don't know how to express what is true for us in the moment. It may feel too vulnerable or too threatening, and so we keep a comfortable distance from other people by talking about our thoughts instead of our feelings.

Here is a typical conversation between two brothers at a family gathering:

Bob: *"I think Mom should get a second opinion before going through with a major operation like this. I just don't think it is right for her to have such invasive surgery based on one diagnosis."*

George: *"Well, I was reading an article the other day on second opinions, and they aren't always such a good idea. It can cost a lot of money, and sometimes getting another doctor involved makes a decision like this more confusing. I think if she feels clear about it, she should just do it and get this over with."*

Both of these men are discussing a situation they probably feel deep emotions about, and they are both demonstrating a concern for the well-being of their mother. Yet the conversation is entirely in the realm of competing opinions. Each has established his point of view, and the only thing left is to convince the other person to change his mind or just drop the subject. The result is likely to be a distancing between these two without resolving their disagreement or touching on the deeper feelings present.

The two brothers in this example have done the only thing many of us know how to do. We approach a difficult situation by forming a judgment or opinion about it. This urge to know and be right comes from wanting a sense of security in dealing with uncomfortable situations that are beyond our control. We learn to come at life with a set of ideas of how and why things work the way they do and armed with solutions that we think will solve the problem.

However, neither man in the conversation above learns how his brother is *feeling* emotionally about their mother's pending operation or what *need* each of them is trying to meet in his proposed solution. Each only hears a static, pre-formulated opinion that he can respond to by agreeing or disagreeing. By keeping the conversation in the realm of ideas, they miss an opportunity to know and support each other on a deeper level.

Perceptions Are Not Reality

The main problem with our opinions and judgments is that we confuse them with reality, and tend to believe that the way we *think* about something is actually the way it *is*. Take a moment now and recognize some of the conclusions your mind has already made about this book. Then make a note of them here:

This book is _____

_____

Now, look at your conclusions and notice how absolute and final they tend to be. You may be thinking, "This book can really help me," or "These ideas are too complicated to be useful." We often make snap judgments like these about our life experiences, before we have given ourselves time to know.

The point here is not what your specific judgments are, but that you have already come to some final conclusions about this book after reading only a few chapters. This is what our minds tend to do. We want to be in a position of knowing the truth so badly that we constantly make it up, even when there is no way we can actually know. At this point, you cannot know what this book is about or how you will feel about it in the end. Any judgments you have already made are premature and will only prevent you from seeing what happens next.

The real tragedy of mistaking judgments for truth is that we miss what happens next. When we draw conclusions, we effectively *conclude* or end our experience. We get caught up in what we think about what is happening and end up missing what is actually going on. This is like going on a trip and missing the actual scenes and events because we are taking lots of pictures. Then, when we get home, we experience the trip through our photographs. We may get some satisfaction from this, but in the end, something essential is missing.

Similarly, when conversations stay in the realm of thoughts and ideas, we can only talk about what *has* been or what we think *will* be and are not able to recognize or communicate to others what is happening for us *right now*. It leaves us still feeling lonely and isolated because no one knows about our experience *while it is happening.*

The way many of us learned to communicate does not express our immediate experience, but rather our judgments and conclusions *about* that experience. Communicating our direct experience usually begins with a feeling or emotion, not a thought or idea. So we need to find a way to focus on what is going on inside of us, in order to first recognize it ourselves, and then share it with another person. The next chapter will explore how to recognize what you are feeling and separate your emotions from those of other people.

Establishing Healthy Boundaries

Chapter 5

Emotional Responsibility

One reason it may be more comfortable to focus on what we *think* rather than on how we *feel* is that we don't know how to handle emotions very well. Talking about emotions and needs can feel vulnerable and messy. So most of us try to ignore our feelings and focus on our judgments and opinions, which seem more defined and easier to manage. We maintain a comfortable distance between ourselves and others and keep emotions from arising by talking about ideas. And relationships can go along well this way, as long as we do not get too close.

As we become more familiar with another person, however, our emotions tend to get stirred up, making it more difficult to simply ignore them. Notice how quickly anger or resentment can arise with a partner, family member, or close friend. These significant relationships are the ones we often find most challenging because they bring up strong feelings that we don't know how to handle.

Letting Down Boundaries

When we first meet someone, or know a person only as an acquaintance, there are formal boundaries most of us maintain that keep the relationship polite and civil, as well as emotionally distant. We tend to keep space between us and allow people more room. As a relationship deepens into friendship or family, however, the boundaries that we normally keep with strangers fall away. As we feel more comfortable, we naturally reveal more of ourselves, which can help us feel connected and not so alone. This kind of connection often feels like a big relief because we can finally let down our protective guards. Yet it can also lead to conflict as we let our hurt feelings and negative emotions surface.

When we are upset about something, we naturally want to release our emotions in order to feel better. Without knowing how to do this effectively, however, we tend to dump them on people with whom we feel most safe. We can easily damage our significant relationships through our unconscious efforts to discharge our emotions in this way, and they quickly become a tangle of old wounds that breed resentment and hostility.

When a relationship begins to feel strained in this way it is often a sign that you have lost the formal boundaries that kept your lives neatly separated. Being close to another person requires that we let go of some social formalities and be more real with each other. However, there are healthy boundaries that are necessary to maintain with *every* relationship that encourage each of us to be responsible for our own emotions and needs.

When Emotions Are Charged

Certain people tend to trigger certain emotions, and the closer you are, the more their behavior is likely to upset you. When this happens, it is easy to think other people are *trying* to hurt you. You may then try to change them or to distance yourself, assuming that they are the cause of the problem.

When you think that someone else is responsible for your feelings, your first impulse may be to get that person to act differently so the emotion does not come up. However, trying to control another person so your emotions are not triggered often causes *more* conflict in your relationships. Most people react defensively when someone tries to get them to change, and this can lead to power struggles that destroy the trust and safety between you. This approach also leads to a feeling of powerlessness and insecurity when you finally realize that you cannot change the other person.

When an interaction with another person brings up strong emotions, you are likely to remember struggles you have gotten into before, and your impulse may be to avoid the situation. Yet these conflicts also present you with the best opportunity to learn more about each other and deepen your understanding and connection. The problem is not the emotions themselves, but that you don't know how to respond effectively.

The skills of Conscious Communication present some new ways to respond when someone is feeling upset. When we react to a person or situation with strong negative feelings such as sadness, hurt, anger, or fear, our whole body becomes charged with emotions. I refer to this as being *emotionally charged*.

We all have emotional charges come up, and there is no way to avoid them. Instead of dumping them on someone else, or trying to deny them, we can learn to respond directly to our emotional charges and those of the people around us in a way that reveals what is *causing* the strong feelings.

Emotional Responsibility is about first separating out each person's emotions in order to respond to them more effectively. Sorting out emotionally charged conflicts works best when we each take responsibility for our own feelings and needs. This first step is essential to all the other relationship skills, however, it is not easy to do because our habit is to deny our feelings or blame someone else for them.

Denial and Addictive Habits

Emotions often appear to be beyond our ability to control or understand. They seem like mysterious energetic states that overwhelm us for no apparent reason and make us do things we do not intend to do. We often think that if we recognize our emotions and speak directly about them, they will grow even larger and more out of control. So, naturally, we struggle to keep them hidden and buried deep in our subconscious where we think they cannot affect us.

Denial of emotions is a common response when something happens that brings up uncomfortable feelings. However, when you try to cover up your emotions in this way, they actually *do* grow more powerful and destructive and can end up damaging you or your relationships. Concealed emotions are what make us lash out at someone we don't mean to hurt, or engage in unhealthy behaviors we know are not good for us.

We each have our own way of trying to dull our painful feelings. Some of these may include compulsive talking, eating, drinking, smoking cigarettes, drug use, sleeping, over-stimulation, sex, or withdrawal. Every day many of us find ourselves doing things that we know may harm us, yet we do them anyway. We know intellectually that these addictive habits are hurting us, but we simply cannot help ourselves.

The motivation behind many such self-destructive habits is to drown out our emotions. We turn to addictive behaviors because they temporarily distract or numb us from our feelings. Yet eventually we discover that avoiding emotions in this way does not work. They always come back with more intensity, and then we need a stronger substance or distraction to make them go away.

Facing Our Emotions

Many of us are afraid of our emotions because they take us over so completely and leave us feeling helpless to do anything about them. We often try to hide this fear by convincing ourselves that showing emotions is a sign of weakness. We mistake the denial of our emotions for strength and believe that courage means never being vulnerable. We mask our complete lack of ability to handle emotions by acting as though we are in control of them.

However, it is not our strength and power that makes us want to ignore our emotions, but our fear and insecurity. It takes much greater courage and strength to turn toward our emotions and look directly at them than it does to turn away from them. And avoiding our feelings in this way actually gives *them* more power over *us* because they remain hidden and beyond our ability to deal with them directly.

The main reason that facing emotions can be so difficult is simply because no one has ever showed us how to do it.

> Few of us have the skills
> to work directly with emotions.
> So we tend to dismiss them as insignificant,
> when actually we tremble
> at the thought of facing them.

When I was a young boy, I played on a local ice hockey team. One day, I was facing another player who was winding up to take a slap shot in my direction. I was afraid of being hit by the hard rubber puck and instinctively turned my back, much like an ostrich puts its head in the sand to avoid seeing danger. I must have thought that if I could not see the puck coming, it would not hurt me.

Later, my coach pointed out that my response to this situation was the most dangerous thing I could have done. He reminded me that I was wearing thick padding and guards on my front side from my waist to my ankles, which could easily deflect a hard puck without hurting me. The backs of my ankles and legs, however, were covered only by my cloth uniform. If the puck had hit me from behind, it could have done serious damage.

Years later, when I was playing on a high school varsity hockey team, another player wound up to take a slap shot right in front of me. I remembered what my coach had told me, took a deep breath, relaxed my fear of getting hit, and faced this player directly. He slapped the puck hard right at me, and sure enough, it hit my leg pads and bounced off without hurting me at all. I then had the puck on my stick with only this player between me and the goal. I skated around him, and with just the goal tender to face, went on to score an unassisted goal that won the game for my team.

~~~~~~

Many of us do with emotions what I did as a young boy with that hockey puck coming at me. We become afraid and turn our backs, thinking if we cannot see them, they cannot hurt us. When we are not aware of our emotions, however, we cannot deal with them. While avoidance can seem like protection, it actually makes us more vulnerable and likely to be hurt.

Turning to face your feelings is the first step in responding intelligently when something has upset you. Emotions are merely a signal that some basic need of yours is not being met. They are sending you a message to take care of yourself, and when you ignore or deny them, they keep growing stronger, trying to get your attention.

Separating Your Emotions from Other People's Emotions

Just as a hockey player has padding, it can be helpful to have some skills that will enable you to face emotions directly without getting hurt. The first skill is to establish a simple boundary between the feelings that belong to you and the feelings that belong to others.

> The first step in handling emotions constructively is to see that your emotional charge is about you, and other people's emotional charge is about them.

We have a habit of assuming responsibility for other people's feelings and likewise blaming other people for ours. This confusion causes much of the damage we associate with emotionally charged situations. We can only deal effectively with *our own* emotions, and when they get mixed up with those of another person, the situation becomes impossible to resolve. You can break this habit by simply acknowledging who has the emotional charge in the present moment. This will encourage both of you to take responsibility for your own emotions and begin the process of taking care of yourselves.

Feeling Emotion in Your Body

To become aware of your own emotional condition, you can ask yourself:

"How am I feeling right now?"

or

"Am I emotionally charged or neutral?"

Answering these questions can be difficult. Most of us have learned to pretend to be neutral when we do have strong emotions, hoping to avoid appearing weak. So it can be helpful to begin by recognizing what emotions feel like in your body. You might have a red-hot face, tight fists, a knot in your stomach, or a pounding heart. Or you might get your first indication of an emotional charge through your behavior. Irregular breathing, crying, yelling, withdrawing, talking fast, moving quickly, or turning to an addictive habit – all of these can be signals that you are feeling strong emotions.

In later chapters, we will explore what these strong emotions indicate and how to release them effectively. For now, we are concerned only with knowing when we have an emotional charge and accepting that it belongs to us, not someone else.

Recognizing the Other Person's Emotions

After checking your own emotional condition, the next question is:

"How is the other person feeling?"

You cannot know for sure how other people are feeling until they directly express their emotion. Yet we can often sense from their behavior, words, or body language whether they are emotionally charged or neutral. Most of us don't know how to talk about our strong feelings constructively, so we tend to either hide them or explode. This question will help you determine if another person is upset, or if they are feeling alright. Once you know them fairly well, it is usually easy to tell.

Staying Neutral in Order to Help

When someone we are close to has an emotional charge, often our first impulse is to assume that we are responsible. We easily blur the boundary between us and get involved in other people's business. We may get defensive or think it is our job to fix the situation, and then we become too caught up in their emotional charge to be able to effectively help them.

If you want to help other people or connect with them when they have a strong emotion, it helps to remain neutral. To be able to do this, you can learn to recognize when other people have an emotional charge and acknowledge that it belongs to them. It can be helpful to say to yourself, ***"That person appears to be upset,"*** and recognize that you are *not* upset at that moment. It is important to remember also that you *don't know* yet why the person is upset. This reality check will enable you to listen and find out more about the problem.

> Staying separate
> from another person's emotional charge
> allows you to take care of yourself
> and offer them real support.

Think of a situation in your life recently when someone you are close to was upset. Remember how you reacted and whether you became defensive or tried to fix the problem. Now try to identify the emotion the person seemed to be expressing, without coming to any conclusions. See what it feels like to simply allow other people to have their feelings without doing anything about it. Try filling in this sentence with a situation, the name of the other person, and an emotion:

When _____

happened, _____ seemed to be feeling _____

(hurt, sad, angry, scared, frustrated, etc.)

The Emotional Well

When someone is having a strong emotional reaction, it is as if they have fallen into a deep, dry well and don't know how to get themselves out. If you assume responsibility for their emotions, or immediately get lost in your own emotional reaction, it is like climbing into the well with them. Joining them in the well can feel like you are supporting them, yet if you are both in the well, it is more difficult for either of you to get out. We often jump into another person's predicament without ever stopping to ask whose problem it is, and who is the best person to solve it.

JUMPING INTO THE WELL

Another option when you notice that someone is having an emotional charge is to try to save them by pulling them up out of the well yourself. It is very tempting to try to pull other people out, especially if you care about them. Yet rescue operations can have negative side effects. This seemingly heroic act often creates an unhealthy dependency in the long run because they never learn that they can do it themselves.

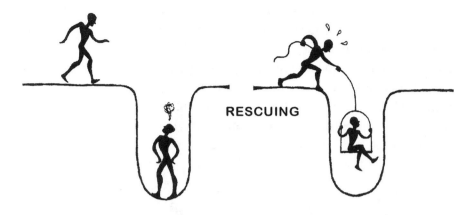

A third common response is to walk away when someone we know is in emotional turmoil. Sometimes we just cannot deal with another person's emotions or we feel overwhelmed with the thought of trying to rescue them. If we think we are responsible for someone else's problem, we often avoid situations that bring up strong feelings or simply deny that they are happening.

None of these responses help the person with the emotional charge to deal with their situation constructively. Another possibility is to stay neutral when someone you know is caught in an emotional well. Staying emotionally neutral when other people are upset is like standing on the ground above the well. It can be challenging because you may feel as though you are abandoning the person below, especially if your habit has been to jump into the well with them.

However, from your position on solid ground above the well, you can throw down a rope and encourage the other person to climb out. This provides support, but leaves the problem solving to them. And, it gives you a way to be helpful without exhausting yourself. Imagine the difference between physically pulling a person up and out of a well and holding a rope for them to climb out themselves. Holding the rope requires presence, patience, and strength, but it is not nearly as much work as pulling them out.

LISTENING SUPPORTIVELY

Climbing the Rope

A thick rope with knots hung from the ceiling in my elementary school gym, and every year we were asked to climb it. The first few years I tried, I could not do it. The ceiling looked extremely high and the task seemed impossible. My friends were stronger and lighter than I was and could easily climb the rope. Year after year, I gave up in despair, thinking I would never be able to do it.

Then, one year, I managed to climb the rope all the way to touch the ceiling. I was ecstatic and full of self-confidence after that experience. Every time I looked at the rope from then on, I knew I could climb it. If someone had pulled me up on that rope instead of encouraging me to struggle to climb it on my own, I never would have gained the inner strength and confidence of mastering a skill.

When you rescue people, you often undermine their ability to care for themselves, which weakens them, as the following Butterfly Story illustrates. In contrast, when people with an emotional charge learn how to care for themselves, it strengthens them. The skills of

Supportive Listening, which we will learn in the next few chapters, show us how to stand on the ground above the emotional well, hold a rope, and encourage the person with the charge to climb out on their own. This is the most effective way to care about other people because it supports their strength and independence rather than their weakness and dependency.

The Butterfly Story *(Author Unknown)*

I was jogging one evening in the park and came to rest, as was my custom, by a large rock. There I noticed a cocoon on the tree close by, and at that very moment, a butterfly was emerging from the cocoon. As I watched the butterfly struggle, I got the idea, "Gee, this is a tremendous symbol for what I do as a minister and counselor: help people out of their bonds. I help them fly."

So I reached up and very, very carefully began helping the butterfly to escape the small hole he had eaten in the cocoon, laid it on the rock close by and watched as the butterfly started to stretch its wings. I felt very happy about stumbling upon this miraculous scene and decided to use this story as the subject for my next sermon. I was greatly excited by this thought and before the day was out I had completed the sermon.

That same evening when I was running again I stopped by the same rock and saw the cocoon and, sure enough, the butterfly was off the rock and had fallen to the ground. I was stunned. I thought perhaps a bird or another insect had attacked it; but I examined it and there didn't seem to be anything damaged on the butterfly; it was just dead.

I was very upset about this, and I went home to look in my encyclopedias to try and determine what had happened. What I found out was that it is the struggle that the butterfly makes by forcing its way out of its cocoon and eating its way through its own bounds that enables it to gain enough strength to emerge whole and strong. The very action of fighting its way through the cocoon is what gives it the strength to fly.

The fact that I had tried to help by assisting the butterfly out of its cocoon had only made matters worse; I had, in fact, limited the butterfly's ability and strength and the butterfly was unable to fly on its own. By helping too much I had enabled the butterfly out of its bounds, yes, but in the process, I had killed it. The sense of my sermon changed. I began to realize how it is that people must not only be willing but also must do the work themselves to become more whole and complete.

Taking Responsibility for Our Emotional Charge

The Butterfly Story demonstrates how we can disable someone when we think we are helping them. It shows us how important it is to allow another person to handle their own difficulties, and underscores the significance of maintaining clear boundaries between our personal challenges and those of someone else. As much as we care about another person or want to shield them from pain, it is not our business to handle their dilemmas for them. And if we take responsibility for their well-being, we may unintentionally be defeating them.

Maintaining a clear boundary between us and remaining neutral when other people have an emotional charge does not mean we don't care about them or want to help them with their struggle. The point is that only by staying separate from their feelings *can* we genuinely help them. In the pictures of the emotional well, this is illustrated by the figure standing above the well holding a rope so the person in the well can climb out on their own. Just as the emerging butterfly had to struggle out of its cocoon, each one of us has to wrestle with our own emotional charges in order to become a whole and complete person.

The main idea of Emotional Responsibility is that the person with the strong emotions is the one responsible for them. This means simply that your feelings have more to do with you than with anyone else, and you are the one who can respond most effectively when you are upset. The chart of Emotional Responsibility below will help you to visualize who is responsible for the emotions in a charged situation, and introduce the primary skills of Conscious Communication that may be useful in responding. Each of these skills will be the focus of later chapters in this book.

Model of Emotional Responsibility

This Model of Emotional Responsibility illustrates four situations that are common in an interaction between two people. (See chart on the next page.) Three of the boxes in the chart represent situations where one or both people are upset. Each of these boxes identifies a specific set of skills that will be introduced later. This chart simply helps us orient ourselves to which situations require which skills.

No Problem Zone

The first situation is when both people are neutral. When there is no emotional charge, relationships tend to be more relaxed, easy, fun, and productive. However, it does not work to fake being neutral. If one of you has an emotional charge that is affecting the relationship, it will diminish your capacity for connection. If you choose to hide it, it will likely strain your ability to care about each other and undermine the trust and safety between you.

When the Other Person Owns the Emotion

Another situation occurs when the other person has an emotional charge and you are neutral. In this case, an effective response is to remain neutral and allow the other to feel their emotion without minimizing it or trying to fix it. You can then help them, if you choose, using Supportive Listening. (Chapters 7 – 12)

When You Own the Emotion

A third situation occurs when you have a strong emotion and the other person is neutral. In this circumstance, it is most effective for you to recognize and "own" your emotion before you do anything else. You may then choose to express it without blame or attack, using an Assertion Message. (Chapters 13 – 16)

When Both of You Are Emotionally Charged

The final possibility occurs when both of you have an emotional charge. These situations are often the most difficult to handle and usually require some combination of Supportive Listening, Assertion, and Collaborative Negotiation. (Chapters 17 and 18)

The purpose
of learning Conscious Communication skills
is to increase the amount of time a relationship spends
in the "no-problem zone."

Model of Emotional Responsibility

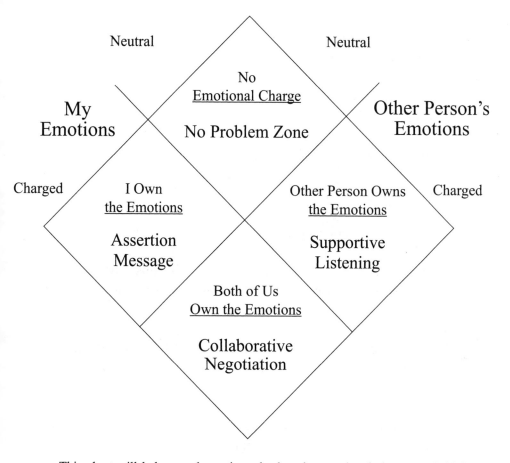

This chart will help you determine who has the emotional charge, and think about which skills to use. When the other person has an emotional charge, an effective response is Supportive Listening. When you are the one emotionally charged, Assertion may be useful. And when both of you are emotionally charged, a combination of Assertion, Supportive Listening, and Collaborative Negotiation may work to maintain the relationship, while you also take care of yourself. Each of these skills will be described in later chapters.

Who Owns the Feelings?

Below is a list of scenarios in which someone may have an emotional charge. See if you can identify who is most likely to have the strong feelings in each situation.

1. Your spouse comes home from work and is upset because dinner isn't ready.

2. You are frustrated with the mailman for driving over your roses.

3. Your son brings home three friends after school, and they eat all the cake you were planning to serve for dinner.

4. Your neighbor comes over very angry because your dog has just bitten his child.

5. Your children are throwing food in the living room.

6. Your friend says that you are never there when she needs you.

7. Your boss is upset because you arrived late to work.

8. You come home and your daughter is really upset because you forgot her piano lesson. She has been waiting for you to take her, and now it is too late.

9. Your six-year-old trips on his shoe lace, falls down, cuts his leg, and starts screaming at you that you should have tied his shoe better.

10. Your work partner forgets to fill out an important document and it means that your paycheck cannot go through this week.

11. A customer tells you that you did not do what he thought you agreed to do, and he wants his money back.

12. A delivery person is consistently late in delivering an important item that your business needs, and it means your product is delayed to your customers.

13. Your son wants to go over to a friend's house for the weekend, and you have already made other plans which mean that he cannot go.

14. Your teacher does not tell you about a pre-assignment, and you arrive for class unprepared.

15. Your employee does not complete a task you gave him on time, and it means you have to stay late to be sure it is done.

16. Your mother feeds your children candy when they go to visit her, and the children come home with too much energy and don't want to eat dinner or go to bed.

Chapter 6

Codependency

Codependency is when we give up our individuality in order to establish a connection with another person. We often blur the boundaries between us in an attempt to feel more connected. Previous chapters introduced some of the ways we do this, such as thinking we have to believe the same ideas, or confusing our emotions with those of someone else. In this chapter we will look at how this habit can lead to confusion and conflict in our relationships as we get our emotions and needs tangled up with each other's.

Until recently, our society was based on codependent relationships that followed a narrow script. Each person had a set role governed by rules of morality and social etiquette. With these clear social expectations came predetermined boundaries that were supposed to apply to all people at all times. For example, it was considered wrong for children to challenge their parents, for a woman to be assertive, or for a man to show emotion. Because our society had such clear notions of what was appropriate, we had little need to establish personal boundaries or be aware of our feelings and needs.

A society that is controlled by social norms and moral codes like this cultivates codependency. Instead of learning individual creativity and expression, we learned to conform to the wishes of other people. The goal was not personal growth or happiness, but simply fitting in with what was going on around us for the sake of uniformity. We learned that if we met the needs of others, our needs would be met. Basing fulfillment in life on being good and pleasing other people is what made this kind of society work.

While these rules of social behavior may create a sense of stability, they tend to stifle individual creativity and independence. Now, as personal freedom and creative expression have become more important, many of us are rejecting these traditional social structures because they do not allow us to become whole and unique individuals. We are rapidly outgrowing the need for society to determine our boundaries and limitations for us, and our primary focus these days is on personal growth and self-determination.

The old ways of conformity and codependency have to fall away if we want to learn new ways. We have taken the first step in this process by refusing to constrict ourselves to fit into a mold of social correctness, wanting instead to do it our own way. However, simply adopting a new ideal of personal empowerment does not change anything. Until we learn how to do things differently, we will automatically fall back into our old habits, even if they undermine what we want in our lives now.

Many of our struggles in relationships today are caused by old habits of codependency that no longer work for us. These familiar ways we use to try to join our lives with other people actually drive us further apart. When we try to get other people to adopt our beliefs, or we blame them for our emotions, it usually results in conflict that cannot be resolved and puts further distance between us. In this chapter, we will look at some of the habits we have learned that may offer a temporary sense of intimacy with another person but do not lead to a deeper sense of trust, safety, or connection in the long run.

Fear of Being Alone

While our shifting cultural values lead many of us now to want independence above all else, most of us still have a deep fear of being alone. This fear can create a sense of urgency to connect with others that takes us back into the murky waters of codependency. The weight of our own lives can feel so heavy at times that we just want someone else to be responsible. It seems that if we could merge with another person we would not have to carry the burden by ourselves. This strategy for trying to get help usually involves an unspoken agreement that we will take care of other people's emotions and needs if they will take care of ours.

Perhaps the root of our discomfort in being alone is our habit of basing our self-worth on what other people think of us. Instead of trusting our own instincts, we defer to the opinions of those around us. This puts us in the difficult position of needing other people's approval to feel good about ourselves. Our focus in relationships is frequently to get other people to like us and agree with our perceptions, rather than finding out what really makes us happy. This can make life feel like a wild roller coaster ride. One minute we are up because someone thinks we are great, and the next moment we come crashing down when they disapprove of us.

While we have a new ideal of individual freedom and independence, we remain stuck in our old habits of referencing to other people for our validation. Many of us do not feel complete unless we are receiving approval and recognition from someone else. We focus on doing things to please other people, fixing their problems, or in some way getting them to acknowledge and respect us. In such situations, however, we are motivated by our own need to be recognized, not by a genuine concern for the other person.

In our quest for recognition from other people, most of us want to be seen as generous, yet we are also afraid we will not get our needs met. We may try to deal with this problem by overlaying our self-concern with selfless giving. We assume that we cannot take care of our needs and care about another person at the same time. So, outwardly, we perform acts of giving while inwardly remaining anxious about our own well-being. This can create an impossible dilemma as we struggle between wanting to please other people and wanting to protect ourselves.

Hiding Our Self-interest

In close relationships, we may try to hide our self-serving instincts by making unconscious deals that we will take care of other people's needs if they will take care of ours. We blur the boundaries between us to make it look like we are caring, while in reality we are still focused primarily on ourselves. The agreement we end up with is that we are responsible for other people's happiness and they are responsible for ours.

The problem with this approach is that trying to hide our self-interest puts us out of integrity with ourselves. We become split internally between our personal needs and our desire for approval. Our attempts to care for others can become tactics to get what we want indirectly, and we may become entirely dependent on other people for our most basic needs. This tends to increase our fears and anxieties because our well-being depends on someone else and is out of our hands. If the source of what we need is another person, we can easily feel trapped and helpless.

When we try to play by the rules of social etiquette and put other people's needs before our own, we are trading politeness for true connection, and no one's real needs get met. We are trying to fit into a formula of goodness instead of actually learning and growing toward greater compassion and generosity. We hide our fear that we won't get what we want instead of dealing with it directly. Nothing changes when we try to be good and do not address our real concerns. Instead of growing beyond our basic fears, we simply ignore them, pretending they do not exist.

This common approach usually fails in the end because it does not heal the wounds we each carry that relentlessly demand our attention. Instead, we fake it and try to look as if we have no needs. Yet we do have needs, and we cannot genuinely offer help to others because we are so emotionally wounded ourselves. Until we deal effectively with our own fear and anxiety, we cannot help other people deal with theirs.

Whose Business Is It?

When we are involved in other people's business, we cannot tend to our own. This creates an unworkable situation where no one is tending to their own business because each of us is so focused on fixing or changing someone else. Then our problems go unsolved, and there is an unspoken expectation that *they* will take responsibility for fixing *our* dilemma because *we* have taken responsibility for *theirs*.

We commonly cross the boundaries of what is our business and what is another person's business with the people who are closest to us. Family, co-workers, close friends, and intimate partnerships seem to offer us a chance to be connected by merging our lives. Then we tend to relax the usual formalities, thinking that dropping the boundaries means we will be relieved of the burden of having to care for ourselves.

Initially, getting involved in other people's business does give us a wonderful sense of connection and belonging. We are part of someone else's life and are no longer struggling with our own problems alone. Letting down personal boundaries can be helpful at times to establish intimacy, yet mistaking our business for another person's often leads to confusion and conflict. This habit we have of taking on someone else's situation as if it were our own is responsible for much of the tension and struggle in our closest relationships.

The Need for Boundaries

It may seem counterintuitive, yet healthy boundaries actually create the safety and trust for deeper intimacy. This is one of those large life lessons that need to be learned from experience. It is similar to how we eventually learn that if we drink too much alcohol, we don't feel well the next day, or if we eat too much chocolate, we get a stomachache and gain weight. It is difficult for most of us to realize the need for clear boundaries in close relationships because it seems to be taking us in the opposite direction from what we want. It's hard to give up the idea that we can merge our life with someone else's and thereby solve the problem of isolation.

Growing a relationship beyond codependency requires that you become aware of what really happens when your emotions and needs become entangled with those of another person. You have to pay attention to the confusion and conflict that results from trying to take care of other people or expecting them to take care of you. As long as you believe it is serving you to feel responsible for each other's well-being, you will continue to do it. Only when you see for yourself that it is not deepening your love or connection are you likely to become willing to try something different.

Your emotions and needs are your own business, and other people's are theirs. It is simply not possible to fix or change another person. No matter how much you care about each other and want to be joined, we all have our separate lives to live. In the process of trying to save the other person, you will inevitably abandon yourself and end up feeling your isolation more painfully than before. In the end, blurring this fundamental boundary creates more disconnection and distance between you.

Allowing Room for Differences

In codependent relationships, the primary focus is on agreeing with each other and sharing the same opinions and preferences. If you like potatoes, then the other person should like them, and if you prefer cats to dogs, you want the other person to think this way, as well. Lining up your likes and dislikes often translates into closeness, because people so often define themselves by what they think is good and bad in the world.

The problem with this approach is that there is little room for individuality. If you have to agree on what is right and wrong in order to feel connected with another person, you may end up forcing yourselves to be like each other and therefore cannot be true to who you are. This attempt to merge with someone else often fails, because it does not allow each of you to be yourself.

> Codependency occurs
> when you sacrifice your need for independence in
> order to be accepted by another person.

This urge to find agreement creates even more tension when someone has been hurt. We tend to approach situations that have triggered an emotional charge by trying to establish what happened and who is responsible. Our legal system is based on finding out who is to blame when something bad happens. We look for a victim and a villain, thinking that if we explain the story of a traumatic event in terms of whose fault it is, we can resolve the situation.

Yet, attempting to resolve issues by reaching a consensus on what happened and what it means usually leads to more conflict. It is rare when our perceptions line up with someone else's. Most of us have different perspectives on the same situation, and trying to get our stories to agree can lead to intense power struggles. We find ourselves insisting that our perception is right and the other person's is wrong, because it is the only way we know how to think about conflict situations.

There is another option besides battling over who is right and who is wrong and trying to determine some absolute truth about a situation. You can let go of your urge to establish what happened and allow for both of you to have your own different point of view. Instead of trying to agree on what took place and who is responsible, you can recognize that each of you has a different perspective. You can allow other people to have *their own* individual way of seeing a situation, at the same time honoring and acknowledging *your own*, knowing there is *not* one right way.

This step is difficult for many of us to take because it seems as though we are giving up our capacity to determine true from false, which is the only handle on reality we think we have. Yet consider that every one of us has a unique interpretation of any situation, and our perspective informs us more about *ourselves* than about what occurred.

The key to taking this step is remembering that other people's stories are about them and have relatively little to do with you. Letting other people have their stories requires that you disengage from your automatic habit of referring their experiences to yours. You have to learn to simply let other people be themselves, separate and apart from you. To do this, it is essential to see that another person can have a very different point of view from yours, and that does not mean that you are wrong. Likewise, it does not mean they are wrong.

> Establishing a healthy boundary
> with another person
> means letting go of having to decide
> what is right and wrong for someone else.

Stop Comparing

If you let go of the habit of comparing points of view and trying to reach agreement, you will be able to see that other people are simply telling a story about how a situation is *for them*. Instead of trying to connect by lining up your perspectives on a situation, you can acknowledge the other person's experience as it is communicated through their story. If you can keep a healthy boundary between you and allow yourselves to have different ways of perceiving a situation, you can accept each other right where you are in the present moment.

This simple act of allowing and accepting is the key to true connection. What we most want in relationship is to be seen and acknowledged for who we are. Our mistake is that we have been trying to do this by getting our beliefs to match up. We have been assuming that acknowledging and accepting means agreeing and sharing the same perspective. Because we so rarely share the same perspective, this process fails most of the time, leaving us less connected than before we started.

The key to this new approach is to be more interested in what is going on for other people, and how their situation is affecting *them*, than in having your own perspective validated. It is usually not possible for both people to receive validation for our experience at the same time. Being conscious in communication begins with taking turns. If the other person has a strong emotional charge, and you can set aside your need for validation for a moment, then you can help them. And, when your emotional charge is dominating your experience, then you probably cannot help another person and you need to find a way to validate your own feelings.

This can be difficult because it requires that you disengage from needing to be right and having a story that neatly explains everything. However, it leads to greater intimacy because each of you is learning about the other person without trying to fix or change anything. Instead of comparing stories, you are simply listening in order to learn more about other people and how they are experiencing life in this moment.

Learning Self-validation

The root of codependency is looking to other people's judgments and evaluations about us to determine how we are doing. Many of us assume that seeking approval and recognition is the only way to receive validation. Yet, other people's perceptions really tell us about *them*, not about ourselves. There is no one right judgment or opinion about anything. Rather, each of us has our own personal truth that is about how *we* see a situation or how it affects *us*.

> Other people's ideas about the way you are
> come from *their* experience of you,
> and have little to do with who you really are.

Even your own judgments about yourself are relatively meaningless, because they change with your circumstances and moods. At one moment, you are the hero in your own story, and at the next moment you are the villain. If you give meaning to these thoughts, your sense of self-worth goes up and down constantly, and your life will be filled with uncertainty.

You can free yourself from the bonds of codependency by learning to accept yourself as you are, without the need for judgment or evaluation. The simplest and most direct way to do this is to recognize your immediate emotions and needs. Through this recognition, you validate your present experience and ground yourself in what is true for you right now. As you learn to do this, you will begin to care for yourself in a meaningful way, and this will allow you to let go of your constant need for approval from other people. Once you relax your demand for other people's approval, you become available to offer them genuine support and nourishment.

Validating Feelings and Needs

We begin to break patterns of codependency by allowing other people to have their emotions and maintaining a clear boundary between *our* feelings and needs, and *theirs*. A next step could be for us to actively *validate* their feelings and needs. The following chapters will show you how to recognize the present-moment experience of other people and help them to accept themselves as they are. When you acknowledge other people's experience without offering your opinions, you are giving them the recognition they seek without creating dependency on your approval.

I call this next set of skills Supportive Listening because it is a way to offer support to another person while strengthening their capacity to solve their own problems. This kind of support requires that we are able to set aside our own feelings and needs for a moment and give ourselves fully to someone else. To effectively let go of your own story and focus only on the other person for a moment is one of the greatest gifts you can give. It may take some practice for you to learn this, and the practical mechanisms suggested in these next chapters will show you how to begin.

This kind of listening also serves to maintain a healthy boundary between you and the other person. Instead of referring back to yourself and your preferences or opinions, you will learn to keep the focus on other people. Acknowledging their individual feelings and needs without comparing them with yours will effectively interrupt your tendency to want their ideas to agree with yours. In this way, you interrupt the habit of codependency and allow each of you the space to be your own person.

When you have your own emotional charge that is dominating your experience, it is usually not possible to support someone else.

The section after Supportive Listening, called Assertion, will describe specific ways you can validate your own feelings and needs, or ask for this validation from another person. Bringing our needs for validation and support out in the open, instead of trying to get what we want from other people in an unconscious way, effectively breaks our habit of codependency. As we learn to use these skills to help ourselves and other people meet our basic needs, the attraction of codependent relationships will simply fade away.

Supportive Listening

Chapter 7

Recognizing Other People's Feelings

Supportive Listening is for situations in which you feel neutral, the other person has an emotional charge, and you want to help them, or simply connect with them in a meaningful way.

> ## Supportive Listening is...
>
> creating a safe space for other people
> to discover their own feelings and needs,
> and begin solving their own problem.

When we think of safety, most of us think of protecting ourselves from physical harm. We have little knowledge of emotional safety. We are well aware of our emotional vulnerability but have not learned how to take care of ourselves effectively so that our feelings don't get hurt.

When we feel emotionally hurt, a common response is to set up permanent barriers around ourselves to prevent other people from hurting us again. Usually this involves attacking or withdrawing from those we believe are responsible for hurting our feelings. These automatic defenses often end up isolating us from other people, and they do not serve their intended purpose of keeping us safe. Instead, they make relationships unstable and increase the possibility for more emotional wounding.

This section will help you support other people who have an emotional charge by showing you how to offer them a safe space to talk about their experience. In the later chapters on Assertion, we will look at how you can make space for yourself when you have an emotional charge.

Being Neutral

An essential element in creating a safe space for another person is your own neutrality. The main reason unconscious communication habits tend to disconnect us from other people is that they contain judgments. In order for other people to feel safe with you, they need to sense that you are fully present and are not judging them. Once people sense that they are being judged, they automatically begin to shut down to protect themselves.

Practicing non-judgment is difficult for most of us because of the habit of reacting to other people by evaluating their behavior. Listening with neutrality means setting aside your own ideas. It is not that you are wrong or your opinions are bad. It is simply that…

> your judgments do not allow other people
> a safe space to talk openly
> about what is bothering them.

Practicing Presence

Another important element in helping other people feel safe is your presence. This can be difficult to learn because we are accustomed to letting our minds wander wherever they want to go. It is often easier to shut out external stimulation such as televisions or radios than it is to ignore your own thinking, which is nearly impossible to stop. Presence means giving the other person your full attention without being distracted by your thoughts or what is going on around you.

You can learn to set aside your own thoughts so you can listen supportively. To do this it may help to acknowledge an idea as it arises and imagine yourself picking it up and setting it to one side. As each new idea or distraction comes up, you simply file it in a mental drawer for later. You won't lose those ideas that are most essential, and after some practice, you will be able to call them up easily when you have a need to do so.

This is not as easy as it sounds because of the habit of giving constant attention to your own story. A practice such as meditation can be a useful way of learning to let go of your running commentary on what is happening, and focus in on a present experience instead. The skills of Supportive Listening offer another way to develop mental presence in your relationships. These tools give your mind something else to do besides thinking about yourself, reacting defensively, evaluating others, or trying to fix the other person's problems.

Setting the Stage

Your job as a supportive listener begins with paying attention to the physical environment. It is important to have some privacy and to minimize distractions. See what you can do to set the stage so the person with the emotional charge feels safe and comfortable enough to open up. You can invite them to go someplace where you can be alone or out of hearing range of other people. You might get physically closer to them, but not so close as to make them uncomfortable. And you can turn off the television, radio, computer, or music, and let the other person know by your body language that you want to be there listening to them. When you try to listen to other people while also focusing on something else, they will sense that they do not have your full attention, and this can discourage them from opening up.

Body Language

Attentive body language is common sense. Think about how you would know if another person was interested in listening to you. Usually this means maintaining an open, upright posture and facing others at their level; not from a higher or lower physical position. Pay attention to appropriate eye contact and the physical distance between you, and notice if the other person appears relaxed and comfortable with your presence. As a listener, always take your cues from other people's comfort. If they look strained, you can change your distance or level of eye contact until they relax a bit more.

It may be useful to notice if your body language is closed or open. When you cross your arms or legs, have a stern look on your face, slouch, or look away, your body signals that you are not open. When you uncross your arms and legs, sit up, and face them directly with a relaxed face, you indicate that you are interested.

Instead of making rules about this, try it out for yourself. When you notice your arms or legs crossed or your posture slumping, change to a more attentive posture and see what happens. You may notice that the other person relaxes, which usually makes them more interesting to listen to, as well.

Opening Questions

If someone appears upset and is not talking about it, you can invite them to talk by offering an opening question. Typical opening questions are:

"You look upset... Do you want to talk about it?" or

*"It looks like something's bothering you;
I've got time if you'd like to talk."*

Once you ask the initial opening question, it is important not to push the other person to talk. Examples of pushing are:

"You should really talk about this. You'll feel a lot better if you do." or

"You know you can trust me. Just go ahead and let it out."

Any pushing on your part is likely to make the situation feel unsafe for other people and may shut them down instead of helping them open up. If the other person does not respond right away to your opening question, it can help to be silent for a few minutes to let them feel it out. They are probably gauging the level of safety before they speak. If you have been pushy with them in the past, it may take some time before they trust that you are simply creating an opening and not trying to push them through it.

If there is no response after some minutes or the person says no, you can leave an opening for them to talk later by saying something like:

"If you want to talk later, just come and find me."

Then leave the situation alone. Talk about something else or leave the room. It is important that people learn to take care of themselves when they have strong emotions and ask for your help if they need it. Asking someone to listen can be difficult, yet it is a big step in beginning to be responsible for our own needs.

Attentive Silence

Sometimes attentive silence is useful, especially when you have just asked an opening question or the other person needs time and space to feel safe. If you are uncomfortable with silence, you may have a habit of filling in the space before the other person has a chance to talk. Pay attention to your comfort level with silence and stretch yourself to wait at least a minute for the other person to talk once you have offered an opening.

Nods and Simple Encouragements

If other people seem comfortable talking, you can show that you are following them by using simple encouragements, like nodding or saying words or sounds that convey your presence without interrupting. Some examples are:

"Oh, wow." "Uh-huh." "Mmm." "Yup, I see."

Basic Listening Skills in Action

Here is an example of a short conversation using some of these basic listening skills:

Imagine you have a teenage son who walks into the living room where you are reading a book. You notice him sit down on the couch, looking troubled about something, but he does not say anything. Common responses to this situation might be:

"What are you so glum about? Is the world coming to an end?" or

"Why don't you do something to cheer yourself up? No sense in moping around the house like this." or

"Look, whatever happened can't be that bad. You'll get over it. Just think about something else."

These are half-hearted attempts to show that you care about your son and want to help him feel better. While your intention may be to help, these statements can sound like you do not care or you want him to go away and take his dilemma with him. Such Disconnects are not likely to encourage your son to open up and talk about what is bothering him, and they tend to put more distance between the two of you.

Instead, you could offer your son an opening question, such as:

"Hey, you look pretty down. Do you want to talk about it?"

He may go right into his story, or he may be silent or say no. In that case, you could say:

"Well, if you do want to talk, I'm here."

This may create just the safety he needs to open up. He discovered you were not pushing or expecting something from him but were simply willing to be there as a neutral listener.

He might then say:

"Well, it's about this teacher at school. She called me up in front of the class to explain a story I had written."

In this case, he appears to want to talk and is opening up and telling you about what happened. Yet you still don't know much about his direct experience of the situation. Once your son is talking, he may only offer a bit of the story without revealing how he *feels* about it. If this happens, and you cannot recognize the emotion behind his story, you can try asking another opening question, like:

"What was that like for you?" or

"How do you feel about that?"

These questions convey interest in your son's experience without adding or suggesting anything. Opening questions allow him to talk about what he thinks is important and demonstrate that you are interested in learning about his experience. They also encourage the focus to stay on basic experiences, like emotions, rather than the facts or judgments in his story.

If he begins to talk more, you can practice attentive silence and open body language to indicate that you are interested and let him get it out without responding. In this example, he might say:

"She asked me all kinds of personal questions, and some of the kids in the back of the room started snickering."

A common response to this might be:

"I had a teacher do that to me once. Teachers can be real jerks sometimes. She's probably new at teaching and just doesn't know how to be sensitive to her students yet. Don't let it bother you."

This kind of response comes from using your head instead of listening to him with your heart, and is usually not helpful. You are making assumptions when you don't yet know how he is feeling or what the real problem is. If you respond to him in this way, he is likely to close up and not tell you more about his experience, and you will miss an opportunity to be more connected and offer him support. This is an example of using these Disconnects: Referring to Yourself, Taking Sides or Blaming, Analyzing, and Advising, with a bit of Reassuring.

Listening for Emotions

Once the stage has been set and a safe place established for someone with an emotional charge to talk, you can begin to listen for how he is feeling. People often tell stories about events in their lives that carry an emotional charge because they want their emotions to be acknowledged. And, if we recognize other people's emotions we can connect more deeply with what is going on for them in the moment.

> We often assume that recognizing
> our emotions will make them grow larger
> and cause us more discomfort.
> However, when we name them directly,
> our emotions actually begin to dissipate.

When you try this out, you will see that listening to other people's feelings and recognizing their emotions can help them let go of their charge. In the example we have been using about your son and his experience at school, you could reflect the emotions that seem to be present in his story by saying:

"It sounds like you felt very uncomfortable."

Hearing the other person's feelings is a matter of listening with your heart instead of your head. You can sense the emotions present by the way your son is talking or the content of his story. You can also take a guess at what he is experiencing based on the emotions you might have in a similar situation. Listening for emotions does not mean that you have to *know* what your son is feeling. Your job as a supportive listener is simply to show interest and support him in recognizing his feelings for himself.

Your reflection of his feelings will not be helpful if it contains judgment or if you have a hidden agenda. Suggesting feelings only works if you have a genuine desire to understand your son's experience without trying to change him in any way. You are simply expressing empathy for his situation. You are *not* telling him what he should be feeling or evaluating his feelings as right or wrong. Moreover, if he does not want to talk about his feelings, that is his business, not yours.

Reflecting the Other Person's Feelings

> Sometimes the most good lies in
> the simplest gestures, such as showing other people
> that we can see how they are feeling.

You can connect directly with another person's experience in the present moment by reflecting back the emotion you hear in their story with a real concern for how the situation is affecting them. Reflective statements begin the process of Supportive Listening. They shift you away from the habit of responding with a judgment or solution and keep your focus on an immediate experience instead. They also help you maintain a clear boundary between the other person's experience and your own.

Here are some helpful phrases for reflecting another person's feelings:

"You sound <u>sad</u>." "It sounds like you are <u>angry</u>."

"You seem <u>upset</u>." "It looks like you feel <u>hurt</u>."

It can be useful to develop a vocabulary for emotions so that you can talk about them more easily. Here is a list of some common emotions that can get you started thinking about what the other person might be feeling.

<u>Emotions</u>

Angry Sad   Hurt Afraid Upset Confused Annoyed Frustrated

Mad Overwhelmed Anxious Concerned Worried Tense Stressed

Alarmed Shocked Ashamed Guilty Embarrassed Humiliated

Exhausted Excited Happy Satisfied Proud Content Elated

Depressed Discouraged Depleted Hopeful Inspired Lost

Jealous Threatened Resentful Relaxed Relieved Vulnerable

Remember that you don't have to be an expert on what other people are experiencing. You only need to show interest, and they will often elaborate and say more precisely what emotions are present for them. The point is for *them* to understand what they are feeling and to know that you have recognized their feelings.

Below are statements that could be charged with emotion. As you read them, listen for feelings, and try writing down a reflection of the emotions you hear using this format:

"Sounds like you feel <u>*(emotion)*</u>**.** *or* **"You sound** <u>*(emotion)*</u>**."**

1. *"My dog got hit by a car today."*

2. *"Yesterday I got a call offering me this job I've been really wanting."*

3. *"Last month, I had some work done on my car and I just got the bill; it's over twice what they gave me for an estimate!"*

4. *"I've been trying to sort out this conflict I've been having with someone at work. We just go round and round over the same issues. I can't figure out whose stuff is whose."*

5. *"It's been going on for too long now; I just want to get to the bottom of it."*

6. *"She had no right to do that, and I'm going to let her know it!"*

7. *"This winter has been too long. I don't think I can take any more of it."*

8. *"What should I do? What would you do?"*

9. *"I've been waiting for this letter for weeks now. I hope it comes today."*

10. *"I hate my teacher! All he does is make fun of me when I can't get math problems right."*

11. *"Can't you figure anything out for yourself?"*

12. *"I just don't understand why he would do something like that."*

13. *"Didn't you ever think about how this would affect me?"*

14. *"Nobody seems to care about what I think."*

15. *"I just found out I got accepted at the university!"*

16. *"I'm just not sure what will happen if I leave this job."*

17. *"I can't believe that I hurt her like that. I am such a jerk!"*

18. *"Why can't you just mind your own business?"*

19. *"The whole class saw me cry when he threw that book at me."*

20. *"Why didn't you tell me about this sooner? What's the matter with you?"*

21. *"My boss drives me crazy. She tells me I'm doing fine, but during work meetings, she is always pointing out things I don't do right. I just don't get it."*

Chapter 8

Connecting Feelings with Facts

When your emotions are charged, it is like having a toxic substance running through your mind and body. It is common to try to rid yourself of an emotional charge by focusing on your thoughts instead of your feelings. Emotions seem fluid, mysterious, and unstable, so you may try to replace them with judgments that appear solid and certain. We often try to explain away our uncomfortable feelings by deciding whose fault it is or by drawing logical conclusions about the situation.

When talking about a difficult experience, we usually express our *judgments* instead of our *feelings* or the *facts* about the situation. This is a familiar way to verbalize an emotionally charged experience, and it follows a scripted formula we have all learned. When we feel threatened, we focus on other people who seem to want to hurt us. We think that we can best protect ourselves by treating others as the problem. So, we direct our judgments at them, instead of focusing on our own wounds.

Using the example from the previous chapter, your son might say something like:

> *"That teacher is a jerk, and those kids are idiots. I'm never going to open my mouth in that classroom again!"*

When he conceals his emotions with his rational conclusions in this way, he loses the ability to think clearly. His judgments are colored by his feelings and become erratic and inaccurate. He is mixing the *facts*, or what actually happened, with his *judgments*, or what he thinks happened, and meanwhile his *feelings* are being ignored.

This kind of response usually intensifies the problem. It can lead to power struggles as each side in the conflict tries to prove that the other is wrong in order to see themselves as right. In the ensuing drama, we often lose sight of what actually happened and do not deal with the real cause of our emotional charge. We come up with a solution that we think will make our emotions go away without addressing our feelings directly or finding out *why* we are having such a strong reaction.

When we rely on our rational mind to control our response we often end up overshooting the immediate problem. We *begin* expressing our concern in terms of *final conclusions,* such as judgments and solutions. This habit undermines our capacity to resolve our own emotional charge because we do not take time to discover what is causing our reaction. Instead we try to solve the situation immediately, before we really understand it.

> When you confuse judgments with facts,
> you are responding to an *idea* you have
> about what happened,
> and not to *what actually took place.*

Separating, Facts, Feelings, Judgments, and Solutions

If you want to support someone who is having an emotional charge, you can begin by helping the person recognize and separate out the facts and feelings from judgments and solutions. Here are some of the facts, feelings, judgments, and solutions from the example we are using:

The facts: The teacher asked him personal questions about his story in front of the class.

His feelings: He felt hurt, embarrassed, and angry.

His judgments: The teacher is trying to humiliate me; the other kids think I am a dork; it is best not to say anything in this class.

His solution: I won't talk in that class anymore.

The most real aspects of a story are the events that stimulated the emotions (facts) and the emotions themselves (feelings). The rest are things we make up, such as our judgments and solutions. We tend to mistake these subjective evaluations for the truth, and then we base our response on them, as though they were real.

> The biggest obstacle
> to solving our own problems
> is that we frequently confuse reality
> with what we make up.

By listening supportively, you can help other people recognize what is real in their story and what part they added, so they can respond more effectively. You can separate out the judgments and solutions from the facts, and then connect the facts with feelings. And you can reflect the facts and feelings back to the other person with phrases like these:

"*So you feel* (emotion) *when* (facts).*"* Or

"*Sounds like you feel* (emotion) *about* (facts).*"*

These responses focus on the raw emotions and the simple event that triggered them, and intentionally leave out any of the speaker's judgments or solutions.

A supportive response to the last comment in our ongoing example might be:

> **"*It sounds like you felt* hurt and embarrassed *when* the teacher asked you personal questions in front of the class."**

Here are some more examples of connecting feelings and facts and leaving out the judgments:

Emotionally charged statement	Neutral reflection of feelings and facts
"I hate this job. All we ever do is try to figure out what that jerk of a boss wants from us, and we end up wasting half the day."	*"It sounds like you feel frustrated and angry when you don't know exactly what your boss wants."*
"I've called her every day for a week, and she just keeps blowing me off."	*"You sound upset about her not returning your phone calls."*
"He can't stand to be around my family, but look at his. What a bunch of arrogant snobs!"	*"Sounds like you feel hurt that your partner is uncomfortable being around your family."*

Emotionally charged statement	Neutral reflection of feelings and facts
"She is so rude. She wouldn't even look at me during that meeting."	*"Sounds like you feel hurt when she doesn't acknowledge you at a meeting."*
"That teacher is an idiot. He never listens to what anyone else has to say and thinks he is always right."	*"You sound really frustrated that you can't seem to get your point of view across to this teacher."*

Discerning Facts from Judgments

Because our habit has been to focus on our conclusions and obscure the actual events, most of us need to learn how to tell the difference between facts and judgments. Focusing on facts is different from asking questions to determine what happened. The facts we are looking for here are simply the most tangible parts of the story the other person has already told us. Facts are relatively simple and can usually be described in a short sentence or phrase. To find the facts, strip away any evaluation that has been added. With practice, you can learn to hear the judgments in a person's story and simply leave them out.

Here are some examples of separating facts and judgments:

Facts (what *actually* happened)	Judgments (what *we think* happened)
"You came home later than usual."	*"You don't care about me." "You forgot about me." "You don't want to spend time with me."*
"You spoke to me in a loud voice and appeared to be angry."	*"You attacked me." "You dumped your emotions on me." "You abused me."*

<u>Facts</u> (what *actually* happened)	<u>Judgments</u> (what *we think* happened)
"You did not do the dishes when you said you would."	*"You don't care about anyone else but yourself."* *"You are lazy and don't want to help out."* *"You don't care about me."*
"You did not talk to me when you came home."	*"You are upset with me."* *"I did something to upset you."*
"You ended our relationship."	*"You abandoned me."* *"You rejected me."*
"You charged me more than we had agreed."	*"You cheated me."* *"You took advantage of me."*
"You didn't show up at our scheduled meeting."	*"You forgot about our meeting."* *"You blew off our meeting."* *"You don't care about me."*

When you break down a story by separating facts and judgments, the story begins to lose its appeal because your conclusions appear less real and solid than you thought. Once your story loses its appeal, you are more willing to let it go. You can then look at it from a distance and eventually perhaps see it with a gentle sense of humor. This gives you room to focus on your own emotional charge and begin to address the real underlying cause of your reaction.

Confusing Feelings with Thoughts

A common way we blur the distinction between our thoughts and feelings is to use the words *"I feel..."* when we really mean *" I think...."* In the previous example, when the boy was talking about his experience in school, he said:

"That teacher is a jerk, and those kids are idiots. I'm never going to open my mouth in that classroom again!"

To help him focus on his immediate experience you might ask:

"How do you feel about that?"

He might say:

"I felt like I wanted to get out of there and never go back again!"

In this statement, he is using the phrase *"I felt like"* to describe what he was thinking, not what he was actually feeling. When talking about an emotionally charged situation, it is common to use the expression *"I feel like..."* or *"I feel that..."* to describe a judgment or conclusion. For example:

*"**I feel that** I am being taken advantage of."* or
*"**I felt like** I wanted to hit him."*

Usually, statements that begin with the words *"I feel like..."* or *"I feel that..."* are not feelings. They are conclusions about what is happening or solutions that try to fix the problem. The feelings indicated by these statements might be *hurt, angry, frustrated,* or *helpless.*

When you confuse the words *think* and *feel,* you blur your thoughts and emotions again and make it more difficult to address the actual problem. Therefore, when separating feelings from thoughts, it is very important to avoid using the words, *"you feel"* when you mean *"you think."* This allows the use of the word *"feel"* to refer to emotions and the word *"think"* to refer to ideas.

Acknowledging Other People's Judgments

Sometimes people insist on asserting their interpretations as facts. In this case, acknowledging their opinions can sometimes help them to feel recognized. In situations where we sense it may be useful to recognize the speaker's judgments, it is more accurate and offers a cleaner perspective to reflect these as *thoughts.* This way they do not become confused with *feelings* or *facts.*

These phrases can be useful for reflecting back judgments:

"You think...", "In your judgment...", or
"From your perspective..."

In the ongoing example, to acknowledge the boy's feelings, the facts, *and* his judgments, you could respond with a statement like this:

*"It sounds like you **feel** hurt and embarrassed when the teacher asks you personal questions in front of the class, and you **think** they were all being mean or insensitive, and don't want to put yourself in a situation like that again."*

It takes practice to recognize the misunderstanding that arises from this common tendency to confuse thoughts and feelings, and so I have provided more examples of these kinds of situations:

Emotionally charged statement	Reflection of emotions, facts, *and* judgments
"I hate that jerk. He cheated at the poker game and took my money from me."	*"It sounds like you feel angry about losing your money to him, and **you think** he didn't play fairly."*
"I can't believe that guy. That is the third time this month he has beat me out of a deal. He has really got it in for me."	*"You sound really angry that he got these deals before you, and **you think** he is doing this to hurt you."*
"That teacher is really lame! He talks all the time and never lets anyone even ask questions. I feel that he shouldn't be allowed to teach here."	*"It sounds like you feel upset with the way your teacher talks in class, and **you think** the school should not hire him again."*
"I feel like we should leave."	*"It sounds like you are feeling uncomfortable and **you think** we should go."*

Listening Supportively

In the ongoing example about your son, you have stayed present with him and acknowledged his emotions and the situation that triggered them. You let him know that you care without trying to solve his problem for him or minimize his feelings. This may help him feel safe enough to open up more. He might go on to say:

> *"Yeah, I was really nervous, and it was hard to look at people. The words kept getting stuck in my throat, and I had a hard time speaking."*

You can continue to use Supportive Listening to let him know you are following him:

> *"So you felt nervous when the teacher asked you those questions, and you had a hard time looking up or just getting the words out."*

He might continue:

> *"Yeah, I started to turn red and could feel myself getting so hot, I was beginning to sweat. The other kids in the class were starting to giggle, and I felt like an idiot, but the teacher didn't notice any of this and kept asking me her stupid questions."*

And you could reply:

> *"It sounds like you felt uncomfortable with the teacher's questions and angry that she was not paying attention to what was happening for you. You also seem embarrassed about your response in front of the other kids, and upset with them for making fun of you."*

These responses let your son know that you care about his situation and understand some of what the experience was like for him. Supportive Listening allows you to join with him in his dilemma so he does not feel so alone, yet it leaves the problem in his hands to resolve. In this way, you are truly supporting him.

In the example we have been using, imagine that your son continues:

"Yes! I could not believe she kept going on and on. I had no idea what she wanted from me. The more questions she asked, the more I stumbled on my words and kept repeating myself. All I could think of was how stupid I sounded, and how much I wanted to leave. It seemed like the teacher was trying to make fun of me."

Try a response using this format: So you felt _____

when _____

and you think_____

Changing Old Habits

The intention of Supportive Listening is to demonstrate empathy for the other person's struggle. Knowing that you see their dilemma and care about them can give other people the strength and courage to take care of themselves and work on fixing their own problem. This simple listening format can offer the other person a hand to hold in their journey through a difficult time.

Sometimes this way of responding by reflecting feelings and facts may seem mechanical and not genuine. It is often so different from how we are used to communicating that it sounds fake or rehearsed. Remember that what seems most natural to you are merely the habits you have learned from other people. Of course, changing these habits now is going to feel uncomfortable and seem unnatural.

The usual response to another person's emotional charge is to fix them or compare their experience with your own. Learning to relate to another person's feelings without comparing, judging, or rescuing naturally requires some practice. Supportive Listening phrases are designed to break these old habits and redirect your attention toward the other person's experience. By using the specific responses suggested in this book, even if they seem artificial, you can effectively interrupt the unconscious habit of making other people's dilemma about you or trying to analyze or advise them.

Guidelines for Reflecting Feelings, Judgments, and Facts

Feelings

- Use words that refer to emotions, rather than ideas (see list in appendix).
- Use one or two words only; more are likely to be overwhelming.
- Avoid feeling words that place blame, like abused, violated, rejected, or abandoned.
- When you find yourself using a blaming word, ask yourself:

"How do I feel when I think someone has <u>abandoned</u> me?"

This will lead you to a more neutral feeling word, like *hurt, sad,* or *angry.*

If you hear yourself saying: "So, **you feel *like*...**" or "It sounds like **you feel *that*...**", **stop and start over.** The most likely things to follow **"*like*"** or **"*that*"** are opinions and interpretations, not emotions. For example:

*"So you **feel like** he cheated you."* or

*"Sounds like you **feel that** she should not be teaching here."*

These reflections tend to reinforce the other person's *story* about what happened and skip over the more immediate experience of their emotional response.

Judgments

If you are going to include the speaker's opinion in your Supportive Listening response, be sure to preface it with **"*you think*"** instead of **"*you feel.*"** Keep the word **"*feel*"** associated with emotions and **"*think*"** associated with thoughts and opinions.

Facts

- Listen for the circumstance or actual event that sparked the speaker's emotion.
- Keep the reflected story factual, and avoid the speaker's interpretations and opinions.
- Keep the facts specific enough to let the speaker know you heard them, yet simple enough not to get bogged down in details.

Listening for Feelings, Facts, and Judgments

Try responding to the following examples by filling in the blanks after each one.

1. *"She is the worst listener! She never hears anything I say and always makes the conversation about her. I don't know why I bother talking to her."*

So you feel (emotion) _____

when (fact) _____

_____

and you think (judgment) _____

_____

2. *"I can't believe he did this to me again! He is so lazy. He doesn't care about anyone but himself. He always leaves the car without any gas and I have to find a gas station before I can go anywhere, and then I'm late."*

It sounds like you feel (emotion) _____

when (fact) _____

_____

and you think (judgment) _____

_____

3. *"Why can't she grow up? She whines about everything we ask her to do and acts like it's some huge burden that we want her help around the house. I am sick of her complaining and sometimes just don't want anything to do with her."*

So you're feeling (emotion) _____

about (fact) _____

_____

and you think (judgment) _____

_____

Chapter 9

Identifying Needs

Once you can separate feelings, facts, and judgments, you can focus on the underlying cause of an emotional reaction. Strong emotions are usually a signal that some need is calling for our attention. Underneath an emotional charge is a basic requirement for health or happiness that is not getting met. Using Supportive Listening, you can often help someone else with an emotional charge recognize their basic need and begin to resolve their own problem by finding a way to meet that need.

Emotions Are Warning Lights

Strong negative emotions are like the red warning lights on the dashboard of a car. When a light comes on, it is a signal to pay attention to some need the car has, such as gas, oil, a battery that needs charging, or a door that needs to be shut. If you pay attention to the light and take a moment to understand the basic need it is pointing to, you can usually solve the problem easily. Owning a car requires learning these basic maintenance skills so you don't damage your vehicle.

Sometimes when a red light comes on, you get an uncomfortable feeling that something is wrong with your car but have no idea what to do about it. If you don't know how to maintain a car, it is easy to see the red warning light *as* the problem, not the *indicator of* a problem. In that case, you may ignore it or even cover it up, thinking that will make the problem go away. Yet, if you do not respond to a warning light, sooner or later something will go wrong with the vehicle and you will have a much bigger problem.

If you think of emotions as the warning lights of your personal well-being, you can see a similar pattern. Many of us see emotions *as* the problem, not as a signal that a basic need requires attention. We try ignoring our feelings or overriding them with our judgments, hoping they will go away. Then our basic needs never get directly addressed or adequately met.

Few of us have skills or experience in self-maintenance. No one ever talked to us about how to take care of ourselves emotionally or identify our own needs. Most of us probably know more about how to maintain our cars than our emotional well-being. Given the lack of knowledge and experience we have, it is natural that our primary strategy for dealing with emotions and needs is to ignore them.

However, when we don't pay attention to the needs that underlie our strong emotions, both the needs and the emotions grow stronger and occupy more of our time and energy. We may try to suppress them, or get someone else to notice and take care of them for us. Yet, if our basic needs are not taken care of, eventually we suffer a breakdown, just as a car would if we never filled it up with oil or put gas in it.

We all have needs, just as our cars do. We may not like having them because they seem to bog us down with maintenance when we just want to cruise. Having needs can bring up feelings of vulnerability and helplessness, especially if we don't know how to get them met. However, having needs is not optional. Our only choice is how we respond to them.

There are basic skills that will help you take care of yourself, which are relatively easy to learn. Once you learn them, your emotions will no longer run your life, and your relationships will become easier and more satisfying. It is like learning how to add window washer fluid, oil, or gas to your car. Once you do it a few times, it becomes natural and effortless. The skills themselves are not complex or hard to remember, but practicing them is difficult because for so long our habit has been to neglect our needs and ignore the emotions that signal them. For this reason, it may take some time and effort to become aware of them again.

Recognizing Needs

I was spending time with a friend one day when she began to sound irritated and upset with me. I became confused, thinking I had said or done something to upset her, but not having any idea what that was. Fortunately, I remembered to let her have her emotions and just be there with her, not knowing what she was upset about.

A few minutes later, she realized that she was really hungry and needed to eat. She also recognized that she had been feeling upset and had directed some of those feelings at me. She apologized and explained how being hungry often emotionally agitates her. We went to get her some food, and immediately she began to feel better.

It is common for us to be out of touch with our basic needs in this way. Most of us learned this habit as infants. When we were babies, we had many needs we could not meet for ourselves. We also had no language to express what we wanted, so we often kicked and screamed, hoping someone else would fix the problem for us.

The parents or adults in such situations have to guess what it is their children need. When they cannot guess, they may get frustrated and react to children's "tantrums" by ignoring them, disciplining them, or offering them treats to get them to stop. Adults often try to get their children to stop crying in any way they can, instead of finding out what their real needs are and helping them meet those needs.

As we grow up, this pattern continues, and we often never learn how to clearly express or meet our needs. We rely on addictive habits that make our emotions go away without addressing the real needs underlying them. Or we pretend that we have no needs, while secretly trying to get other people to take care of them for us. So, the first step in caring for ourselves is accepting that we *have* basic needs. Once we recognize what our needs are in this moment, it is much more likely we will find a way to get those needs met.

> Many of us get stuck repeating
> the same strategies that never really work
> because we don't take time to
> understand what we need.

Self-maintenance

Some time ago I bought an old farmhouse in the country, and after moving in, I realized that it was a complete wreck. The pipes in the basement were squirting water, windows and doors were broken or missing, the roof leaked, the cellar had holes to the outside, and there were rats living in the walls. I felt overwhelmed and depressed and wondered why I had done such a foolish and impulsive thing. I had only a few skills and tools to repair a home, and the situation seemed hopeless.

Once I got over being sorry for myself, I began by doing the only thing I could: taking the problems one by one and focusing on each until it was solved. I learned about copper water pipes and how to fix them, found out how to keep the cellar from freezing, and got a trap for the rats. To my amazement, I discovered that, taken one by one, the problems were not too much for me to solve. When I focused my attention on a particular problem, instead of on all of them together, the solution often became obvious and relatively simple to implement.

The same is true for our personal needs. Taken as a whole, they can seem overwhelming and impossible to attend to. Yet each need in itself is relatively simple, and the solution is often obvious, if we try to handle only one at a time. The challenge for most of us is to recognize our needs as they arise and take the time to focus on each one until it is resolved. Like my friend who was hungry, or my house that needed so many repairs, if we take time to learn the specific need, a logical solution often presents itself.

> The only thing
> that resolves the tension of an unmet need
> is to find a way to meet it.

Some Basic Human Needs:

Food   Water   Air   Clothing   Shelter   Warmth   Sleep   Recreation   Exercise

Appreciation   Connection with other people   Recognition   Support   Love

Money   Transportation   Work   To feel useful   To help other people

Safety   Security   Stability   Respect   Solitude   Peace   Health   Comfort

Connection with higher self - source - God   Self-esteem   Sense of belonging

Independence   To feel powerful   To contribute to another person's well-being

Intimacy   Personal space   Inspiration   Rest   Purpose   Meaning   Joy   Energy

This list is just a suggestion. You may recognize some of these, while others may not be true for you. The list is meant to simply encourage you to think about what is essential for your health and happiness so you can take better care of yourself. Needs are different for each person and each situation, and your needs change constantly. You have to be able to sense what your basic requirements are in the present moment because no one else can do that for you.

Basic needs are different from the endless list of things we desire. Usually, our cravings are for things we think will help us *meet* our needs. We may need love, for example, and feel a desire for sex. Or we may need comfort and feel a desire for sweet or fatty foods. We frequently confuse our needs with ways of meeting them in this way.

When we confuse needs with desires like this, we often make life much more difficult for ourselves. We tend to put all our energy into what we think will make us happy instead of focusing on getting our real needs met. We become obsessed with getting the *solution* we think will work, while tending to forget about the *actual need* we were trying to meet.

While needs vary and change, we all share the same basic requirements for survival and fulfillment. You can know you have identified a basic need when it is something most people want. Identifying needs can bring you closer to other people, because you can recognize the other person's need as similar to your own. The benefit of learning about your basic needs and how to meet them effectively is that, once your needs are met, you tend to relax and feel happy. Learning how to get your own needs met gives you a sense of confidence and trust in life.

Physical Needs

The most obvious needs we have are our physical requirements for survival. Everybody needs water, air, food, sleep, and some protection from the elements to keep the body alive. We cannot ignore these for long without tangible consequences. Noticing these needs as they arise and being responsible about getting them met, is a good way to begin taking care of ourselves.

We can learn what kind of food is good for us and how much to eat so that we feel nourished but do not harm ourselves. We can pay attention to how much sleep we need, how warmly to dress, how much water to drink, and even how deeply we breathe. Given how obvious these basic physical needs are, it is surprising how often we neglect them because we are busy with other concerns, or don't think they are important. If we do not learn how to meet our physical needs, however, our physical health suffers, and we have bigger problems to deal with.

The consequences of not eating healthy food, drinking water, getting exercise, or tending to other bodily needs are fairly obvious. In this way, the body is much like a car. It needs fuel, fluids, and maintenance, and without them it stops working well. Most of us have some experience with this and can recognize the importance of meeting these basic needs on a regular basis. Still, it often takes some focused effort and practice to tend to our physical well-being.

Emotional Needs

The rest of our needs are less obvious because they have to do with how we feel inside. I call these emotional needs because we feel more relaxed and fulfilled when these needs are met. While the first set of needs are requirements for physical health, this second set are requirements for emotional health. Emotional needs are often more difficult to identify, easier to ignore, and the consequences for disregarding them harder to notice.

When we are feeling afraid and needing support and do not find a way to meet this need, the fear usually grows larger. It can generate stress and tension in the body and color our thoughts. We may find ourselves worrying obsessively or trying to formulate a plan that will dissolve the fear. And if the emotion becomes too overwhelming, we often try to numb ourselves in some way, just to get rid of it.

Our emotional needs, like support or understanding, are what make us different from machines. Taking care of ourselves is not as simple as feeding and clothing our bodies, and these inner needs often complicate our lives and cause us pain. While some of our relationships are about meeting our physical needs for food or shelter, many of our interactions with other people are about meeting our emotional needs.

When we are unconscious of our basic needs, relationships become more difficult because we don't know how to ask for what we want, and it is not clear how to help and support each other. We end up indirectly approaching our needs by hinting or trying to control other people, and we often have emotional charges that keep recurring without resolution.

When we are aware of our needs and able to express them clearly, we build honesty and trust with other people. It creates a solid foundation for our relationships and frees us from recurring emotional charges. Communicating more consciously strengthens our connections because it helps us meet each other's needs effectively. Helping another person also meets our need for belonging and gives our lives a sense of purpose. We are all interconnected in this way. Knowing what we want from other people aids this process and keeps our relationships healthy and nourishing.

Separating Needs from Solutions

As we discussed earlier, our needs can seem obscure or complicated because we often confuse needs with solutions, which are *ways to get those needs met*. Most of us express our needs initially as solutions. For example, if a woman is feeling frustrated with the way meetings in her workplace drag on and drain her energy, she might begin talking about it by saying:

"I don't want any more meetings!"

Normally, this kind of statement is accompanied by body language and vocal tones that let us know there is an emotional charge behind it. She may have a scowl on her face, and her voice may be loud and express frustration, resentment, or anger. The words she is using, however, do not tell us about her emotions or needs. They tell us about a solution that would solve her problem, but do not tell us what the problem is.

Not having any more meetings is a *solution*, not a need. A solution is a strategy for meeting needs. When we are trying to release emotion or solve a problem, we often begin by describing the outcome we want. Talking about solutions seems safer and more certain than expressing basic needs.

Like the habit of expressing our judgments instead of our feelings, communicating solutions allows us to appear sure and decided, while voicing our basic needs leaves us open and vulnerable. We usually prefer being seen as strong and knowing what we want out of a situation, rather than as people who have needs we don't yet know how to fix.

The problem with this approach is that it does not work very well. When we grasp onto a solution before we have identified the need the solution is trying to address, there is little chance of actually getting the need met. We are putting the cart before the horse. Although it makes little sense, this habit of jumping to solutions is the most common way we respond to uncomfortable emotional charges.

As supportive listeners, we can translate a comment like the previous one about meetings at work into basic feelings and needs. We have already learned how to listen for feelings and the situation that triggered them. So we can begin hearing and reflecting back what is going on for her by saying something like:

> *"It sounds like you are really frustrated with meetings at work."*

Listening for Impacts

As you have seen, listening in this way can enable you to understand the woman in the example and help her to feel supported. If you want to further support her, you can try to understand the need of hers that is not getting met. To do this, pay attention to the *impact* the meetings at work have on her.

Often a simple Supportive Listening response like the last one encourages the other person to tell us more. She may say something like:

> *"Yes, they just go on and on, and after they are over, I feel so exhausted I just want to go home and go to bed!"*

In this statement, we can hear more about how the situation is affecting her. She acknowledges that her *feeling* is frustration and the *fact* that is triggering her emotions is that there are meetings at work. Her *judgment* is that these meetings are too long, and the *impact* on her is that she feels exhausted.

The important information to listen for is the impact the situation is having on her, instead of her judgments or conclusions. This helps her to discover her basic needs that are not being met so she can find a way to meet them, and thereby resolve her emotional charge. In some cases, as we discussed earlier, it may help to acknowledge the other person's judgments. However,

> judgments often make it harder to solve a problem because they block us from seeing things from a different point of view, and thereby limit our options.

So, a complete Supportive Listening response usually includes only the **feelings, facts,** and **impacts**, and leaves out the judgments.

To reflect back to her all this information in a complete Supportive Listening response we might say:

> *"So, **you feel** frustrated **when** you have to attend meetings at work **because** you feel exhausted afterwards."*

The format for this three-part listening statement is:

Feelings: *It sounds like you feel* (emotion)

Facts: *when* (situation that stimulated the emotion),

Impacts: *because you* (tangible impact this situation has on the person speaking).

When you reflect back the impact the situation is having on the person telling the story, you help her connect with her need. Until you can see clearly how a situation is affecting you personally, you cannot find an effective solution because you don't know what you need. Once you recognize the tangible impact a situation has on your life, you can figure out what basic need is not being met and start thinking about how to meet it.

In the example we are using, the woman's need might be for more energy during meetings at work. This perspective opens up the situation and reduces the sense of hopeless struggle. Once she shifts her focus to basic needs, instead of one particular solution (which often seems impossible to attain), the problem is clearer and other solutions can come into view.

Three-Part Supportive Listening

Supportive Listening is intended to help other people recognize:

1. **Feelings**: the emotions they are having
2. **Facts**: the event that stimulated those feelings
3. **Impacts**: the tangible effect of that event on their lives

Here is how listening for these three parts could work in another situation where a man comes to us with this statement:

"I can't believe my boss did this to me. I am quitting this job right now, and never going back there to work!"

This statement is obviously loaded with emotion, and it also contains an instant solution for dealing with that emotion. The emotion is something like anger, frustration, or hurt, and the solution is to leave his job.

Leaving the job may offer some temporary relief from the emotion by eliminating the situation that triggered it, but this solution will not resolve the problem because it does not recognize the need that is not being met. If he does not find the basic need connected to his feelings, he will have little chance of resolution and will likely experience the same conflict again in a new situation. This is why we tend to repeat the same relationship patterns in our lives and often feel powerless to do anything about them.

We help this person the most by listening for and reflecting his emotions and the impact the situation is having on him. Then he can more easily recognize his basic needs and explore ways to meet those needs.

In this example, a three-part listening response could be:

*"It sounds like **you feel** angry **about** what happened at work today, and you don't want to go back there **because you** don't feel comfortable with what your boss did."*

He might respond:

"Yeah, that jerk of a boss of mine told me I was not pulling my weight right in front of the whole department. I just wanted to haul off and punch him."

And you might respond:

*"**So you felt** hurt and embarrassed **when** your boss said you were not pulling your weight in front of your co-workers **because** you didn't feel respected?"*

If you are getting a close enough reflection of the other person's experience, he might say something like: "You got that right!" or a respond with a loud. "Yeah!" Often there will be some sign of relief, such as a more relaxed tone of voice or body posture. This indicates that his basic emotions and needs are being recognized. Then you can move on, knowing that you have helped him to better understand his problem.

Notice that nothing done so far in the example involves opinions or judgments. Supporting the other person does not mean evaluating his situation or offering him solutions. Any such attempts on our part to fix his problem would involve *our* emotions and needs, not *his*. All we are doing here is helping him recognize the basic elements of what he is dealing with so he can more easily find his own solution.

Here is another example of Supportive Listening. Suppose someone you know has a small business, and one day she says to you:

"This stupid business isn't ever going to make it. Every year we end up losing money. I feel like throwing the whole thing out and going to look for a real job."

You could respond:

*"**You sound** really frustrated and discouraged **when** you keep losing money in this business, **because you** put a lot of work into it that you are not getting paid for."*

Here are more examples of this kind of listening:

Emotionally Charged Comment	Three-part Supportive Listening
1. *"I hate that teacher! Today she laughed at me when I did not know the right answer. It made me feel like such an idiot."*	*" So, you felt hurt when she laughed at your mistake, because you lost confidence in yourself?"*
2. *"I don't like it when you take my coat without asking me first. I had to find something else to wear and I was cold all day."*	*"You sound angry that I borrowed your coat without asking you first, because you had no coat to wear and you got cold."*
3. *"He's such a jerk! He always yells at me for no reason. I don't want to talk to him again."*	*"It sounds like you are upset that he raised his voice when talking to you because you felt bad about yourself and did not feel safe being around him."*
4. *"I can't do this homework assignment! The teacher never explained anything and I don't even know what I am supposed to do."*	*"You seem frustrated when the teacher does not explain homework assignments clearly, because you don't know what to do."*

Here are the feelings, facts, and impacts for the above examples separated out so you can see them clearly:

Feelings	Facts	Impacts
1. Hurt	someone laughed when you made a mistake	you lost confidence in yourself

Feelings	Facts	Impacts
2. Angry	I borrowed your coat without asking you first	you had no coat to wear today and you were cold
3. Upset	he raised his voice when talking to you	you felt bad about yourself and unsafe with him
4. Frustrated	the teacher did not explain the homework assignment clearly	you don't know what to do

In the following examples, listen for emotions, facts, and impacts, and write a response using this three-part format:

So you feel (<u>feelings</u>),   ***when*** (<u>facts</u>),   ***because you*** (<u>impacts</u>).

1. *"This homework is stupid. I can't even figure out what the teacher wants me to do. I am just going to tell her tomorrow she is a lousy teacher and doesn't know how to give assignments."*

So you feel _____

when _____

_____

because you _____

_____

2. *"I hate that coach. I can't believe he cut me from the team without even talking to me. He is such a jerk. I never want to see him again."*

So you feel _____

when _____

_____

because you _____

_____

3. *"I don't know how to deal with my husband. He never talks to me anymore and acts like I don't even exist most of the time. I'm just going to ignore him and see how he likes it if I don't talk to him!"*

So you feel _____

when _____

_____

because you _____

_____

4. *"My father never listens to me. He always thinks he knows what is right and he just lectures at me all the time. I can't wait to get out of his house. Meanwhile, I'm just going to pretend to listen so he doesn't go ballistic on me, but I won't hear a word he says. As far as I'm concerned, he can take all that moralistic crap and shove it!"*

So you feel _____

when _____

_____

because you _____

_____

5. *"If she thinks she can get away with that, she better think again! Nobody treats me that way without paying for it! I am going to show her. When I get through with her, she'll wish she never said anything about me to those jerks!"*

So you feel _____

when _____

_____

because you _____

_____

6. *"I can't believe he left me for that woman! After seven years of marriage, he just walked out without a word. I never want to see that jerk again. If I ever get a chance to hurt him, he better watch out. He'll be sorry for treating me this way!"*

So you feel _____

when _____

_____

because you _____

_____

7. *"I'm so worried about this test coming up in my accounting class. I haven't had time to really study for it because my seven-year-old has had the flu and has been home sick in bed for the last three days. I'm afraid I might not pass this class. I don't know how I would handle that!"*

So you feel _____

when _____

_____

because you _____

_____

8. *"My mother-in-law thinks I'm being a bad mother and wife by going back to school. She keeps hinting that I should be home to take care of my children and husband all the time. I could just scream at her sometimes! She just doesn't get that I want to do something more with my life than staying home all the time."*

So you feel _____

when _____

_____

because you _____

_____

Chapter 10

Developing Listening Skills

One of the most challenging situations in relationships is when other people direct their emotional charges at you. When it appears that someone is blaming you, it is difficult not to become defensive or put up a wall of protection. When you react defensively or attack the other person, however, you end up in a tangle of hurt feelings that can quickly undermine the sense of trust and safety in the relationship.

The most common response most of us have to feeling hurt, afraid, or angry is to make it someone else's fault. We think that somehow we can resolve our discomfort by making another person responsible for it. This approach can't solve our problem, however, because our emotional charge is not the other person's responsibility. When we blame someone else for our wounds, we take our attention away from our own needs and make it more difficult to find a real resolution to our situation.

Likewise, when other people blame you, they are not able to focus on their own wound and take care of themselves. Instead of reacting defensively, as your common instincts may tell you to do, you can listen to other people's concerns and try to understand them, without taking their judgments about you personally. Remember that when someone else is judging or criticizing you, they are really giving you information about themselves.

Deflecting Blame

Listening supportively keeps the focus on the person who has the emotional charge, and allows you to keep your heart open and not shut the other person out. It establishes a gentle but firm boundary between you that allows you to redirect instead of absorb the power of their emotions. You will then be better able to reflect their feelings and needs back to them, and the two of you can begin to establish a connection based on understanding.

Listening to other people's concerns in this way allows their emotions to settle and opens the door to resolution. Instead of seeing each other as a threat, this approach can bring you into alignment and enable a more collaborative kind of problem solving. It can be helpful to use this skill even if you can see some way that you have contributed to the other person's wound. Once the emotions have dissipated and you can see the situation more clearly, it will be easier for you to acknowledge your part and make amends.

Here are some examples of situations in which people are blaming someone else for their emotional charge, followed by Supportive Listening responses. Notice how these responses encourage the people with the charge to take responsibility for their own emotions, while helping the person being blamed express empathy and concern.

Emotionally charged statement	Neutral reflection of emotions and facts
"You never get the car fixed when you say you will, and I end up having to find other rides at the last minute. What do I have to do to get you to fix the car?"	*"It sounds like you feel frustrated and angry when the car is not ready when you need it, because you have to scramble to find other ways to get where you are going."*
"How could you do this to me? You knew I had that report due this week, and you took the computer into the shop, anyway. Did you ever stop to think about how that would affect me?"	*"You sound really upset and angry that I took the computer in to be fixed when you needed it for your report, because you could not get your work done."*
"You never think of me when you invite friends over to watch TV."	*"So, you feel upset and hurt when I invite friends to watch TV at our house because you don't feel included?"*

Often, expressions of emotion come across as sarcasm or indirect blame and include harsh judgments, such as:

"I hope you had a nice time flirting with all the girls from your office tonight. I had a really exciting evening cleaning the house by myself and fixing the stupid vacuum cleaner."

These indirect expressions of emotion can be confusing and difficult to understand, especially if they seem to direct criticism at us. They can hurt and leave us wondering what the other person is trying to say. This is where it is especially helpful to translate what the other person says into simple emotions, facts, and judgments.

You can begin with recognizing that the other person seems to have an emotional charge and reminding yourself that the charge belongs to them, not you. Then, you can ask yourself what emotions the other person is feeling, what specific situation is stimulating them, what tangible impact the situation is having on them, and what judgments they have about you. A reflection of the statement above might be:

"Sounds like you felt upset and hurt when I was out with people from my office tonight because you were home alone, thinking that I don't care about you." or

"You sound angry and hurt about me going out tonight with people from my office because you ended up doing housework and fixing the vacuum cleaner without my help, and you thought I was flirting with other women?"

Imagine that someone says to you:

"What do you think I am, your housekeeper? How come you never clean up after yourself? Do you like living in a pig sty?"

Listen to this statement for feelings, facts, judgments, and the impact on the other person, and write a Supportive Listening response using this format:

So you feel (non-blaming feeling words) _____

when I (facts without interpretations)_____

_____

because you (how the other person is affected by my actions)

_____

and you think (any judgments the other is expressing)

_____

Learning to Witness

Once, when I was in a long distance romantic relationship, my partner told me in a phone conversation that she was feeling upset and overwhelmed with jealousy. I had been telling her about a woman I was interviewing for a position at the business where I worked. She told me that the time I was spending with this woman was making her feel very uneasy.

I felt an urge to fix the situation by talking my partner out of her feelings. I wanted to convince her that there was no threat to our relationship, that my affections were purely devoted to her, and that this concern was all in her head. I was starting to feel afraid that she would pull away from me, and frustrated because there was no real cause for her feelings of jealousy. Yet I could sense that no manner of explanation or reassurance would resolve her dilemma. Her feelings were arising from something going on inside of her that I could not see and had little to do with me.

I sensed how difficult her dilemma was for her on many levels, and I could see that she was struggling. I realized that I needed to stay separate from her story in that moment, and not get my emotions involved. It was challenging for me, because I could see no basis in reality for her feelings. Yet I knew this was her dilemma to fix, and the best I could do was to recognize her discomfort and care about her. I chose to listen to her supportively and be aware of the discomfort she was experiencing. I said something like: "It sounds like you are feeling anxious about the time I'm spending with this other woman because you are afraid I will become attracted to her and lose interest in you?"

By focusing on her emotions, I immediately felt empathy and saw how uncomfortable her feelings of jealousy were for her. A few moments later, she asked me for reassurance, and I tried in every way I could to let her know that her perceptions were not true and that I had no interest romantically in the other woman. When I had finished, she told me that it hadn't really helped, and that she was still feeling jealous. We ended the conversation there, and I chose to let it be, not knowing what would happen next.

The next morning she called to say that she had realized something about her feelings of jealousy. She had recognized that our relationship was going well for her and that she was having the kind of deep intimacy she longed for in her life. She had seen that this was actually frightening her a bit, because she was not familiar with relationships working out well.

Her feelings of jealousy, she realized, were a way for her to separate from me and sabotage our relationship. Somehow this felt more familiar and comfortable than having the intimacy she longed for. She recognized that this was a hidden agenda that had interfered with her relationships for much of her life.

She sounded open and happy on the phone. She told me that as soon as she had seen her own hidden wish to find something wrong with our relationship, a great weight had been lifted, and she found herself feeling deeply in love with me again. Knowing she did not want to feed this pattern, she was able to let it go because she could see it for what it was. This insight helped the jealousy disappear, and she was flooded with love and gratitude for our connection.

I had not understood her feelings and was afraid that she would end our relationship because of them. Yet, if I had somehow convinced her not to feel jealous, she might not have come to her own insights. By acknowledging and allowing her feelings, I offered her the space and support to discover a deeper truth for herself, which set her free from a pattern that had limited her throughout her life.

Hearing Another Person's Experience

When you hear about what you did that upset another person, it is common to want to argue about what actually happened. Usually, other people's stories contain their interpretations of the event, as well as judgments about you. And, there is a tendency to focus on their *story* instead of on their *feelings or needs*. You are then more likely to defend yourself by telling your version of what happened or by judging the other person's behavior in a similar way.

In the previous example of my partner feeling jealous, she said something like:

> *"You said you would call me in an hour, after you had a meeting with this woman, and it has been three hours. I knew you were going to spend more time with her!"*

I felt upset and thought she was accusing me of being irresponsible, so my urge was to defend myself by saying:

> *"It has not been three hours, and I never said I would call you in exactly one hour!"*

This would most likely have led us into an argument about exactly what I said, and how much time had passed before I called her back. And we never would be able to determine those things because we both had a different memory of the event. This demonstrates why it is futile and often so destructive to get into debates over something that has already happened.

I also felt a bit angry because it seemed that she was attacking my character, so I could have retaliated by attacking her like this:

> *"Well, look who's talking! You **never** call me right when you say you will, and I end up waiting around by the phone when I could be doing other things!"*

Of course, this would have triggered her defenses and could easily have led to a verbal battle that left each of us feeling hurt and distant from the other.

A more effective way to approach a situation like this is *not* to focus on the story about what is happening and to remember that other people's judgments of you do not describe what is really going on for them. Most likely, they are reacting in a habitual way to an emotional charge, which is simply a signal that some basic need of theirs is not being met. If you stay focused on the story, you miss a chance to help the other person discover what they really want.

In this situation, my partner seemed to think that I was attracted to someone else and was not being honest about it. Her story was that I told her I would call in an hour and then blew her off because I wanted to pursue a relationship with the other woman. I really wanted to argue with her story because I knew that was *not* what was happening.

Fortunately, I recognized that her story about *me* was not important. She could never have known for sure what I was feeling or thinking in the situation. Rather, her story was telling me about *her*. If I listened in this way, I could learn about her emotions and the basic needs they indicated.

The best way I could care about her and offer support in the situation was to set aside my defensive reactions and respond to what was really going on for her with empathy and compassion. So, I said something like:

> *"You sound upset that I didn't call you back when I said I would, because you think I am attracted to this other woman, and you are afraid you will lose my love?"*

Reflecting the Other Person's Feelings and Judgments

It can be helpful in these situations, if you are going to reflect back any of the other person's judgments or opinions, to preface them with the words, *"you think,"* or *"in your judgment."* Doing so allows you to acknowledge parts of the story that may seem very important to them, without agreeing or disagreeing. You can thus avoid an argument over who is right or wrong by simply recognizing the other person's thoughts and judgments for what they are.

Obviously, a conversation with someone you care about would not end there. Using this format is simply a way to begin to hear other people's concerns and acknowledge their feelings without avoiding the conversation or having it become overheated. Once you understand how the other person feels and what need is underneath their emotions, you will be in a better position to respond. You may be willing to change your behavior or help the person in some other way. Or you may simply understand that person better. Diffusing resentment and blame in this way can help greatly to restore trust and respect, especially in your closest relationships.

To practice this, think of a situation in your life where someone blamed you and write down what you remember that person saying.

_____

_____

Now write a Supportive Listening response:

It sounds like you feel _____

when I _____

_____

because you _____

_____

and you think _____

Listening with Your Heart Instead of Your Head

If other people are blaming you, it is not helpful to tell them they are responsible for their own feelings. Usually, it only fuels the conflict and makes resolution more difficult. Each one of us has to recognize that we are responsible for our emotions on our own, and blaming someone for blaming us makes no sense. In listening to another person's strong feelings, the most important thing is to simply remember this idea of emotional responsibility so that you do not take on the blame and are able to stay open and listen to their concerns.

It may help to imagine that you are listening with the ears of your heart instead of the ears of your head. You can then take in the stories of others as information about them, not about you. When you hear with your heart, you can translate their judgments and solutions into emotions and needs. By acknowledging their immediate feelings and how the situation is affecting them, you can help them understand their dilemma and begin to resolve it.

This undefended listening also enables you to see how your behavior impacts other people and be more aware of their feelings and needs. When you listen to understand how you have affected someone else, without immediately springing forward to defend yourself or fix the other person, your behavior toward that person is usually affected in a positive way. Once you see where other people are sensitive and learn about what they need, you may be more able to avoid hurting them again in the same way.

Shifting Into Problem Solving

When other people have been heard and their immediate feelings and needs have been recognized, often they pause and look more relaxed. Sometimes an empathetic response is enough, and the conversation ends there or moves on to another topic. This usually happens when the other person's primary need is for recognition and release of emotion.

This was the case in the earlier example of the phone conversation with my partner. She needed to be heard and have her feelings recognized and accepted. Once this happened, the work of resolving her dilemma was hers, and no action was needed on my part. This became clear when I did reassure her of my love and devotion to her, and she told me it did not help.

At other times, an unresolved problem requires a solution. In this case, once the emotions and impacts have been acknowledged, it may be helpful to move into Facilitated Problem Solving. This can help the speaker stop circling around the same issues and provide a way for the listener to offer a deeper, more tangible kind of support. The key to this skill is that the person with the problem is the one solving it, while the listener is simply providing support and encouragement. The next chapter will describe how to do this.

Chapter 11

Facilitated Problem Solving

When I was a boy, I really wanted a tree house, and my father said he would build one with me in our backyard. I felt excited because I wanted to spend time with my father working together. I assumed that he would show me how to use tools and that I would help with the project. Instead, he just built the tree house while I watched. He didn't ask for my help or show me how to use any tools. When he was finished, I had a great tree house, yet I felt deeply disappointed because I didn't get to participate and never learned how to build something.

Many years later, when I bought an old farm house that needed a lot of repair, I had to teach myself how to fix things. It took years to learn how to use tools because I had never fixed or built anything when I was younger. All this would have come much easier for me if my father had taken the time to include me in building the tree house. While my father thought he was helping me by giving me the great gift of a tree house, the result was that I felt weak and ineffective because I could not help him do it. And years later, I had to struggle to learn how to build things on my own.

Allowing Other People to Solve Their Own Dilemmas

To return to an earlier metaphor, solving another person's problem is like pulling them out of a well with our own strength. There may be times when this is necessary, such as when they do not have the capacity to find their own way out. However, we often rush in to rescue other people because it gives us a feeling of power and strength to save someone who appears to be floundering. We assume they are weak and cannot do it themselves, instead of trusting their capacity to learn and grow from their mistakes.

The problem with rescuing other people is that it can make them weaker and more dependent in the long run. We may end up damaging them, just as the minister inadvertently killed the emerging butterfly in the story from Chapter 5. While saving others can put *us* into the hero's spotlight, it can also make *them* feel helpless and unable to take care of themselves.

Rescuing another person can be especially damaging when we do it automatically, without being aware of the specific need the other person is trying to meet. When the basic need has not been revealed, solutions offered by a listener tend to be quick fixes that take care of symptoms without addressing the root of a problem. Our tendency to fix other people also interrupts their natural capacity to problem solve for themselves and does not allow them to develop this essential life skill.

In this chapter, you will learn skills for helping other people come up with their own solutions. Facilitated Problem Solving is a way to offer the person a rope so that they can climb out of an emotional well, while allowing *them* to do the climbing. It encourages the other person to build strength and self-reliance while not having to face a challenge all alone. In the end, this approach makes for healthy, strong people, and relationships based on mutual respect, shared strength, and deep trust.

> There is a way to let other people know
> that we simply recognize their dilemma
> so they don't feel so alone.
> This often gives them the courage
> to face their problem by themselves.

Open Problem-Solving Questions

To begin to help other people solve their own dilemmas, it can help to ask one or more of these open problem-solving questions. An open question is different from digging for facts or asking a question that can be answered with yes or no. Open questions prompt other people to think about their emotions or needs, while leaving as much room as possible for them to express these in their own way. Such questions are open-ended prompts that nudge other people to begin thinking of what they can do to help themselves, without leading them toward a specific solution.

We have already discussed other open questions such as; "How do you feel about that?" or, "What was that like for you?" These questions help other people think about their emotions and express their direct experience. This next set of problem-solving questions helps other people move toward finding an effective response to their emotional charge.

1. ***What do you want?*** (possibly followed by):
    a. If a solution is offered instead of a basic need:
    What will you get if you get (<u>your solution</u>)?

    b. If a basic need is offered: ***What would that look like?***

2. ***What have you tried?*** (possibly followed by):
    How did that work?

3. ***What could you try?***

4. ***How do you think that would work?***

5. ***What else could you try?***

6. ***How can I help you?*** or
    What kind of support do you need?

7. ***Do you want some ideas?***

The idea is to simply make an opening for the person with the problem to generate effective solutions. We provide assistance and support in the form of questions that may help other people think more clearly about their dilemmas and come up with some new ideas for resolving them. Sometimes it works to ask these questions in the sequence above and listen supportively as other people formulate their own solutions. Other times, one or more of these questions may not apply or may be more appropriate in a different order.

1. *What do you want?*

Too often people get stuck repeating the same story, and there is no sense of movement. This can make it difficult for you to stay interested in listening. And for the person with the emotional charge, the situation can begin to feel hopeless. The question, *"What do you want?"* encourages other people to look beyond the story to what they would like to change, and gets them moving toward resolution. Sometimes, gently nudging the person toward finding solutions can be the most helpful way to offer support.

We have to know what we want before we can solve our problems. When listening supportively, you have already learned to identify the tangible impact the situation is having on the other person. Following up with this question, you can now help them connect the way the situation affects them with a basic need of theirs that is not being met.

Frequently, the speaker will respond to this question by stating a solution, not a need. Returning to the situation from an earlier chapter in which someone was talking about quitting his job because of the way his boss pointed out his mistakes in front of the other workers, a Supportive Listening response might sound like this:

> *"It sounds like you were hurt and angry when your boss*
> *pointed out your mistakes in front of your co-workers because*
> *you felt so vulnerable and exposed."*

If you ask him what he wants, he might say:

> *"I want to quit that job!"*

This is a *solution* that might take care of his need, but it does not tell you what his *need* is. Effective problem solving begins with considering a variety of strategies, which enables the other person to choose the ones that work better. Knowing the basic need is essential to this process of coming up with new solutions because it defines what the solutions are trying to do. So to find out the need in this example, you might ask:

> *"What will you get if you quit your job?"*

This question can prompt him to consider what he is trying to accomplish. It gets him to stop and think about what his need is, often for the first time. Because people are so accustomed to focusing on solutions rather than on their basic needs, it may take them a little time to realize what they really want. In response to this question, he might say:

"I won't get yelled at that way in front of other people anymore."

This answer tells you what he does *not* want, but not what he *does* want. It is usually more helpful in getting your needs met to express them as something positive that you want, rather than something negative that you do not want. As a supportive listener, you can help the other person by hearing and reflecting back what it sounds like his need is. So in this example, you might respond:

"It sounds like you want to be treated more respectfully at work."

Notice that this statement does not add a new idea. It simply translates his statement into more of a need. He said what he *didn't* want to happen, and you are translating that into something it sounded like he *did* want. This can help him to think of trying to get what he does want, instead of simply avoiding what he doesn't want. It encourages him to focus on solving his problem instead of getting stuck in blame or avoidance.

It is all too easy for us to blame our problems on other people or situations beyond our control. Many of us have developed this tragic habit of putting responsibility for our happiness onto someone else. This seems to relieve us of the burden of taking charge of our own lives, yet it leaves us with a sinking feeling of being helpless and disempowered. Facilitated Problem-Solving questions help other people by not allowing them to reside in this powerless place.

Remember that these are simply questions or suggestions you are making in an attempt to clarify what he is trying to say. If you don't get it right, it is important to leave plenty of room for him to correct you. This process will not work if you have your own agenda or think *you* have the answer to *his* problem.

If the other person describes a basic need like "respect," it can be helpful to encourage him to define what respect would look like. To move from a basic need toward a specific strategy to meet that need, it can be helpful to ask a second question like:

"What would that look like?"

This question asks him to be more specific about what he is looking for. Most of us have different ideas of what respect is and what it looks like. It can be useful to help the speaker think about what would feel respectful to him in this situation. This stimulates imagination and creativity and helps him move beyond defensiveness.

Until he thinks about what tangible actions would meet his needs for respect, he may still be waiting for you to guess. This approach makes getting his need met unlikely, and it usually leads to frustration and a sense of being a helpless victim. Once he has identified what respect would look like to him, he can formulate a direct request.

The person in the example might answer this question by saying:

"I want him to talk to me privately if he has complaints about my work, and not in front of everyone."

Once the basic need or want has been identified, it is tempting to jump into finding new ways to meet that need. Before you go there, however, it can be helpful to review what has already been tried. It is likely that the person with the dilemma has already been trying to solve it, and this next open question invites him to review what he has done so far.

2. *What have you tried?*

This question gets him to think about what, if anything, he has already done about the situation. It can reveal a number of creative solutions he has tried, which clears the way to move on to new ideas. If the other person discusses things he has already tried, it might be helpful to ask him: **"How did that work?"** This will help him think through what he is already doing and evaluate how effective it is.

Question number 2 could also reveal that he has not tried anything, which can prompt him to begin thinking of what he could try. This leads into question number 3:

3. *What could you try?*

This question simply gets him to think of options. It seems such an obvious question to ask, yet often it can help to have support from another person to take this step toward solving our own dilemma. If he seems stuck here, you could elaborate, using the information he has already given you:

> *"What could you try to get your boss not to talk to you that way again in front of your co-workers?"*

Notice that this question does not add any of your own ideas or agenda. You are simply combining this open-ended problem-solving question with something he has already said he wants. All this question does is to help him connect these two.

If the other person begins to generate some creative ideas, the next helpful question might be number 4:

4. *How do you think that would work?*

This question encourages the other person to think about his proposed solution a bit more deeply and talk through the possible outcomes. It can be especially useful if he offers a solution that seems ineffective or harmful, such as:

> *"I could go into his office and tell him what a jerk he is."*

When someone makes a proposal like this, it is usually about venting some emotion instead of really trying to solve the problem. A common reaction, especially if this is a child, is to moralize and explain why this is a bad idea. However this kind of corrective response can make the situation feel unsafe and shut the other person down because it contains judgment. Instead of criticizing such a proposal, you can encourage him to think of more ideas by simply asking the question:

> *"How do you think that would work?"*

This question can work if you sincerely want to understand what the person is thinking and are not being sarcastic or tying to make a point. It is important to remember that your role is to assist, and the other person has to sort this out on his own. Question number 4 can help him troubleshoot possible solutions before trying them out. It also can bring some humor into the situation, giving him the opportunity to laugh at his own dark side. Then he has a chance to admit for himself that it is not such a good idea, and laughing together about it may relieve some of the tension of his situation.

This next question could be helpful to gently keep him moving forward toward a more workable solution.

5. *What else could you try?*

Questions 2 - 5 form the core of open problem solving. They assist other people to generate new solutions to their dilemmas and think clearly about the potential effectiveness of each. These questions can be asked in different combinations until the other person comes up with a solution that feels workable, or realizes that he is stuck and needs help. At that point, this next question might be helpful:

6. *How can I help you?* or *What kind of support do you need?*

Most of us want to help, and we like the feeling of strength and purpose it gives us to assist another person. The problem with this attitude is not the desire to help, but the impact of solving other people's problems for them. The Facilitated Problem Solving process offers a way to help other people help themselves, which will give you both a sense of power and purpose.

Offering help in this way is most effective after other people have gone as far as they can go in trying to solve their own dilemmas and now appear to be stuck. It would only be appropriate if you genuinely want to do more than you already have done to help them. It communicates your willingness to help, yet it leaves the specific direction of that help in their hands.

If other people request your help, they are still in control of their own problem solving. For many of us, asking for direct assistance from another person is a big step. Question number 6 can help them to feel more comfortable asking for help, and it allows you some room to negotiate your involvement in their dilemma. If they make a direct request, you can evaluate your willingness or ability to do it.

In the example we have been using, the other person might ask:

"Would you talk to my boss for me?"

You might not be comfortable with this, or you may sense that it is too strong an intervention and could weaken the other person in the long run. If so, you can respond:

"I'm not comfortable doing that. Is there another way I could help you?"

He might then come up with another request like:

"Would you let me practice talking to my boss with you?"

And you might respond:

"Sure, I will be happy to do that."

If the other person appears to be stuck and unable to come up with any ideas or requests for help, you could ask this next question:

7. *Do you want some ideas?*

This is the moment many of us have been waiting for. As other people are speaking, we often get ideas about what they could do to solve their problems. It is natural to want to jump in with your solution because it makes you feel useful, and this is the way many of us habitually respond to someone who is having a difficult time. We assume that our role is to offer solutions.

As you have already seen, rescuing other people in this way is not necessarily helpful to them in the long run. If you resist your temptation to offer your ideas and continue with the problem-solving process outlined here, quite frequently the other person will think of the same ideas themselves. If they come up with the solution themselves, they are more likely to follow through with it and come out of the process stronger and more confident than before.

However, if other people seem truly stuck, and you have an idea, it could be useful at this point to ask if they want to hear it. This question leaves room for them to say yes or no and keeps responsibility for the process in their hands, allowing them space to think about what they really want from you. Sometimes people say no, realizing that they want to figure it out on their own. And if they say yes, it is more likely that they really do want to hear your suggestion.

In the ongoing example, if the other person had said yes to this question, you could respond:

> *"It might be helpful for you to talk directly to your boss about your concerns. Perhaps you could ask for a private meeting to discuss what happened and how you felt about it, and to ask him to do it differently next time."*

Now, he can think about this idea and whether it might work to meet his needs in the situation. It is still up to him to create his own solution and he might take parts of your idea and leave others out. He might end this process by saying:

> *"That makes sense. I really don't want to talk with him, but I probably should give it a try. And, it would help me to have your support. What if I write down what I want to say, and then maybe you could listen to me say it out loud, to see how it sounds?"*

Staying on Track

During the problem-solving process, the speaker will often reveal new emotions, facts, or impacts. It can be helpful to reflect these as they come up, using Supportive Listening. This may change the problem-solving process by revealing a more central problem, or it may add more information to the situation at hand.

Reflecting what people have said as they go deeper into their story also helps to keep them on track. Many of us have a tendency to jump around to different problems, especially when someone is listening to us. However, it is usually not possible to solve more than one problem at a time. Skipping from one dilemma to another can result in a lot of talk with no resolution, and it is often frustrating and discouraging for both the speaker and listener.

Be careful not to add an entirely new problem to the discussion before resolving the initial one. If the speaker appears to be jumping from issue to issue, it can be helpful to acknowledge the new issue and suggest that it is a different problem that may better be explored at another time. Helping the speaker stay focused until one issue feels complete is one of the greatest gifts a supportive listener can give.

Suppose a friend of yours is having some conflict in her marriage and says to you:

> *"I don't know what to do. He keeps on charging things to our credit card without checking with me first, and we keep having these huge bills just to pay off the interest. If this keeps up, we're going to go bankrupt!"*

You might respond:

> *"You sound frustrated about your partner buying things on your credit card without talking to you, because you are afraid of getting so far in debt that you can't get out."*

When the other person hears that you are actually listening and paying attention to what she is saying, sometimes she just wants to unload all that has been troubling her. In such an instance, she might go on to say:

> *"I also hate the way he talks to our kids. He doesn't take time to listen to them and always seems to be in a rush to do something else."*

This is a new and different issue. If you let the conversation go and simply keep reflecting, it is likely to turn into a scattered dumping of emotions with no sense of resolution. So you could respond:

> *"It sounds like you are also upset about the way he communicates with your children because you are concerned that they aren't getting what they need. Let's stay focused on the financial issue for now. I think you will come out feeling better if you can get clarity on one issue at a time."*

Other phrases that might be helpful in cases like these include:

"I think I can listen more fully to you if you stay with one issue at a time."

"I am getting a bit confused here. Can we go back to the first issue and deal with that one before bringing in any others?"

"I see that there is more than one issue up for you at this moment. Which one feels the most urgent to talk through first?

"I think it will feel more productive to both of us if we stick with one issue at a time."

Or simply suggest: *"Let's get back to the issue of the credit card debt."*

Completing the Listening Process

It is helpful to end the listening process with care. Conversations of this nature require a lot of focused attention and are usually not sustainable beyond half an hour or so. If it goes on for too long, both people may end up overwhelmed and exhausted, so it is important to bring the discussion to a timely conclusion. Of course, it can be disturbing to just cut off a conversation or change to a new topic without any acknowledgment of the sensitive issues that are on the table.

As the listener, it is your job to sense a point of completion. It may be when the other person has a solution they are going to try. If so, you may conclude the process with a reflection of what the speaker plans to do, using the specific details they have already described. In the earlier example of the man who was upset with the way his boss treated him, you might say:

"So, you are going to try talking directly with your boss about what happened, and you want to write out what you want to say and practice saying it to me first?"

You can then offer continued support, if you want, by suggesting that he talk to you after he tries his solution and let you know how it went. In this example, it might be appropriate to say this after he has practiced with you and before he goes to talk to his boss. You might say something like this:

"I would be interested to hear about what happens. If you want to talk about it afterwards, I'll be happy to listen."

This leaves the door open for continued support, which can be very helpful to the other person, especially if he is feeling anxious about what he has decided to do.

Leaving a Situation Unresolved

Often people dealing with an emotional charge will not come to a clear resolution of their dilemma while talking to you. Sometimes the situation is just too big or too complex, one of you runs out of time or energy, or neither of you can come up with a good solution. It can be difficult to leave a conversation in these instances, especially if you think it is your job to fix it.

Supportive Listening does not aim at finding neat and tidy solutions. It simply helps other people think about a situation from a new perspective. Even if they don't complete the process of problem solving during one conversation, they often go away with more clarity and come up with a solution on their own later.

You can know it is time to end a conversation if you notice that one or both of you are losing interest, if the speaker keeps repeating the same information, or if ambiguity seems to be creeping back in. The exchange can begin to feel labored, and one of you may be getting distracted repeatedly. When you are the listener and sense that it is time to bring closure to an issue, you can acknowledge an end to the conversation by saying something like:

"This feels complete to me; is this a good place for you to stop?"

"I need to go now. Do you feel comfortable leaving this here?"

"Do you feel complete?"

"Are you willing to leave this here for now? I will be happy to listen to you again if you want to talk more at a later time."

"It seems like you have opened up a complex situation that may take some time to work itself out. What if we leave this conversation here for now and visit this subject another time if you want to?"

Clear conclusions help the speaker move on to a different topic and leave the conversation with a sense of feeling supported. They help the listener acknowledge what has happened and let go of the role of assisting. A simple statement of conclusion can help both people honor the deeper sharing that has just occurred and the vulnerability of the process.

Chapter 12

Helping People to Help Themselves

There is a traditional proverb that goes something like this:

> Give people a fish and they will eat for a day.
> But teach people to fish,
> and they will eat for the rest of their lives.

Many of our familiar ways of responding to people who are struggling with a problem aim at fixing the problem or making them feel better right away. This is like giving hungry people a fish. It can set up a pattern in which they come to you for another fish as soon as they are hungry again. Just so, the next time they need to get out of an emotionally charged dilemma, they are likely to look to you to rescue them again.

Instead, if you take the time to teach people to fish, you help them learn how to help themselves. This is exactly what the skills of Supportive Listening are for. They help other people see their own dilemmas more clearly and use their own problem-solving ability to find their own solutions. A key to making this approach work is having faith that other people *can* solve their own problems.

Holding Space for Another Person

Supportive Listening is essentially holding space for other people to explore their feelings and needs and begin taking care of themselves. It works by accepting them where they are, without trying to change anything. This helps them to be present with themselves and calmly focus on getting out of their dilemmas.

The usual way of listening is to offer opinions or suggest solutions. We think we have to add something to be helpful. Holding space for another person is quite different. When you listen supportively, you are simply allowing them room to explore their own situations. Instead of doing the thinking or problem solving for them, your part is to be present, adding only your attention.

By listening without adding any of your own judgments, you create an opening for another person to relax into. This can be a tremendous help for someone who has a strong emotional charge. It allows them to step outside of their emotions and see their situation from a new perspective. And doing so often leads to them solving their own difficulty, because they can see new possibilities that were not visible before.

As you are listening, it is helpful to convey a sense of trust that things have a way of working themselves out in the end, even if we cannot see how that will happen in the moment. Believing other people can solve their own problem is different from offering them verbal reassurance or praise. Remember that these attempts to make the other person feel better often sound hollow and do not usually work. Instead, you can simply hold a positive image in your mind of the other person being able to pull themselves up and out of their emotional slump.

A Language of the Heart

The Supportive Listening skills presented in the previous chapters often don't sound natural and may seem too clinical or contrived. Keep in mind that what seems natural is what we copied from the adults around us when we were learning how to talk. Rejecting these skills because they don't feel right is like refusing to learn to swim or ride a bicycle because you were not born knowing how to do it.

Learning new habits of communication is like learning a foreign language. When you first try to talk to someone in your new language, it can feel uncomfortable. The new word or sentence sounds artificial and odd, and you can hardly believe that anyone could understand it. However, if you keep trying, eventually you realize that people who speak that language do understand, and that creates an immediate sense of connection between the two of you.

When you learn a foreign language in the classroom, you learn how to speak in formal sentences and use grammar correctly. As you begin to use your new skills with people who are native speakers of the language, you soon drop the formal structures in favor of the common street language. It is the same with communication skills. In the beginning, it is important to use the formal structures offered here in order to make a clear shift away from your old habits. Once you understand how they work, you can relax and use language that works with the person you are listening to.

The phrases presented in this book are artificial structures and are meant to redirect your attention to present-moment experiences, instead of to conclusions or interpretations. They are like the training wheels on a two-wheeled bicycle. Once you learn to balance the bike yourself, it does not make sense to keep the training wheels on; that would make riding the bike cumbersome and restrict your freedom. Likewise, once you learn to focus on present-time experiences, such as feelings and needs, you will no longer need the structures in this book and will be able to speak more freely and creatively, using your own style.

Conscious Communication could be considered a language of the heart. In many ways, it is as foreign as another country's language. This is because we tend to reference our experiences through our heads, processing them through our rational judgments and opinions. Naturally, it feels foreign to change such a basic orientation and refer to our emotions instead of our thoughts. With time, however, this new language will feel as natural and effortless as swimming or riding a bicycle.

Offering a Clean Mirror

Using the Supportive Listening format can remind you that *your* personal story is not the focus at that particular moment. It is also an effective way to help other people help themselves, simply by holding up a mirror so they can better see the dilemma they are facing. A key ingredient in making Supportive Listening effective is your sense of compassion for the other person.

When someone shares an emotionally charged experience, our impulse may be to say, *"I know how you feel,"* or simply, *"I understand."* While these comments are motivated by a desire to be supportive and show that we care, they often don't work. When someone makes either of these comments we have a tendency to think, *"No, you don't understand."* It can sound like the other person is just trying to gloss over our emotional charge and doesn't care enough to listen or understand our dilemma in a genuine way.

Supportive Listening is a more direct way to convey understanding.

Instead of telling other people *that* you understand, you tell them *what* you understand. Then they know exactly what you are hearing, and if you are not getting it right, they can clarify their experience. It is a way to be involved in other people's dilemmas without taking over or undermining their capacity to solve it for themselves.

This can be difficult to practice because simply witnessing and reflecting other people's experience can seem like a weak and ineffective response, especially if you are used to trying to solve their problems. However, showing emotional empathy for the other person may be the most powerful and caring way you *can* respond. Once you have reoriented your approach from thinking you have to rescue other people, to realizing that *they* are responsible for their own dilemmas, this non-intrusive listening makes more sense and flows more easily.

Sometimes this kind of listening is called mirroring because you are simply reflecting back what you hear the other person saying, without adding anything of your own. Holding a mirror for the other person may not feel like you are doing much, yet consider the benefit of seeing your reflection clearly in a mirror.

A physical mirror shows us what we look like, and it enables us to take better care of ourselves. A person mirroring back our story and reflecting our emotions and needs can show us what is going on inside of us. When we are aware of what is going for ourselves in this way, we can begin to find our own way out of an emotionally charged place.

It is not easy to provide a clear reflection. Our habit is to respond to other people by telling them our opinions, which impairs our ability to reflect them. Only when we relax our judgments and set aside our conclusions can we hear what is going on *for them*. Letting go of our own ideas is like cleaning the dirt or fog off a mirror. The more our own opinions are cleared away, the cleaner the mirror is.

The Power of Compassion

Listening supportively is more than mechanically repeating what the other person says. It can begin with reflecting back the feelings, facts, and needs that we hear in another person's story. However, the support that is most helpful when we are in an emotionally charged state comes from other people empathizing with our situation and showing that they care. This validation of our experience can then give us the courage we need to face the issue for ourselves.

Imagine that you are walking alone in the dark. Perhaps it is on a dark street, in a dark room or hallway, or out on a trail at night, and you likely feel some discomfort or fear. Then, imagine that a friend is there with you, and notice what happens. Just having a companion with you in the dark can give you strength and courage, and magically, the fear disappears. Nothing has changed: you are still in a dark and unknown place. Yet having another person beside you can give you enough courage to continue forward.

When you are in an emotionally charged state, it can feel like being in the dark alone. Often the most caring response you can receive from another person is simply their presence beside you in your pain and discomfort. It is amazing how much better you can feel as soon as you know that you are not all alone in your trauma, and that someone else knows and cares about it. This can change the whole situation and motivate you to face your difficulty directly, so that you can begin to resolve it with your own resources.

Developing Your Capacity for Compassion

Compassion is the ability to relate to the other person's struggle, *without making the story about you.* Caring for yourself provides the foundation for this kind of response. When you are overwhelmed or distanced from your own pain, it is hard to recognize or be comfortable with another person's struggle.

The more you care about yourself and are able to recognize your own fear and pain, the more capacity you develop for being fully present with other people who are dealing with difficult emotions. Tending to your own healing makes it possible to support the healing of a friend or loved one in a truly caring way. Compassion arises naturally when you take care of yourself, let go of your judgments and solutions, and are simply present with another person's dilemma with an open heart.

True compassion or empathy is different from sympathy or pity. These latter attitudes tend to separate us and convey that the person with the emotional charge is weak and in need of caretaking. This can make other people feel more isolated in their dilemma because it highlights the differences between us, instead of our similarities.

If you approach someone with a problem as if you have no problems, the other person often feels more separate and alone. This is common in traditional helping relationships, such as psychotherapy, and often limits the effectiveness of these counseling situations because the patient is left with a sense that there is something fundamentally wrong with them.

The aim of Supportive Listening is to convey that you can understand another person's experience, while keeping the focus on them. Compassion comes from a recognition that we both have difficulties and we both experience pain because of them. Instead of referring to your own struggles, however, you simply recognize silently within yourself how it is to be hurt, afraid, or angry. From this place you can relate to the other person's situation with a deeper sense of understanding and caring.

> True compassion is
> the ability to care about other people's suffering,
> while trusting that they have
> the capacity within themselves
> to find a way out.

Are You Available to Listen?

In any situation where another person has an emotional charge and seems to want to vent, it is important to be honest with yourself about your capacity for listening in the moment. If you cannot be fully present and neutral, you are not going to be able to offer real support and are more likely to use Disconnects. Here are some reasons that this may occur:

You may not be able to offer Supportive Listening when:

You are physically tired or overwhelmed with your own life dilemmas.

If you have had a long day or are bogged down with an emotional charge about something happening in your own life, most likely you will not be able to be present for another person. Sometimes you can gather the energy to listen, however, if you find that you are not able to stay focused on other people's stories and hear their emotions, it can be useful to let them know that you cannot listen right then. You may set another time to listen if you think you will be able to do so later. Here is a response that could be useful in such a situation:

> *"I see how upset you are and know you want to talk to me about this. I want to hear you, and this is not a good time for me; I am too tired and overwhelmed right now. I would like to listen to you later this evening, after I have had some time to myself. Can we talk around eight o'clock?"*

An emotional charge is triggered in you by the other person's story.

If you are close to other people, their emotional charges may bring up your own emotions. You can try to set aside your reactions and bring yourself present to listen. If your emotional charge is strong and keeps coming back, however, it is more effective to acknowledge that you cannot listen well at this time. Again, you may set another time if you want to help and think you can be more neutral later. Meanwhile, you could choose to take care of your own emotions so you can be neutral when you meet again. Or you might ask the person to think of others who may be able to listen supportively and be more neutral. Here are some responses that may be helpful in such a case:

> *"You sound upset about this situation, and I see that you want to tell me about it. I am getting too upset listening to you right now and cannot be very present or clear. I would like to take a break and come back to this in an hour when I have had a chance to take care of myself."*

> *"I know you need to talk about this and get it off your chest. It is just bringing up too much of my own emotion for me to listen to you right now. Is there another person who you could talk to about it? Let's think together about who that might be."*

You don't trust other people
to find their own solutions.

If you are convinced that other people cannot solve their problems on their own, you will not be able to listen supportively. This may be a time to be more active in directing them or to refer them to someone who may be more qualified to help. This is often the case in situations involving small children or adults dealing with substance abuse, domestic violence, disabilities, or suicide. In this situation you might respond by giving direction, or a statement like this:

"I am concerned about you and I don't know enough about what you are dealing with to help you. I would like to help you find someone who is trained in helping people who are in situations like this."

You don't have time.

If there is something else you need to be doing, or you have a time limit, you may not be fully present for other people. Again, the most honest response in this case is to let them know you cannot listen because you don't have time. It may be helpful to include that you really do want to listen, and then set another time when you are not going to be rushed. This could sound like:

"I see that you want to talk to me, however, this is not a good time for me. I do want to listen to you. Can we find a time to talk when I don't have another task to focus on?"

You do not feel connected enough
with the other person to want to help.

If you don't feel a sense of connection or a desire to help another person, you won't be able to listen to them supportively. It can be difficult to express this directly. Yet pretending to care about someone when you don't only undermines their sense of trust and safety. Other people can usually sense when this is going on, and it can do more harm to fake interest than to be honest about your feelings toward them or their situation.

Most often we get ourselves out of situations like this by avoiding the other person or withdrawing from the relationship. These more subtle responses often work when another person wants our attention and we are not interested in giving it to them, and we don't have to say anything. Yet in some situations it may be necessary to be more direct. In this case you might say:

> *"I have too much to deal with in my own life right now and can't give you the attention you need. Would you be willing to find someone else to talk to?"*

Taking Care of Yourself

Although you may have good intentions of wanting to help other people, or think that it is your responsibility to listen to them, you are not always in a position to offer real support. If you try to listen when you cannot, the other person will usually sense that you are not there and the connection between you will be weakened. If you can be honest about what is going on for you at the moment, it builds trust and establishes a stronger relationship in the long run.

When you recognize that you are not able to fully listen to another person because you have your own needs to take care of, it is helpful to stop and focus on yourself for a moment. You can ask yourself what you need and consider how you might go about getting that need met. Sometimes you can do this by yourself, and can then be present with another person and offer them support.

Other times, however, you may have a bigger emotional charge that is blocking your connection with a particular person or keeping you from being present. In the next chapters, which focus on Assertion, you will learn ways to approach these situations by communicating directly with the person you are reacting to.

Supportive Listening

Creating a safe place for other people to discover their own feelings and needs, and begin solving their own problem

Opening Questions:

"You look upset, want to talk about it?"

"Looks like something's bothering you; I've got time if you want to talk."

"What was that like for you?"   or
"How do you feel about that?"

Attentive Silence: Eye contact, full attention, open posture.
Simple Encouragements: *"Oh." "Uh-huh." "I see." "Then?" "Wow!"*

Three-part Supportive Listening (connecting feelings, facts, and impacts):

It sounds like you feel... (feelings)   *"It sounds like you feel upset*

when... (facts)   *when he makes decisions without talking with you first*

because you... (impacts)   *because you don't feel included"*

<u>Open Problem-Solving Questions</u>:

1. ***What do you want?*** (possibly followed by)
        a. ***What would you get if you get*** (<u>your solution</u>)?
        b. ***What would that look like?***

2. ***What have you tried?*** (possibly followed by)
  How did that work?

3. ***What could you try?***

4. ***How do you think that would work?***

5. ***What else could you try?***

6. ***How can I help you?*** *or*
  What kind of support do you need?

7. ***Do you want some ideas?***

<u>Reflecting Proposed Solutions</u>:

"***So, you are going to try***
(<u>specific solution the other person described</u>)"

Assertion

Chapter 13

Recognizing Your Own Feelings

The previous chapters have focused on responding to other people when they have a strong emotional charge and you are available to listen. Now we are going to shift gears and look at situations in which *you* have an emotional charge.

Our Habit of Blame and Attack

When wild animals feel threatened, they usually respond by threatening back. They might show their teeth, growl, or lunge aggressively at the other animal to show that they are capable of self-defense. They do this when they are scared or wounded and need space to heal. Once an animal has defined its personal space in this way, it tends to retreat and take care of itself.

We humans, however, do not usually stop at protecting our personal space and tending to our wounds. We have a habit of plotting against our enemies, believing that we can never be safe as long as they have the capacity to hurt us. Instead of taking care of ourselves, we often spend our energy trying to hurt people who we think are trying to hurt us.

We have a tendency to justify our attacks on other people as self-defense. This habit is as common in relationships between nations as it is with our family and friends. We can easily perceive an intimate partner, family member, or friend as a threat and begin unconsciously treating that person as an enemy. Once we have convinced ourselves that they are out to get us, trying to hurt the other person for our own protection seems so natural we don't even realize we are doing it.

Threatening an enemy may work well for our animal counterparts, yet it is highly destructive when used by humans. With our capacity for memory, future planning, and technology, our ability to hurt each other is enormous. When we rely on our animal instincts for our defense against each other, this natural urge can quickly turn into a nightmare of violence and overwhelming destruction.

The impulse to destroy our adversary has led nations to develop weapons of immense destruction, like nuclear bombs, deadly chemicals, and viruses capable of killing whole populations. In our personal relationships, it can lead to sophisticated and disguised ways of hurting each other that destroy the trust and safety between people. It seems that those who know us the most intimately are also able to hurt us the most deeply.

Aside from the obvious insanity of hurting those we love for our own protection, this approach simply does not work. Instead of establishing safety and security, as it seems to do in the animal kingdom, retaliation only makes our world more dangerous. Each attack only increases the likelihood of retaliatory attacks. In relationships between people, the capacity to do more harm has not lead to greater peace or stability, but has made our lives more uncertain and dangerous.

If It's Not Working, Stop Doing It

Thankfully, we humans *do* have the capacity to change our basic conditioning. We often resist the process of our own growth and maturity, however, until we are motivated by a dramatic failure. When we see for ourselves that an approach is not working, we become open to a new one.

> If you are relying on a defense mechanism
> that consistently makes your world
> more dangerous and unsafe,
> it may be time to recognize
> that this response is not working,
> and try something new.

Take a moment and review the way you have dealt with a situation in which you felt threatened or hurt by someone else and did not feel safe. It is likely that you eventually blamed the people involved or tried to hurt them in some way, either in your thoughts, words, or actions.

Now, ask yourself – did it work? Did your response result in greater safety or security for you? If the answer is yes, then what you did appears to have worked. If the answer is no, then it did not.

A lot of us get stuck in repeating the same approach over and over, thinking that if we can muster just a bit more force or appear more threatening, we will be safe. Or we have given up completely and taken up the strategy of avoidance, thinking this will protect us from harm. We may see ourselves as innocent victims of bad people trying to hurt us and believe our only chance for safety is to make ourselves less visible to our attackers. In either case, we do not feel safe, and we live in a state of low-level anxiety and defensive alertness most of the time.

It is difficult to resolve feelings of fear and insecurity if you continue to blame other people or circumstances for causing them. Seeing another person as responsible for your feelings relieves you for a moment of the emotional burden, yet it also means that the problem is out of your hands. While this may lift some weight off your shoulders, it often leaves you with a residue of resentment and powerlessness.

Making other people responsible for your emotions gives *them* power over *your* happiness and well-being. Placing responsibility for your emotions outside of yourself sets up a situation in which you have to control someone else in order to feel better. And most people respond to attempts to control them with resistance and defensiveness, which is why this approach can lead to endless conflict. No one likes to be controlled or manipulated, and no amount of control or manipulation of others can guarantee that you will be safe.

> It is not possible to change another person
> or to control a situation
> so that it does not aggravate your wounds
> and trigger your emotions.

When your primary aim is to protect your sensitive places, you create uneasy truces with the people closest to you, or are engaged in a constant struggle for power and sovereignty. Focusing your efforts on changing something external to you also sets you up for failure. You can easily begin to feel helpless and depressed, thinking that the world is out to destroy you and that there is nothing you can do to protect yourself.

Once you question this habit of aggression as a defense, the attraction of violence as a remedy for violence begins to diminish. You can see that it may not make sense to hurt the person who hurt you so that they can't hurt you anymore. The solution to feeling vulnerable and afraid does not come from focusing on and trying to control those who appear threatening. If you can suspend your urge to strike back for a moment, you may discover that there is a better way to meet your need for safety.

Focusing on Our Own Wound

It is common to mistake justice for self-care, as if establishing what is right and wrong in a situation will heal our wounds or take care of our needs. Once we have made these judgments we tend to react impulsively, trying to protect ourselves from a person we think is bad. Yet, in following the impulse to control or avoid others, we often completely neglect ourselves.

When you have an emotional charge that seems to be triggered by someone else, focusing on that person drains the energy required to take care of your own needs. As we discussed earlier, an emotion is simply a signal that a basic need requires attention. When you let go of the urge to blame and attack for a moment, your own unmet needs come into view, and you can begin to take care of them. Instead of focusing on the other person and what they have done wrong, you can focus on *yourself* and begin to pay attention to your emotions and the basic needs underneath them.

No one situation or person is fully responsible for the magnitude of our emotional charge. That person or situation has usually caused an emotion to surface that was already there, connected to some hurt that occurred in the past. One of the consequences of our habit of ignoring emotions is that they tend to pile up. So most of us have a backlog of emotional wounds connected to situations that we never dealt with or resolved.

When someone does or says something in a certain way, it can stir up this old emotional baggage and bring it to the surface. This is what is usually happening when we have a strong emotional charge, and why it is so important to take responsibility for our own feelings. They really *are* ours, and actually have only a little to do with the person or situation that triggered them.

To respond more effectively when an old wound has been irritated, the first step is to recognize that you have an emotional charge. We are so accustomed to ignoring our emotions and jumping directly into solutions that we may have lost the ability to know when we are upset. This may sound elementary, yet many of us are not aware of our emotional states. So we begin by learning how to feel our own feelings.

As we discussed earlier, an emotional charge often has a

corresponding bodily sensation that is observable. It may be blood pressure rising, a hot face and hands, a loud and fast thumping heart, a sweaty brow, shaking, a knot in your stomach, or irregular breathing. Take a moment now and make a list of physical signs that you recognize in yourself when you are upset.

When I am upset, angry, hurt, scared, or anxious, I often feel in my body…

_____

_____

There are no right or wrong answers to this question. Each of us tends to have different physical sensations related to different emotions. Writing them down for yourself can help you to recognize when you are having strong feelings. Once you are aware of your own emotional condition in the moment, you can make choices that increase your chances of getting what you really want.

Basic Self-protection

In order to address a threatening situation more effectively, the first step is to shift the focus away from the other person and let go of blame and attack. Your primal self-defense instincts may suggest that this is the worst thing to do, because it lets the other person off the hook and leaves you feeling defenseless. However, focusing on your own feelings does not mean you do not protect yourself. It simply means not trying to hurt others in order to achieve safety.

Surrendering your aggressive impulses does not require giving up your ability to establish boundaries for your own safety. In a situation where your physical or emotional well-being appears to be threatened by someone else, the first step in self-care may be to establish a boundary. This can look like saying no, asserting your needs firmly, or removing yourself or the other person from the situation.

One difficulty many of us face in protecting ourselves is that we don't know how to set a boundary *without hurting the other person*. We tend to either sacrifice our personal safety in the name of being a nice person or to attack the other person with more force than necessary in order to protect our personal space. Assertion is a skill that enables us to meet our need for safety without attacking someone else. Here is a story that illustrates this idea:

The Hermit and the Snake
A Folk Tale from India

Once in the jungle outside a small village in India, there lived a hermit. He was known to be very wise and would often receive visitors from the village who were in search of counsel. One summer, the hermit began to notice that no villagers were visiting him anymore. He became curious and concerned about this, and decided to make the journey into the village to see what was going on.

Along the way to the village, he discovered the problem. A large, venomous snake had taken up residence beside the trail to the hermit's hut. The hermit realized that this snake had been biting villagers, which made them too afraid to walk along that path. The hermit had the power to talk to animals, and he asked the snake to stop biting people so the villagers would feel safe to visit his hut. The snake held a lot of reverence for the hermit and agreed to his request.

Some weeks later, things had returned to normal and the hermit was making his way back to the village to get some rice. Along the path, he noticed some village boys holding the snake by its tail and beating it against trees and rocks. The hermit rushed over in distress and asked the boys to leave the snake alone. The poor snake was all bruised and beaten and barely alive.

The hermit asked the snake what had happened and why the boys were treating him so badly. The snake replied that it had done what the hermit requested and stopped biting people. Gradually, the villagers became less frightened, and eventually some of them started attacking it in retaliation for all the times the snake had bitten the villagers. The snake said that now these village boys came every day and beat it up. The hermit bent down to soothe the snake's wounds with his healing hands. And he said to the snake: "I told you not to bite, but I didn't tell you not to hiss."

Most of us have not been taught adequate methods for protecting ourselves, so we either tend to go overboard and hurt other people, as the snake did in the beginning, or do nothing and let people hurt us, as the snake did in the end. Assertion is about learning how to adequately protect yourself *without* hurting someone else.

Mistaking a Mouse for a Lion

We all know the old expression, "Making a mountain out of a molehill." This is exactly what our instinctual defense mechanisms urge us to do when someone's behavior triggers an old wound and an emotional charge comes up. We make a story about how the other person is a monster who is out to destroy us, and then use this story to justify our attempts to disable them.

I once found a baby mouse that had lost her mother and was crying to be fed. She was tiny and had not opened her eyes yet. I took her in and began to feed her with an eye dropper. After some days, she began to grow stronger. One day, I reached into the nursing pen to pick her up, as I always did, and she reacted by trying to bite me. Suddenly, she was all mouth and teeth, and I became startled and afraid.

Taken by surprise, my immediate thought was to punish her so she would learn not to bite me again. I had done this with other small animals and it seemed to work. So, I hit her on the nose with my finger. Immediately, she went limp and began to shake, and I realized that I had seriously hurt her. I felt terrible as I had not intended to harm her; I simply wanted to teach her not to bite.

When I calmed down, I realized that I had reacted to the mouse as though she were a lion who could really hurt me. The truth was that she was no larger than the end of my thumb, her teeth were barely developed, and she still had not fully opened her eyes. Her attempts to bite me could not even break my skin and did not really hurt at all. I was astonished as I saw how I had made this helpless tiny creature into a monster, and then attacked her as if my own safety depended on showing her that I was bigger and more powerful.

What really happened was that the mouse's sudden attempts to bite me had frightened and upset me because I thought she trusted me. My feelings were hurt, I was scared, and I needed to take care of myself. This had little to do with my mouse friend at this point, but I made it about her in my mind. Instead of caring for myself, I had lashed out at her, as we often do when we are afraid. In this situation, I could have recognized my hurt and scared feelings and taken a few deep breaths or sat down to calm myself. I would have realized that I was not in serious danger, and then I could have responded to the situation more intelligently.

After I did calm down I was able to see that, by picking the mouse up suddenly, I had probably frightened her. She did not recognize who I was and was only trying to defend herself by biting me. At the next feeding, I put my hand in her cage and waited until she came out to climb onto it, instead of grabbing her as I had been doing. Sure enough, she came over to my hand and willingly climbed up. I handled her like that every time afterwards, and she never tried to bite me again.

When someone attacks us, it is often because they feel threatened in some way and are only trying to defend themselves. If we attack back, the conflict escalates, leaving little chance of a positive resolution to the situation. If we take care of ourselves for a moment, it gives us a chance to see the other person's vulnerability and understand their behavior, as I finally did with my mouse friend. Then we can try a different approach that may be more effective.

Self-empathy

The most certain way for us to get help and support when we are upset is to give it to ourselves. Yet many of us have no idea what this means or how to do it. We have somehow lost the ability to care for ourselves, and we do not even consider it an option when we find ourselves in a difficult situation.

Once, I was in a lot of emotional pain because of the end of a significant relationship. Recognizing the sinking feeling of disappointment and deep hurt, I decided to take a break for a few days and take care of myself. I put my canoe on my truck, loaded up my fishing pole and tent, and set out to explore a river I had wanted to visit for some time. I spent several days in nature, doing things I loved. This did not resolve the situation, and I still had to work through my own healing, yet taking time out made the process much gentler and easier.

It took some years of paying attention to my feelings and needs and committing to care for myself before I could even think of doing something like this when I was emotionally hurt. Most of us learned to simply ignore our emotions and disregard our inner well-being. Often we feel too ashamed or afraid to admit to having hurt feelings, and have no idea how to nourish ourselves. Or we do not see ourselves as worthy enough to pay attention to our own needs.

In order to resolve our basic needs when a strong emotion is stimulated, it is helpful to do something that is truly nourishing. Self-nourishing activities are simple and immediate things that allow us to feel better and do not harm us. Taking care of ourselves in this way gives us a chance to feel what is going on inside and respond intelligently. Here are some examples:

writing   talking to a good listener   physical exercise

creative activities   venting in a way that is not destructive

taking a bath   going for a walk   being in nature

listening to music   cleaning the house   crying   laughing

singing   physical affection   physical work   meditation

Take some time now and make a list of things you can do for yourself that are nourishing when you are upset.

When I feel upset about something going on around me, I can take care of myself by:

_____

_____

Addictions Numb Feelings

A common impulse when feeling hurt is to reach for something that will numb the emotional pain. These automatic habits make us feel better momentarily yet they often have damaging effects on us or our relationships in the long term. These addictive behaviors temporarily block out our emotional charge, yet they make us weaker and less able to resolve difficult situations effectively. Some habits that do not nourish but rather deplete us over time may include: cigarettes, overeating, drugs, alcohol, television, sex, or even violence.

Numbing our emotions is not the same as discharging them. Burying emotions through addictive habits is as ineffective as an ostrich putting its head in the sand to make itself safe from danger. By avoiding our emotional charge in this way, we never reveal the underlying needs, and the problem does not get resolved. While another person's actions may have stimulated an old wound, when we respond with an addictive behavior, we are directly hurting ourselves.

Addictive habits may offer immediate relief from discomfort, yet the price we pay is a decline in our well-being. We fool ourselves into thinking these habits will somehow solve our problems by ignoring the long-term consequences. And, when we realize that these behaviors are not healthy, we often turn to discipline and will power to overcome the attraction of our addictions.

When we approach addictions as a challenge to be overcome through will power, we set ourselves up for a constant struggle. Essentially, we are pitting one part of ourselves against another, and there is little chance of resolution to this internal conflict. The rational mind sees the addictive behavior as a problem and thinks it can be overcome by self-discipline. Yet, at the same time we are still drawn to the behavior, because it is the only way we have of dealing with our uncomfortable emotions.

To resolve the problem of an addiction, you have to look honestly at its cause. You need to understand what purpose the addictive substance is serving and find more effective ways of accomplishing that purpose before you can free yourself from its grip.

Addictions are ways of numbing your emotions so you
do not have to feel them.
These harmful habits will fade away
once you learn how
to effectively discharge your emotions.

Tending Emotional Wounds

The only way to release emotions is to deal with them directly. Once you learn to respond to your emotions in an effective way, the attraction of addictive behaviors begins to diminish. There are no shortcuts in this process. However, you can learn simple skills that will help.

Just as physical pain is a signal of a physical wound, emotional pain is a signal of a wound in your deeper being. To resolve physical pain, you need to know where you are hurt and care for your body in a way that helps it heal. In a similar way, discharging emotions involves paying attention to your hurt feelings. It may help to do an inventory of what you are feeling by asking questions like these:

What does the hurt feel like, and where do I feel it?

What are my emotions, and what do they feel like?

What do I need now?

Self-inspection is a natural response when you feel physical pain. If you cut yourself while using a knife, it is normal to stop what you are doing, rinse off the wound, and examine it. It is common sense to find out how deep the wound is and whether there is dirt in it, and to gauge the level of pain you are feeling. With this basic information, you can take care of your cut effectively.

For emotional wounds, it is the same. Simply being present and paying attention to what is happening inside you usually reveals what is wrong and how to take care of it. Just as physical pain is a signal of a physical need, emotional pain is a sign of an emotional need. You simply have to listen and use your awareness to discover what you need at that moment.

Of course, even taking care of a physical wound is not always so easy. Sometimes it takes a crisis to teach us the importance of tending to our wounds. I once got a cut on my leg and just tried to ignore it, hoping it would take care of itself. I did not pay any attention to it at all, and several days later, I noticed that it was not healing by itself. In fact, the skin around it was becoming swollen and turning white, and the wound began to hurt all the time.

I asked someone to look at it with me and discovered that the wound had become infected and was getting worse. The infection had moved inside my body, and I had to see a doctor and get a prescription for an antibiotic. Resolving the infection cost a lot of money and involved taking strong medication for several weeks. I learned through the pain and discomfort of this experience that it is much easier in the long run to tend to a wound carefully when it first occurs, than it is to neglect it and have to deal with a more serious situation later.

This pattern of denial occurs even more frequently when it comes to our emotional wounds. They are less visible than a cut or bruise, and easier to hide. Emotional well-being is hard to define, and we have little training or experience in dealing with hurt feelings. Because we don't know how to take care of ourselves emotionally, neglecting ourselves and blaming other people when we are hurt has become a habit. And the consequences are the same as when we neglect a cut.

Like physical wounds, emotional wounds fester and grow bigger if we do not tend to them. They can impair our ability to care about other people and lead to emotional instability and depression. An emotional wound that is disregarded typically hardens into a contracted place in our memory and continues to haunt us throughout life. Whenever we get close to a situation that is similar to the one that hurt us originally, we tend to become overemotional and lose our capacity to think clearly.

The more we neglect our hurt places inside, the more these unhealed wounds pile up and impair our ability to respond intelligently to life's challenges. Oversensitivity cripples us, and we go through life emotionally handicapped. We develop complex ways of avoiding our wounds and hiding them so that no one else can see where we are hurt. Eventually, unhealed emotional wounds disappear from our awareness, which makes the injuries nearly impossible to heal.

Built-up emotional wounds make relationships difficult because we carry them around hidden below our own awareness. To keep the wounds hidden, we have to control other people so they don't get near our painful places. We also try to make other people responsible for our emotional wounds as a way of getting someone else to fix them. Both of these strategies cause confusion and struggle and put distance in our relationships. And most of this happens subconsciously, which means we never address the problem directly.

There is growing evidence in Western medical science that stress and other emotionally charged conditions cause physical illness. It seems that when we bury emotional charges in an attempt to get rid of them, they often express themselves as long-term physical diseases. If you think of charged emotions as a pot of soup on a hot stove, you can see that if you put a tight lid on and ignore the soup, it is likely to boil over and cause damage.

However, if you pay attention to the soup on the stove and notice when it is boiling, you can remove the lid in a timely manner, releasing the pressure so the liquid does not come spewing over the top. In a similar way, you can learn simple ways to discharge your strong feelings so they do not build into an internal crisis. The next chapters will examine how to express emotions and needs to another person in a way that helps you heal, and strengthens rather than damages your relationship.

Chapter 14

Withdrawal, Attack, and Assertion

The two choices most often considered when we are feeling emotional pain triggered by another person are either attack or withdrawal. Fight or flight is our instinctual response to danger, and in the animal kingdom it seems to work well. In the world of human relationships, however, these habitual responses tend to cause more problems than they solve.

Withdrawal

Withdrawal, avoidance, and submission are all ways of trying to deal with emotions by *not* dealing with them. When you are uncomfortable with conflict, this option can look appealing. It may seem that if only you could ignore your emotions and act like you are doing fine, you might be able to avoid a confrontational situation. Many of us like to see ourselves as nice people who don't make waves and try to make everyone else happy. Submissive behavior also allows us to portray ourselves as innocent victims of other people's mean behavior, which means we do not have to take responsibility for our part in a conflict.

There are many reasons we might want to avoid confrontation. We may have been hurt by conflict, or it may have damaged our relationships, and it can seem that conflict will only lead to more pain and loss. Some of us have been taught that surrender to another person is the right thing to do. Submission can seem noble, and we may take pride in being nice and giving in, so that relationships remain harmonious.

Submission can also be a way to manipulate a person or situation to get what we want, without having to ask for it directly. By appearing to be helpless and under attack, we may get people to rescue us. We get a lot of attention by evoking the concern of others, and this can be used as leverage to get our way.

For some of us, playing the role of the innocent victim is the way we approach life. We get our sense of power from seeing ourselves as unjustly wronged by others. Thus, we lock ourselves into a pattern where the only way we can feel strong is by appearing weak and helpless. And the only time we feel energized and motivated is when we are opposing someone we think is trying to hurt us.

The Benefits and Costs of Submission

Withdrawal, avoidance, or submission can be healthy and effective responses in some circumstances. If you are continually being hurt by another person, it may be smart to take space in order to gather yourself together. Stepping out of a difficult situation can be useful so that you can allow emotions to cool and get some perspective. If it is an important relationship, you can go back later and address the issue directly with the other person once you feel your strength return.

However, the price you pay for withdrawal is that you may not get to release your emotions, and your needs often do not get recognized. If withdrawal becomes a habit, you may lose respect for yourself, and the other person might also lose respect for you. Another cost of avoiding conflict is that the situation does not get resolved and is likely to come up again in your life. And, when withdrawal or avoidance becomes your primary response to conflict, you do not learn how to take care of yourself and thereby limit your capacity for healthy relationships.

Withdrawal can also cause damage to relationships. If you do not talk about what happened at some point, but instead hope that the problem will resolve itself or go away, you undermine the intimacy and trust between you. When this becomes a habit, you may end up isolated from each other and feeling a chronic sense of discomfort in the relationship.

Attack

Attack, aggression, and retaliation are other common responses when our emotions are charged. We make other people wrong, punish them, or try to render them powerless. This approach assumes that the other person is responsible for our emotions, and that controlling or defeating that person will make us feel better. Some benefits of attack are that we get to vent our emotions and have a sense of power and control in our life. We also tend to get more of what we want and to think of ourselves as being right and winning.

We may choose this approach when we feel threatened because it seems to be the quickest way to regain our confidence and provide for our own protection and security. Some of us have been taught to be aggressive in order to appear strong and powerful. Our culture tends to glamorize competition and evaluate people on their ability to win. It equates might with right, and often the dominant person is seen in the best light.

While competition may have a place in games, it can be very destructive in personal relationships. When we compete with the people we are closest to, the relationship often loses. If people do submit to our aggression, it is out of fear rather than respect, and this can breed resentment, hostility, and rebellion. The price we pay for attack is that we usually alienate other people and find ourselves isolated.

The sense of strength and security we gain momentarily through aggression depends on our ability to dominate other people. This feeling of power can quickly turn into fear and insecurity as those others begin to resent and resist us. Attack tends to create more conflict and instability in our lives as the defeated struggle to get their power back. Dominating another person also can leave us feeling badly about ourselves in the long run. It does not really feel good to defeat another person or to get our way at someone else's expense.

When we want something from another person, a common first approach is to be nice and hope they will take care of us. We hide any feelings of anger and resentment or thoughts of blame. If our attempts at being pleasant fail, we may then flip to the opposite approach and lash out, aggressively demanding what we want. This makes for a highly unstable dynamic, and it damages trust and security in relationships.

Assertion

We have been focusing on effective ways to respond to strong emotions because they are the fuel behind most conflicts. Consider again that emotional storms do not arise randomly and without any reason, as it may often appear. The emotions we feel indicate how well we are meeting our needs. If we feel positive emotions, it means we are getting what we need. If we feel negative emotions, something essential to our well-being is missing. So, a skillful way to respond to an emotional charge is to learn about the basic need it is indicating.

When we face a situation where it looks like another person is threatening our well-being, we naturally have a need for safety.

Submission and aggression are the most common ways of trying to feel safe, yet they often do not work very well in the long run. Both of these approaches may achieve some level of safety in the moment, but they build relationships based on fear. Either we remain afraid of other people, or we try to make them afraid of us.

Submission focuses on the *other person* getting what they want, and aggression focuses on *us* getting what we want. Assertion, on the other hand, focuses on *both* of us getting what we want, and offers a way we can both meet our needs. It enables us to protect ourselves without weakening the other person, and maintain a boundary without violating the other person's boundary. It establishes our relationship as one of shared strength and power, without one of us dominating or submitting to the other. And it takes relationship out of the realm of competition, so that no one wins or loses in the end.

Real safety comes from building relationships with other people that are based on mutual respect and caring. Instead of blindly resorting to these instinctual reactions of submission and aggression, we can learn what we really need when confronted with a situation that charges us emotionally.

Setting Personal Boundaries

A basic skill in self-care is learning to set personal boundaries when we feel threatened. Most of us have no idea how to do this. We have been taught either to attack the other person or submit to them, as the snake demonstrated in the story from the previous chapter. Our options seem to be to meet our needs and sacrifice the relationship, or to stay connected and sacrifice our own needs.

Assertion gives us a third option, which is to stay connected *and* meet our needs. It offers us a way to set a personal boundary *while* maintaining our connection with the other person. Staying connected through the conflict does not mean we surrender our personal safety, as we would if we submitted to the other person. It simply means not attacking them in order to make ourselves safe. Assertion enables us to establish and maintain clear boundaries without making the other person wrong or blaming them.

Once we learn how to be assertive and create healthy boundaries for ourselves, the need for withdrawal or attack diminishes. Eventually we can learn to use withdrawal as a temporary time-out that gives us the space to collect ourselves in order to come back and resolve the situation. With skill in setting personal boundaries, the need for attack can be relinquished altogether. This is what the hermit taught the snake to do in the earlier story when he told him to hiss instead of bite.

Assertion skills allow us to take risks and open our hearts to people or circumstances that appear dangerous. Many times we perceive a threat where there is none, and our defensive responses get in the way of seeing the situation as it really is. Once we trust our ability to set personal boundaries as needed in the moment, we acquire a freedom to explore territory that we may previously have avoided for fear of being hurt.

The Importance of Personal Boundaries

In our closest relationships we inevitably hurt each other without realizing it. Most of us are too focused on meeting our own needs to always be aware of how our behavior impacts another person. We also don't know where the other person's wounds are, and if we spend a lot of time together, it is likely we will bump up against them often, without intending to do so.

It is not that we *want* to hurt each other. We are merely trying to protect our space and get our needs met, and most of us have not learned how to do this effectively. So we often try to manipulate or control another person to get what we want, without realizing what we are doing. This naturally tends to upset other people and can cause distance in our relationships, especially if we are not aware of how the other person is feeling.

Because we all tend to hurt each other without intending to do so, it is important to learn how to make personal boundaries for ourselves in relationships. No one can guess what our needs are at any given moment, because they change according to our emotions and the circumstances at hand. It is unrealistic to expect other people to know when they have hurt us.

> Other people cannot know
> where our personal boundaries are,
> *unless we tell them.*

Communicating Our Needs

The expectation that *"if you loved me you would know what I want"* is the cause of much unnecessary stress and conflict in relationships. No matter how long we have lived with other people, or how well they know us, they simply cannot know our moment-to-moment needs. It is *our* responsibility in a relationship to know our own needs, and communicate those effectively to the people around us.

Much of our time and energy is devoted to meeting our basic needs. And, because we have so little training or experience with meeting our needs, we often try to free ourselves from them by pretending that we don't have any. All this really accomplishes is that we become unaware of our own needs, and end up acting unconsciously to get them met through manipulation or indirect means.

We may be unwilling to recognize and respond to our needs because we have been taught to think of that as a selfish act, and believe that taking care of ourselves is somehow wrong. Yet denial of our basic needs makes them go underground and surface in unconscious ways. When we do not take care of our own needs we have less capacity to help others, or our helping has invisible strings attached to it, as in codependent relationships.

For example, one of your needs might be for recognition and feedback. Perhaps you have spent a lot of time or effort taking care of something for another person, and that person has not thanked you or appreciated your efforts. If you feel guilty for having this need, or think it is wrong, you may push the need into your unconscious where you can no longer feel it. Then you are stuck trying to meet a need you are no longer aware of.

You may find yourself feeling resentful toward that person, avoiding them, or expecting them to do something for you in return. This can end up being a game where you expect the other person to know your need and fill it for you, without asking directly. You may drop hints or even keep trying to please that person so they will notice your efforts.

And if they do not, you may become angry with them, thinking they do not care about you.

It may seem safer to indirectly get the other person to recognize you because you do not have to make yourself too vulnerable and risk rejection. Yet, this approach usually does not work. It can cause confusion in your relationships and end up with you feeling disappointed and isolated.

A cleaner way to approach this need would be for you to ask directly for appreciation from the other person. This can be difficult because it puts you in a vulnerable place, and you risk that they will not be able or willing to recognize and appreciate what you did. However, asking directly for what you want makes it far more likely that it will happen. In a situation like this you could express your need in this way:

> *"I'm feeling frustrated because I spent time and effort helping you, and you did not notice or recognize my work. It would help me to feel more connected to you if you could let me know how you are feeling about what I did."*

Direct Requests and Fear of Rejection

Taking care of ourselves does not mean we do this in isolation. Many of our basic needs get met in our relationships with others, and by asking clearly for what we want we *are* taking responsibility for our own needs. Yet asking for help or setting personal boundaries is risky, because the other person could say no, or refuse to honor them. We often are afraid to make direct requests because we don't want to risk rejection.

Expecting help without asking for it is like trying to win the lottery without buying a ticket. If we don't ask directly for what we want, our chances of getting it are pretty slim. It also puts a strain on our relationships. Other people have to guess what we need, and this can lead to a sense of insecurity and uneasiness between us.

Direct requests offer a chance for the other person to help us meet our needs, without attaching conditions. And, if they say no, we can still be responsible for our need, and look elsewhere to try to meet it. This may challenge us to broaden our range of solutions, and let go of having our need met in one specific way. Yet, once we know that we can take care of ourselves, we are not lost and do not have to abandon ourselves if the other person cannot meet our need.

Informal Assertions

The simplest Assertions are everyday messages meant to convey a boundary or express a need, without being demanding or attacking the other person. This involves telling other people how their behavior affects you, or what your specific needs are in this moment.

A direct request tells other people exactly what you want, and gives them the choice to meet your need. Giving other people the room to say *"yes"* or *"no"* to your request is a way to respect *them* and honor *their* needs. Requests communicate that you care about yourself, and you care about the other person. Here are some examples:

> *"I'm afraid I will be late for work, can you help me?"*
> (followed by a specific request, if the other person says yes)

> *"I don't feel comfortable doing that."* or
> *"I am not comfortable with* (specific situation).*"*

> *"Will you do the dishes tonight?"* or *"I have a lot of homework to do before tomorrow; can you help me out by cleaning up the kitchen after dinner?"*

> *" That hurts!"* or *"Please don't step on my toes like that – it hurts."*

> *"I don't like it when you talk to me like that."* or
> *"Would you make a request, not a demand?"*

> *"I am feeling uncomfortable now and need to take a time out."* or
> *"I am not comfortable with the way this conversation is going."*

> *"I need help lifting this television, can you give me a hand?"*

> *"Would you be willing to make this call to the electric company about our last bill?"*

"I could really use a hug."

"I need someone to talk to about this situation at work. Are you available to listen to me?"

"I am trying to make a decision about what kind of car to buy. It would help me to think out loud about it. Would you be willing to listen to my dilemma?"

"There is something I need to talk with you about; is this a good time for you?"

"Can you please turn the television down?"

"I am confused about what you are asking me to do. Would you be willing to meet with me to discuss my project?"

"I am feeling overwhelmed at the amount of things I have to get done today. Would you be willing to help me?" (followed by a specific request)

"I can't seem to figure out how this program works on the computer and I need to use it for my homework assignment. Can you help me understand how to use it?"

"I feel uncomfortable when you tell me what you think about my situation or what I should do about it. Would you be willing to help me recognize my basic feelings and needs instead?"

"Would you be willing to tell me what you hear me saying so I can find out if I am communicating clearly?"

These informal Assertions are important to practice so you learn to ask for what you want, without demanding or being indirect. The more you practice asking other people for help, the easier it becomes, and the more you can accept when they say "no."

Write several of your own requests here, thinking of specific people and situations in your life now. Below are some prompts that may help you word your assertions.

"Would you be willing to _____

_____ *?"*

"I am uncomfortable with _____

_____ *."*

Chapter 15

Formal Assertion Messages

Formal Assertion Messages can be useful when we have made repeated requests or set informal boundaries with another person, and these have not worked. It is always other people's choice to respect our boundary or meet our need, yet if they choose not to repeatedly, the connection between us is likely to break down. We get a sense that they do not care about us, and the relationship is not important to them. Often at this point, we either become aggressive and demanding, or withdraw and put a distance between us. And both of these responses tend to weaken the relationship further.

A clear Assertion Message can help both of us address our emotions and unmet needs, and result in strengthening the relationship. In this message, you let the other person know the emotions you are feeling, the situation that stimulated those feelings, and the tangible consequence to you. You can follow the same three step format as Supportive Listening, with the focus on yourself, rather than the other person. The key ingredients in this message are: **feelings, facts,** and **impacts.**

A typical three-part Assertion Message sounds like this:

"I feel (<u>feelings</u>), *when you* (<u>facts</u>) *because I* (<u>impacts</u>)."*

Practice writing an Assertion Message now, using a live situation in your life. Think of someone who has done something that upset you. It may be a small event that happened once, or a large repeated occurrence. Try to pick something current that you still have feelings about. Then use the spaces below or another sheet of paper and fill in the three parts as we go along.

Feelings

I feel ...

Use one or two words that indicate the basic emotions that come up when you think about what the other person did.

This part is relatively simple and straight forward, once we accept that we have emotions and are able to identify them. (See list in appendix) Avoid emotional words that immediately place blame like: *used, abused, violated, attacked, abandoned,* or *rejected.* These words are more likely to spark a defensive reaction, and we can usually find more neutral words that do the job like: *hurt, sad, scared, angry, or discouraged.* To find these more neutral feeling words, ask yourself how you feel when you think someone has used (violated, attacked, etc.) you.

If you are giving this message you still have strong feelings about what happened. Keep the emotions in present time if you can, and name the feelings you are having now. If you cannot feel the emotions present for you now, you can begin your message with " **I felt...**"

Facts

when you...

Describe specifically what the other person said or did, using neutral language with no value judgments or interpretations.

This part of the message is about giving the other person specific information about what affected you. It is useful to state other people's behavior or words as accurately as you can, and not to assume that they know what you mean. Keep the facts simple and honest, so you don't get into an argument over what happened. Describe only the actual events, so they know what you are talking about, and can agree with your description.

Assertion works by staying connected with other people as you tell them how their behavior has affected you. Offering a simple, accurate description that you both can agree on helps you to focus on your similarities, rather than your differences. All you are trying to do at this point is give them clear information about what triggered your emotional reaction.

Recognizing Your Own Judgments

Seeing our own judgments can be more challenging than recognizing those of another person. When we have an emotional charge our response typically involves judging someone else as wrong. We often describe what happened using exaggerations and interpretations as a way of venting our emotions. And, we tend to mix our interpretations with the facts in order to make it look like the other person is responsible for our feelings.

When we mix emotions with facts, our story ends up full of judgments and accusations. This unconscious venting usually evokes a defensive response from other people, because they hear our message as an attack against them. If we do not separate our emotions from the story, our judgments tend to dominate, and it is more difficult for the other person to hear us. The conversation then turns into a battle over who is right, and our real needs do not get addressed.

If we can resist the temptation to vent our emotional charge while describing what happened, our message will be more accurate and truthful. This makes it more likely that the other person will hear us and respond to our feelings and needs. To keep this message clean we can keep our emotions separate from describing what happened. That is why we begin with stating our feelings, and then the facts.

Separating our story about what happened, from what *actually* happened, is a key to getting our message across clearly to the other person. Remember how we learned to separate these when listening to another person in Chapter 8, and do the same for yourself now. Notice what part of your story is a neutral description of an event, and what part contains your evaluation. Then simply leave out the evaluation.

This can be difficult because it appears that we are abandoning the truth, and leaving ourselves open to being hurt again. We often think that morality can protect us, assuming if everyone just knew right from wrong we would be safe. We confuse justice with safety so often, that to let go of sorting out good from bad can appear like a careless disregard of our own self- interests.

We often think that if we could just get all people to follow the same rules everything would be fine. Yet we have never been able to all agree on one moral code to follow. Individual freedom means we each have our *own* idea of what is right and what is wrong. There *is* no final authority that we can all turn to who will decide who is to blame. In the end all of our judgments that seem so absolute and final, are merely personal opinions. When we try to make these apply to everyone, we only increase the distance between us and create more tension in our relationships.

Distinguishing right from wrong does not make us safer or more secure. In fact, it does the opposite. When we are in conflict we *all* see ourselves as right, and the other person as wrong. If we focus on proving that the other person is wrong, it only sets us up for a fight and creates *more* conflict in the long run. So in this part of the message, we attempt to set aside any notion of blame toward the other, and simply state the basic information about what happened that triggered our emotional charge.

These examples illustrate the difference between judgments and facts.

Judgmental Interpretation	Factual Description
1. When you ignored my request and left a mess in the kitchen.	*When you did not do what I asked and left dirty dishes in the kitchen.*
2. When you acted like such a jerk and abused me in front of the whole department	*When you told me what you thought I was doing wrong in a loud voice in front of the people I work with.*
3. When you don't give a hoot about anyone else and act like everyone is your personal servant.	*When you tell me to write a report on this by Friday, and don't ask about my current projects to see if I have time.*
4. When you attack me for no reason and vent all your pent-up aggression on me.	*When you talk to me in a loud voice, tell me what you think I do wrong, and call me an inconsiderate jerk.*
5. When you are selfish and just do whatever you want.	*When you don't respond to my request for help with the dishes.*

Judgmental Interpretation	Factual Description
6. When you are rude and inconsiderate.	*When you interrupt me before I have finished talking, and do not seem interested in my point of view.*
7. When you've got your head in a hole and act like you are the only one who lives here.	*When you don't ask me how my day was, and don't acknowledge what I do to contribute to our household.*
8. When you act like a know-it-all and use that psycho babble on me like I am an ignorant child.	*When you tell me what you think my problem is and how to solve it.*

Impacts

because I...

State clearly the impact of the other person's behavior on you, without evaluations of right or wrong.

Think about how the situation you just described above actually impacted you. Look for immediate and basic consequences, like costing money, interfering with work, or physical or emotional pain. And, describe these specific impacts as clearly as you can, in a short sentence or phrase.

The intention is not to make other people appear wrong or feel guilty. In this part of the message, you are simply letting them know something about you that they may not be aware of. You are describing the real impact on you, so they can see your need and have a chance to help you. In doing this, you also become clear about your needs, which puts you in a better position to meet those needs, regardless of how the other person responds.

Sometimes the impact on you is something material like costing money, or physical pain. At other times the impact is more emotional, and may be about the relationship itself. These can be expressed as more feelings or thoughts, as long as you don't evaluate the other person's behavior as wrong. Once judgments are included, the other person is more likely to shut down and not hear your message.

Our normal impulse is to refer to a moral or legal system to prove that we are right and the other person is wrong. This may seem to be the best way to protect ourselves, yet as we have seen, these judgments usually lead to more intense conflict as each of us tries to prove our innocence by making the other guilty.

Let's look at some of the tangible impacts in the examples from the previous section. Here are some possible three-part Assertion Messages for these scenarios. See if you can understand the impact on the speaker when you read these statements.

1. "I feel upset when you leave dirty dishes in the kitchen after I asked you not to, because *I have to clean up the kitchen myself and don't get my other work done on time.*"

2. "I feel hurt and angry when you tell me what you think I am doing wrong in a loud voice in front of the people I work with, because *I feel embarrassed and unsafe with you.*"

3. "I feel frustrated when you tell me to write a report on this by Friday, and don't ask about my current projects to see if I have time, because *I don't get to complete what I am already working on, and it throws off my work schedule.*"

4. "I feel angry when you talk to me in a loud voice and tell me what you think I do wrong, because *I feel bad about myself, and I am not comfortable being around you.*"

5. "I feel upset when you don't respond to my request for help with the dishes because *I have to do more work and end up resenting you.*"

6. "I feel hurt when you interrupt me before I have finished talking, and don't seem interested in my point of view, because *I don't get heard, and think you don't care about my thoughts and feelings.*"

7. "I feel discouraged when you don't ask me how my day was, and don't acknowledge what I do to contribute to our household, because *I feel invisible and taken for granted.*"

8. "I feel uncomfortable when you tell me what you think my problem is and how to solve it, because *I don't get to solve my own problem, and end up feeling weak and helpless*."

Tuning in to Your Needs

Stating the impact on you can help you discover a basic need of yours that is not getting met. When you are able to describe how you are being affected by a situation, your need often becomes obvious. Some needs we can hear in the previous Assertion Messages include:

1. personal time, cleanliness, and order

2. respect, safety

3. recognition, independence

4. self-esteem, safety

5. personal time, support

6. respect, understanding

7. respect, recognition

8. independence, self-reliance, support

Needs, like emotions, are not fixed and absolute realities. They change from moment to moment, depending on our inner experience and outer circumstances. Different words will have different meaning for each of us, so we don't have to get bogged down with exact definitions. The point is to have a clear sense of our basic need in the moment. Then we can go about meeting it, and thereby resolve the emotional charge that signaled the unmet need in the beginning.

Writing Three-Part Assertion Messages

Three-part Assertion Messages are intended to help you to release your emotions in a constructive way, recognize what you need, and ask another person for help in meeting your need. Try writing three-part Assertion Messages in response to each of these situations below. Put yourself in the role of the person facing this dilemma, and see if you can discover some of the needs that are indicated in your message.

If you would like a review, you can find a list of basic needs in the appendix.

1. Your father has said, "When will you get a real job!" several times when you are telling him about your interest in helping people in poorer countries get adequate health care and food for their children.

I feel _____ when you _____

_____

because I _____

_____

(and my need is) _____.

2. When making plans to get together, your friend is often tentative and will not make a commitment. He usually says "let's wait and see what happens" instead of saying yes or no.

I feel _____ when you _____

_____

because I _____

_____

(and my need is) _____.

3. Your family member has borrowed your car and returned it several times without any gas.

I feel _____ when you _____

_____

because I _____

_____

(and my need is) _____ .

4. Your son has a habit of leaving food and dirty dishes on the counter after he is done eating.

I feel _____ when you _____

_____

because I _____

_____

(and my need is) _____ .

5. Someone you do business with has a habit of arriving for work meetings twenty minutes late.

I feel _____ when you _____

_____

because I _____

_____

(and my need is) _____ .

6. Your employee often does not complete their paper work after doing a job, and you end up doing it for them.

I feel _____ when you _____

_____

because I _____

_____

(and my need is) _____.

Summary of the Three-Part Assertion Message

I feel...(feelings)

Beginning an Assertion Message with a disclosure of emotions does several things. It interrupts your habit of blame and attack by shifting the focus off the other person and back to yourself. It establishes what is true for you now, and locates you in the present. And, the other person is not likely to argue with your basic emotion, so there is little room for disagreement or controversy.

Opening with an emotion also makes you vulnerable, which can feel very strange and uncomfortable at first. We usually approach someone who we think has hurt us by armoring ourselves, assuming it is going to be a win or lose contest. By making yourself vulnerable at the outset, you signal that your intention is not to make this a competition, but rather to see if you can cooperate. It also invites the other person to set down their defensiveness and become vulnerable, too.

when you...(facts)

Establishing the simple facts that triggered your emotions lets other people know exactly what you are referring to, and helps them focus on the same situation with you. Because these data reports have no judgments or interpretations and do not indicate blame or induce guilt, the other person can still hear you without becoming too defensive or shut down. Arguing over what happened or who is to blame wastes energy and diverts the communication away from your basic needs.

because I...(impacts)

Bringing the message back to the tangible impact on you again takes the focus off the other person, and encourages you to discover and tend to your basic needs. It offers information for the other person to know how their behavior affects you. And, it indicates what the real problem is, so they can help you if they choose to.

The key to the effectiveness of an Assertion Message is:

- *Describing a specific situation that brought up an emotional charge*

- *Taking responsibility for your own feelings and needs*

- *Asking other people to understand how you are affected by their actions, and inviting them to help you find resolution*

An Assertion Message is a way to take care of yourself. Its strength depends on keeping the focus on *your own* feelings and needs, instead of what other people are doing. If your focus is to get *them* to change, this often finds expression in subtle ways like sarcasm or hints. The other person is then more likely to become defensive, and you are less likely to get your needs met.

Chapter 16

The Assertion Process

Writing an Assertion Message can help you define your emotions, separate the facts of a situation from your judgments, and identify your needs. Sometimes this is as far as the process goes. There may not be an opportunity to deliver the message, or you may choose not to do so. In considering whether to use your message, it is helpful to look at the relationship more closely.

When to Use Assertion

Formal Assertion Messages are intended for the significant relationships in your life, and they focus on situations that have repeated themselves and are likely to continue if you don't say anything. This is a major tool for maintenance and repair of major relationships. The time and effort required for this process is an investment you make. It brings you closer when you are moving apart and allows each of you to have your feelings heard and your needs met when emotions are running high.

This kind of in-depth process would not be appropriate for many of your casual relationships, business contacts, or acquaintances. It is not likely to work in situations where you do not both have an investment in the relationship. Without a deeper bond or ongoing commitment to each other, it may not be possible to hear and understand each other's feelings and needs.

Even in our closest relationships, most of us feel uncomfortable or afraid to share an Assertion Message. When other people act in a way that offends or hurts you, it is easy to assume they don't care about you. You may think that if the other person cared, they would not have acted as they did. In these situations, it is common to believe that it will not make a difference if you explain your feelings and needs.

In all relationships, we hurt each other frequently. We rarely intend to harm another person, and often we are not aware when that is happening. When you resist giving your message to other people because you think they should already know how they hurt you, you never give them a chance to learn about you. Other people cannot know what your emotions, needs and boundaries are, until you tell them. And, even if you have already told them, they can care deeply about you and still forget what you need or want from them.

A formal Assertion Message will help you *find out* if the other person cares about you enough to respond to your concerns. If the relationship is valuable to you, it is important to give this a try. If you express your feelings and needs clearly without judgment or blame, and the other person does not respond to your concerns, then you might conclude that they don't care about you. However, if you have not tried a formal Assertion Message, you owe it to yourself and your relationship to do so before deciding that the other person simply does not care.

What Do You Have to Lose?

It may be helpful to consider both the risk of sharing your assertion and the risk of not sharing it. When you tell other people about your emotions and needs, you take a chance that they will not care about you enough to respond. They might even become hostile and react aggressively. If there is already uneasiness between you and you use Assertion, you might generate more conflict and lose the relationship entirely.

Yet, if the relationship is strained because of an emotional charge you are carrying, not speaking about it is likely to increase the distance between you. If you do not assert yourself, the other person cannot know what you are feeling or needing. And, if you have a basic need that continues to go unmet, the relationship will eventually come apart.

An Assertion Message is designed to address a specific situation that is bothering you, while affirming your interest in staying connected with the other person. This approach *could* result in the other person hearing your concerns and responding in a positive way. When Assertion works, it can bring you closer together and increase the trust, safety, and sense of caring between you.

Setting the Stage

Once you have decided to give the message, it is important to think about where, when, and how to do it. People often want to assert themselves right when an emotional charge comes up. However, that is usually the worst time to do it. In the middle of a traumatic situation, you may be too emotional to think clearly, and your message is likely to be distorted by your strong feelings. You are more apt to use harsh, judgmental language, place blame, and attack the other person, even if your intention is not to do so.

~~~~~~

Soon after I moved into that ramshackle old farm house, it rained hard, and I discovered that the roof leaked in several places. I did what I could to remedy the situation, placing buckets under the leaks and emptying them out from time to time. And, I made a mental note to go up on the roof and put tar on the leaky places next time it was warm and sunny out.

Of course, the next time it was warm and sunny out, the last thing I thought about was fixing my roof. I forgot all about the leaks until the next time it rained. Again, I put out the buckets and vowed to fix the roof on the next sunny day. And again, when the sun came out I forgot about the roof. This pattern repeated itself a number of times until, on one sunny day, it finally occurred to me that I had to fix the roof then, even though I did not want to. I made myself go up on the roof and fix it, and the leak problem was solved.

~~~~~~

Delivering a formal Assertion Message is like fixing a leaky roof. When your emotional charge is being triggered by the other person, it is too stormy and unstable a time to address it clearly. And, when that situation is not happening, you tend to forget about it or not want to bring it up. Yet if you want to be heard, the time to address the situation is when things are relatively calm and the problem is not occurring.

It is helpful to find a time when you and the other person are somewhat relaxed, and there is time and space to talk. When you recognize this time, begin with a direct request like this:

"There is something I need to talk to you about.

Is this a good time for you?"

Then wait for the other person's response before you begin. If they say "yes" then you have their consent and they feel included in the process. If they say "no" then ask when a good time would be, and do not leave this interaction until you have decided on a time and place to talk.

This question needs to be asked firmly so that you will be taken seriously, yet in a way that is not too demanding, which might make them defensive. Keep in mind also that a question like this signals that something is bothering you and is likely to make the other person feel uneasy. It is common for the other person to ask what it is about and want to get right into it. Most people begin to feel guilty or defensive as soon as someone says they need to talk to them, and they either want to avoid talking or get it over with right away. It usually works better, however, not to jump in too quickly and instead stay with the simple question, "Is this a good time?"

The Assertion Process is likely to bring up strong emotions for both of you, and it is important to maintain a sense of safety by doing this in private where other people cannot hear you. It is also important to minimize distractions. Turn off the television or radio, and ask the person to sit and face you so that you can have each other's full attention. Tending to these details lets the other person know that you are serious and want to be taken seriously.

Prepare for Defensiveness

A lot of careful preparation has already gone into your formal Assertion. You have recognized a persistent emotional charge that was triggered by another person's behavior which is affecting your relationship with them. You have formulated a response to that person based on your emotions, the actual events, and the impact on you. And now you have found a time and place that seem appropriate, asked the other person to listen to you, and delivered your message. It is important to pay close attention to what happens next so you can use your skills to increase the likelihood that your message will be heard.

In most situations, the other person will become defensive and try to get you to stop. No one likes to hear that we have hurt or upset someone else, and when we do get this kind of feedback, it usually comes in the form of criticism, blame, or attack. The most common and least effective way of communicating in situations like this is to use "you" messages that make the other person responsible for your emotional charge. These old habitual messages sound like this:

> *"You always get mud on the carpet. Don't you ever pay*
> *attention to where you are walking with those boots on?"*

Although the words you are using and the attitude you are conveying with a formal Assertion Message is *not* one of blame and attack, this is what other people are most likely to think you are doing. They will usually hear something like the Disconnect used above, no matter what you actually say. So, in order to be successful, it is important to anticipate a defensive response. If you know the person well, you might be able to guess how they will defend themselves, and this can help prepare you for the next step.

If other people respond to your message by defending themselves, or by blaming and attacking you, your impulse will likely be to defend yourself or blame and attack them back. If you give in to this urge, the conversation will usually turn into a downward spiral of negativity, with each of you defending and attacking in turn.

These conversations are all too familiar, and most of us know how hurtful and destructive they can be. If you do find yourself in this situation, ask to take a time out. Stop the conversation and separate from each other for a while before addressing the issue again. Once you give in to your urge to defend yourself, the chance of a successful Assertion Message is lost. It is best at this point to abort the process and come back to it at another time.

Listening Supportively to the Other Person's Concerns

When other people begin to defend themselves, or appear to be attacking you, it is easy to take this as a confirmation that they don't care about you and want to hurt you. This line of thinking encourages retaliation, and the conversation can become quite destructive. Instead, consider that they may be reacting out of habit, because they think you are attacking them. If so, the other person is not hearing your message, but is hearing an accusation instead.

If you can restrain yourself when other people become defensive or verbally aggressive, you have a chance to listen to them. You can give them your full attention and reflect back what you hear them saying with an earnest desire to recognize their feelings and needs. By listening supportively, you learn what is going on for them and can often hear what is motivating their behavior. Once you discover this, you have a better chance of reaching some resolution to your dilemma.

Supportive Listening allows other people to be heard and lets them know that you value them and are not just trying to get your way. It helps them to feel respected and included in the process, and often it will calm the emotions they are feeling. Once their emotions are calmer, there is a better chance that they will hear your message in the way you are intending it: as information about you, and not an accusation of them.

Repeating the Assertion Message

Once you have reflected back the other person's concerns and they sound calmer, it is important to bring the focus back to your original issue. An effective way to do this is to simply repeat the same Assertion Message that you began with. It may seem odd to repeat yourself, however, in most cases the other person did not really hear you the first time.

By repeating the message, you are letting the other person know that you are serious and want to be heard. Often an Assertion Process requires numerous repetitions of the same basic message, followed by several Supportive Listening responses. The idea is to do this until other people hear you and acknowledge your concerns, and you have heard them and acknowledged their concerns.

Completing the Process

The process is near completion when the other person says something like:

"Well, what do you want me to do about it?"

This may sound defensive, but it indicates a willingness to get involved in a solution. At this point, it can be helpful to move together in the direction of problem solving. You might ask:

"What do you think you could do?" or

"I don't know. Let's think of some ideas together."

Or, if you know what you want, you could make a direct request such as:

"Would you be willing to (<u>direct request</u>)?"

Guidelines for the Assertion Process:

- Prepare a simple, clear message that you can easily repeat.
- Choose a neutral time and place where you have privacy and no distractions.
- Say: *"There is something I need to talk to you about. Is this a good time for you?"*
- Be prepared to listen and reflect the other person's response.
- When the other person appears less defensive, repeat your message.
- Limit your responses to either Supportive Listening or Assertion.
- Repeat this process until you are satisfied that the other person hears you.
- Move together into problem solving, if appropriate.

Formal Assertion in Action

I once lived with someone who had a habit of leaving her shoes or boots right in the entry way to our home. I tripped over them a number of times and began to feel irritated. As soon as I noticed that this was a problem for me, I asked her not to leave her shoes there using this informal Assertion:

"Would you be willing to leave your shoes away from the doorway, where I don't have to step over them to get into the house?"

I made this request on several occasions, and still she often left her shoes right in the doorway. I began to feel resentment and anger toward her and noticed that it was creating a distance between us. I realized that this issue was a problem for me because the resentment began to creep into other parts of our relationship.

I decided to use a formal Assertion so the relationship did not grow farther apart. I looked for a time when I was not upset, her shoes were not in the doorway, and we were both relatively relaxed and available. Then I approached her to talk, and the conversation went something like this:

<u>Me</u>	<u>Other Person</u>
(setting the stage)	
There is something I need to talk with you about. Is this a good time for you?	*Yes.*
(formal assertion)	
I feel frustrated and annoyed when you leave your shoes in the front hallway, because I often trip over them when I come in.	*I can't believe you are making such a big deal out of this. Can't you just move them if they are in your way?*
(supportive listening)	
It sounds like you feel upset because you think I am making a big deal out of nothing, and you want me to move your shoes if they are in my way.	*Well, where am I supposed to put them, anyway? There isn't anyplace in the hallway to put them.*
(supportive listening)	
So you are frustrated because there is no other place to put your shoes in the hallway?	*Yes.*
(reassertion)	
I still feel frustrated and annoyed when you leave your shoes in the front hallway because I often trip over them when I come in.	*Well, what about when I come in and trip over your shoes?*

Me	Other Person
(supportive listening)	
It sounds like you are uncomfortable because you think I am asking you to do something for me that I don't do for you?	*Yes.*
(reassertion)	
I still feel frustrated and annoyed when you leave your shoes in the front hallway because I often trip over them when I come in.	*So, what do you want me to do about it?*
(problem solving)	
What do you think you could do?	*Well, if we had someplace to put shoes in the hallway, I would put them there.*
(problem solving)	
So you are saying if we had a good place to put shoes out of the way, you would use it?	*Yes.*
(problem solving)	
What if we go together right now and look at the hallway to see if we can make a place for shoes that is out of the way?	*Okay.*

When I used Supportive Listening in this example, it helped me stay calm and focused and not get sidetracked away from my concern by the other person's defensiveness. Her initial defensive responses were smoke screens. They were aimed at getting me to drop the issue by blaming me for the situation.

After I reflected these responses and reasserted my message, I then learned that she did not know where else to put her shoes. That seemed to be the root of the problem. In my mind, I had made up a story that she did not care about my needs and was intentionally disregarding my request in order to hurt me. When I listened to her and got beyond her defensiveness, I learned that there was a practical consideration that needed attention.

By calmly and directly dealing with the emotions and needs of both of us, we were able to come up with a relatively simple and practical solution. Not only was the shoe problem solved for me, but our relationship was strengthened. We discovered that we could have a conflict and move through it together, instead of competing with each other to see who would win, as we had in the past. In this case we both won, meaning that both of us got our emotions recognized and our basic needs met.

Deciding to Use a Formal Assertion Message

In most relationships, we unconsciously step on each other's toes in a lot of ways, and it is not practical or wise to use formal Assertion every time this happens. Many small hurts happen throughout the day, and part of being in relationship is learning to take care of ourselves and forgive the other person. Taking into consideration that other people do not intend to hurt us, and not taking their actions personally, is a good way to free us from anger and resentment without getting into a longer process. Healthy relationships require that we be flexible, learn to take care of the needs underlying our emotions, and let the feelings go when we can.

However, because many of us have had a habit of ignoring our emotions, we have to use caution and know the difference between genuine release, and denial. It is wise to try letting go of an emotional charge as soon as you realize that a situation is bothering you. You can set the feelings aside, discover what you need in that moment, and take care of yourself. However, if you find yourself dwelling on it, or if the emotional charge is causing distance in the relationship, it is a signal that you need to address the situation with the person directly. Otherwise, you and the other person are likely to grow apart.

When you have an emotional charge related to another person's behavior, it is usually wise to try an informal Assertion first. This requires that you be in touch with your emotions and needs and are willing to ask the other person for help. Letting people know what you want on a regular basis, especially with your most significant relationships, tends to reduce the need for formal Assertion, because it keeps your emotions and needs from piling up. Informal Assertions can be used frequently because they do not take a lot of time or effort.

The signal that it may be time to use a formal Assertion is usually a sinking feeling in your stomach. You may be avoiding the other person, or carrying resentment that is putting distance in your relationship. When you need to deliver a three-part Assertion Message, you may feel afraid and uneasy because you don't want to initiate a confrontation that could lead to a larger conflict. It is common to rationalize that the problem will take care of itself if you leave it alone. This is the very time to muster your courage and assert yourself.

Getting Outside Support

Sometimes the thought of doing an Assertion Message with a particular person is too overwhelming. Even though you know it needs to be done, you just can't bring yourself to do it. As you have seen, the choice not to assert may mean the relationship grows more distant or comes apart. Therefore, if you are in a relationship that you don't want to lose, yet you cannot talk directly to the person about an emotional charge, a good option may be to involve a neutral third party. This person could be a professional mediator, counselor, minister, community or family member, or a neutral friend.

A third person to witness and guide the process can create safety and help both people stay focused and hear each other. This person can also interrupt attacking or defensive communication and use Supportive Listening when one or both people are not able to do so. Before you involve other people in a conflict like this, however, be sure they are willing to help. They also have to be able to remain neutral, maintain confidentiality, and use basic communication skills.

As uncomfortable as it can be to deliver a formal Assertion Message, the results are often worth it. If the other person does hear you and you are able to come to some resolution that you both agree on, the sense of accomplishment and relief can be tremendous. This process can result in deeper trust and intimacy and a more alive and satisfying connection with the other person. Going through Assertion successfully can strengthen a relationship by creating a new pattern for dealing with emotional charges and give both people the courage to face these tensions directly again.

Assertion is a better way to get your needs met than being aggressive or demanding because, in the end, you can feel good about it. It maintains your connection with the other person, and in many cases strengthens it, so you don't lose a relationship in order to get what you want. Assertion also offers a better way than surrender to achieve stable peace and security. When both people are heard and have their needs met, the tension of conflict dissolves because the underlying cause has been addressed.

Positive Assertion

So far, we have been talking about using Assertion as a remedy when someone has done something that hurts or upsets you. You can also use a formal Assertion Message to give positive feedback. It is a good way to let someone know that they have done something that helps you, and is an effective way to express appreciation that does not rely on evaluation or praise.

As we discussed earlier in Chapter 3 on Disconnects, the problem with praise is that it can weaken other people by encouraging them to value themselves based on what *you* think of them. If you use praise or positive evaluations habitually with other people, it may create an unhealthy need for them to seek approval and recognition outside themselves, instead of trusting their own feelings.

Giving a positive Assertion is more strengthening and supportive because it refers to your *emotions and needs* instead of your *judgments or evaluations* of them. It is a way to tell other people who have made a positive impact on your life exactly what they did and the specific way in which it helped you. Here are several examples:

> *"I feel relieved when you leave the kitchen clean, because I can cook without having to clean up first."*

> *"I am grateful when you set your shoes aside because I don't trip over them when I walk in the door."*

> *"I feel better when you give me feedback about my work in private because I don't feel so uncomfortable and exposed."*

Try writing some positive Assertions for the role-play situations below. Put yourself in the role of the person speaking and think of how you might feel, what the other person did, and exactly how it helped you. Then fill in the three-part positive message below:

1. A colleague at work took an important detailed message for you while you were away.

I feel _____

when you _____

_____

because I _____

_____

2. Your spouse packed a lunch for you in the morning before you left for a business trip.

I feel _____

when you _____

_____

because I _____

_____

3. Your child was sick and your parent took care of them while you were at work.

I feel _____

when you _____

_____

because I _____

_____

Think of someone in your life now who has done something to help you, and try writing a positive Assertion Message to let them know exactly how their actions affected you.

I feel _____

when you _____

_____

because I _____

_____

Assertion

Expressing your feelings and needs honestly without blame or attack

Informal Assertion:

"Would you wash the dishes tonight?"

"I'm afraid I will be late for work, can you help me?"

"I don't feel comfortable with that."

"I feel scared when you talk to me in a loud voice."

Three-part Assertion Message (connecting feelings, facts, and impacts):

I feel...	(feelings)	*"I feel hurt and lonely*
when you...	(facts)	*when you go away on your day off,*
because I...	(impacts)	*because I miss spending time with you."*

Delivering an Assertion Message

"There is something I need to talk with you about. Is this a good time for you?"

You   Other Person

Assertion Message ⟶ Defensive Response

Supportive Listening ⟵ Defensive Response

Supportive Listening ⟵ Less Defensive

Assertion Message ⟵ Hears the message and responds to your concerns

(repeat until...)

Possible Conclusion Statements

"Would you be willing to...(direct request)?"

"So, you are going to... (what the other has offered), and I am going to... (what I have offered)."

Conflict Resolution

Chapter 17

Conscious Conflict

Think of the idea of conflict for a moment and make a list of as many words to describe it as you can:

Conflict is _____

_____

The exercise above should help to illustrate that most of us view conflict in a negative way. We associate it with stress, frustration, tension, hurt feelings, relationships ending, destruction, and violence. These are the most common consequences of conflict in our lives. We have an assumption that conflict is a struggle and causes great damage. It is no wonder, then, that many of us either avoid conflict at all costs or try to overcome opposition quickly and decisively.

We tend to see our options as running and hiding from conflict or throwing ourselves at it with as much force as we can, in order to win. Our common approach is to either avoid or control whoever we think is causing the conflict. Yet these immediate responses only deal with the symptoms, and not the cause of the tension. Rarely do we take the time to resolve the issues that are at the bottom of a conflict, so it usually returns at another time in a different form.

Conflict itself does not create the problems normally associated with relationship tensions. It is our lack of *skill* in dealing with our differences that makes these situations so difficult. Instead of avoiding conflict or trying to force a resolution, you can learn how to respond more effectively by paying attention to the predictable patterns that underlie it and expanding your range of responses.

Ingredients of Conflict

The first step in resolving conflict is to understand its basic components. Here is a simple recipe for conflict that will help you understand what is happening:

1. Two or more people

2. A perceived threat to your values and/or needs

3. An emotional charge

The key word above is *perceived.* Conflict happens when you *think* someone is blocking you from getting a need met or challenging your beliefs. In such situations, it can appear as if your very existence is threatened by the other person. And, it is this sense of being violated or discounted that often generates the strong feelings associated with conflict.

Emotions in Conflict

An emotional charge is often the first signal of conflict, and it is the strong emotions in a conflict situation that usually lead to the destructive outcomes you have learned to expect. When you are emotional you cannot think clearly and are likely to react from your survival instincts rather than your intelligence. There are very practical reasons for this.

When you perceive a threat, the physical chemistry of your body changes. You are charged up with adrenaline to give you added physical strength in order to defend yourself or run for safety. The energy in your body is being directed to your physical capacities, and not to your brain, so you cannot think effectively. With your capacity for rational thought diminished, it is easy to make impulsive decisions that hurt yourself or others. And, often these are the responses you most regret later on.

Earlier chapters in this book have focused on emotions and how to work with them because this is so essential for maintaining your relationships with other people. Using Supportive Listening, you can hear another person's emotions and acknowledge them. And, you can get in touch with your own emotions and express them constructively through Assertion. Once the emotions have been recognized, they tend to diminish, leaving you calmer and more able to think clearly.

Values in Conflict

A second component of conflict is values. These are the beliefs and judgments that form the core of our personality. Our values are what we think is right and wrong, and we often use them to define who we are. A common cause of conflict is when one of our values appears to be threatened by other people. It may be that they have an opposite opinion, or their actions violate what we believe is right.

Our identity is so dependent on our values that we often mistake these ideas for reality. We tend to hold tightly to them because they seem to give us fixed reference points. We often use our ideas of right and wrong to guide us through life, so when our beliefs are challenged, our whole world can seem uncertain. When another person criticizes something we believe in, we take it as a personal attack and often react defensively. This is why values can be at the root of many conflicts.

> The problem with conflicts of values
> is that a final resolution
> is unlikely.

Resolving values conflicts would mean that both you and the other person would have to embrace the same idea of what is right and wrong. An agreement like this is not likely to happen in many situations because of our need for individuality. We each have a different set of values, and this is part of what makes us unique. When other people try to change our values, most of us get defensive. And, the more they try to change our mind, the stronger we hold on to what we believe in.

A conflict of values is a losing proposition. The more you fight, the worse the situation becomes. That is why seemingly simple values clashes can lead to such violence and never reach a conclusion. Once opposition has been expressed and emotions are charged, an agreement over what is right and wrong becomes highly unlikely because of the individual nature of human beings and the very personal nature of values.

Conflicts of values often play out on a large scale and can be the cause of wars. The Civil War in the United States happened largely because one part of the country believed strongly that slavery was necessary and good, and another part believed that it was wrong. Sometimes wars are fought over differences between religions, or different sects within one religion. Violence has simmered for decades in northern Ireland between Catholic and Protestant Christians, and in parts of the Arab world between Sunni and Shiite Muslims, to name a few.

Some major values conflicts going on today within the United States concern abortion and homosexuality. There are people on both sides of these issues who feel strongly that they are right and the other side is wrong. And these conflicts can continue indefinitely because of the impossibility of one side convincing the other side to change its beliefs.

In the end, our values tend to be a complex layering of personal experiences and conditioned beliefs that are never exactly the same for any two of us. If you scratch the surface of two people who share a belief in vegetarianism, for example, you will find that they have different reasons for that belief and different ways in which the value of not eating meat expresses itself. One person may be vegetarian because she does not want to harm animals, and the other person because he wants to be more healthy.

People who consider themselves vegetarian also have differences in their diets. For some, vegetarianism means eating a standard diet of commercially packaged, chemically processed foods without any meat. For others, it means eating whole foods that are organically grown and locally in season. Some vegetarians eat fish and eggs, while others do not. This is an example of how subtle and varied individual beliefs can be, and it explains why trying to get other people to agree on one set of ideals and express them in the same way is nearly impossible.

The Longing for Certainty

Most of us long to find something absolute and certain in life that never changes. We want a place to stand that is solid and sure. However this constantly changing world does not seem to offer such a place, so we often try to create it ourselves in the form of beliefs. Making a clear distinction between right and wrong establishes fixed reference points in the constantly shifting landscape of our lives. We think that if we hold tightly enough to these ideals, it will give our lives a sense of certainty.

Our values are ideas that we place beyond question, in order to create that sense of certainty. We look at them as things that are final and cannot be changed. Then it becomes important that the people around us agree with our beliefs in order to validate that we are right. If other people do not agree with the point of view we hold, it tends to create tension between us, and we often end up in competition with each other to see whose value will prevail.

> When your idea of what is right and wrong
> is the *only* way,
> it is sure to create conflict in your relationships.

The problem with trying to distill truth by comparing our opinions is that these are merely personal beliefs that are true for us now, and tend to change over time. Ideas of right and wrong can never provide the certainty we seek because they are only *ideas* and are not real. If we pay attention to our thoughts it becomes clear that our ideas change frequently and dramatically from moment to moment. They are far from the fixed reality we think they are, and they cannot provide a solid foundation.

There simply is no measure of good and bad that applies to all people at all times. Relying on personal beliefs for certainty is like trying to hold a wild song bird in your hand to keep it from flying away. You have to hold on tighter and tighter, and eventually the only way to be sure it will not leave is to kill it. Values are like this, too. If you try to make them permanent, you end up killing them and finally have nothing but dead and lifeless ideas to hold on to.

To maintain your values as absolutes, you have to continually assert and reaffirm them. Like the foundation of a house built on sand, they require constant maintenance, adjustment, and shoring up to keep them in place. However, because you are looking to them as final reference points in your life, there is *no* room for variation or disagreement. Any different set of values tends to pose a threat as you struggle to defend your beliefs against opposition.

This is why values are at the center of so much conflict. Each side is trying to prove that they are right and the other side is wrong in order to establish *their own* beliefs as the absolute truth. In a values conflict, both sides are trying to force their beliefs onto the other and the result is a self- perpetuating cycle of opposition and struggle. The more one side asserts their beliefs, the more the other side is compelled to defend their own. You have to do this if you think you *are* your values and if your values are the only reference point you have.

> We defend our values
> as if they are the only thing we have
> to validate our existence.
> Yet, instead of making us more secure,
> this habit creates tension and instability in our world
> as we end up constantly competing with each other
> to see who is right.

There is no way to win or resolve a struggle over beliefs, and the more you try, the worse the situation becomes. When you try to attain peace by making your values apply to all of humanity, you actually create more conflict in your life and your world. You end up caught in a self-defeating pattern where the only method you know for creating security results in making the world you live in more threatening and uncertain.

Conscious Communication offers an alternative to this blind habit that results in so much struggle and never reaches a satisfying conclusion. Instead of looking for truth and certainty in thoughts and ideas, we can reference to our experience of the present moment. Our feelings and needs are the only things we can be truly certain about. By distinguishing between our emotions, values, and needs, and learning a simple way to communicate these to other people, we ground ourselves in what *is* really happening now, instead of our ideas about what *should* happen.

Do Our Values Define Who We Are?

There was a time in my life when I thought computers were not a good idea because we would become too dependent upon them and they would have a negative impact on our lives. However, when I saw how a computer helped me to run a small business, write books, and stay in touch with the people I cared about, my belief changed. I no longer see computers as bad. Instead, I see them as tools that can enable me to do good things in the world more efficiently.

We tend to assume that our values make up who we are, yet this is simply not true. You can recognize this by looking back at your life and finding a significant value that has changed.

Think of a belief you were certain about that has now changed. It may help to think in terms of something you were sure was right and now think is wrong, or something you were sure was wrong and now think is right. Take a moment now to see if you can find a shift like this that has happened in your own life.

I used to believe...

_____

_____

_____

And now I believe...

_____

_____

_____

Cultural Values

Our beliefs about the world come largely from the culture in which we were raised. Beliefs tend to be invisible to us because we began learning them when we were children and now they are so familiar we don't notice them. A major benefit of values conflicts is that they bring to light our unconscious beliefs.

> In our conflicts with other people,
> our values become visible to us.
> We can then ask ourselves
> if they are still serving us
> and if we want to keep them or let them go.

I was raised in a suburb near a city, and now live out in the country. Many of my neighbors grew up here, and because of our different backgrounds, we naturally have different values. One summer a large pack of coyotes was hanging out in the woods nearby my house. Night after night, I heard them howl. I loved to hear them because they reminded me of how wild and free this land is compared to the crowded and overdeveloped neighborhood where I grew up.

One day, I was visiting a neighbor and mentioned the coyotes howling at night, and how wonderful it was to hear them so close by. He responded passionately, saying that he hated hearing them and they were much too close for comfort. He said he kept his gun loaded by the door in case he ever saw one of them close enough to shoot.

On a different occasion, I was visiting another neighbor, a kind and gentle older man who I respected for his love of the land and detailed care of his old farm. I commented to him excitedly about a family of foxes I had been observing near my house. He then told me he had discovered a mother fox with pups living in a culvert under the road near his home. He proudly explained how he had closed in the end of the culvert and piped in exhaust from his car in order to kill them.

Both situations left me shocked and speechless as I realized how differently we each saw these wild animals that lived around us. To my neighbors, these animals were dangerous and threatening, while to me they represented an untamed wildness that filled my heart with joy. My first impulse was to judge my neighbors as bad people. I wanted to argue with them and try to convince them they were wrong about the coyotes and foxes that shared our woods. Yet I knew this would probably result in alienating us from each other, and it was not likely I would change their deeply held beliefs.

In order to make peace with myself and stay connected in my heart with these people I cared for, it helped me to put myself in their shoes for a moment and view the situation from their perspective. They each grew up in the country, had farm animals, and knew firsthand how violent and destructive coyotes and foxes could be. They had likely seen livestock under their care being killed or taken by wild animals, and they saw these predators only as a threat.

I understood that there was no point in trying to change either of my neighbor's minds on this issue. Our continued friendship and caring about each other depended on letting go of this issue and seeing it as only a superficial part of who each of us were. Even as I felt sick to my stomach at the thought of my neighbors killing these beautiful wild animals that I loved so much, I knew that the only way to resolve this conflict was to let it go. I had to see myself as more than my ideas of right or wrong in a particular moment, and recognize that in different circumstances, I might agree with their point of view.

Dealing With Conflicts of Values

The most effective way to deal with the values component of conflict is to recognize it and let it go. After enough pain and struggle, we can finally recognize that trying to make our beliefs apply to all people creates irresolvable conflict in our lives. We can learn that we are bigger than our values and beliefs, and that they do not provide the certainty we think they will.

However, letting go of our opinions is not usually easy. Setting aside our beliefs and considering them temporary requires courage and vulnerability.

> To allow for other people to have different values,
> we have to expand our definition of ourselves
> beyond our ideas of right and wrong,
> and root our identity
> in an inherent connection with all of humanity,
> instead of in our personal convictions.

Ironically, allowing other people to have their own beliefs is often more difficult with the people to whom we feel the most connected. We tend to expect those closest to us to share our ideas of what is good and bad and look to them to support our beliefs. Often, we form relationships based on the assumption of shared values. However, when we discover that the other person does not share our judgments, it can be very disturbing.

If we define ourselves by our ideals, we can easily become mired in power struggles, trying to get other people to believe as we do. Our basic identity seems to depend on lining up our judgments and opinions with the people around us to prove that we are right. Yet if we can see that our attempt to create security by forcing a common value system is actually *causing* more conflict, we may become willing to try something different.

Values Conflicts within Families

I was with my family one Thanksgiving, when someone asked to hear our opinions about the recent United States invasion of Iraq. That began a heated argument which ended with my brother and I almost yelling at each other over the dinner table in a formal restaurant. I was passionately expressing my opposition to the war, while my brother was equally passionate about his support for it. The conversation ended with both of us feeling separate and mistrustful of each other because neither of us had convinced the other to budge from his point of view.

I felt terrible later that night as I reflected on the distance between me and my brother and the futility of our argument. I was especially disappointed with myself because I had abandoned my training in conflict resolution and communication skills, resorting to old habits that I knew did not serve what I most wanted. As I thought about what happened, I realized that I was not able to stay separate from his story and see that it was about him. I had taken his opinions as a personal challenge to mine and proceeded to get into a struggle over who was right.

I began to see that his story contained information about his experience that I had not recognized. He described how, on the day of September 11, 2001, his wife was in New York City working when two commercial passenger jets were deliberately crashed into the World Trade Center buildings. No one knew what was happening and it seemed as if the whole city was under attack. He lost contact with her for the entire day and was home with their infant daughter, wondering if his wife was still alive.

The terror that my brother felt that day turned into anger and he wanted to strike out against any possible enemy who might have been responsible. He had been convinced by our President, as so many people in the United States were, that Iraq had something to do with the attacks of September 11th, and was planning to attack us again. So, he naturally supported the President's plan to destroy the government of Iraq and disable their capacity to hurt us again.

Once I let go of my need to be right and gave up trying to align our perspectives on the war, I could step back and see that he was telling me something about him that was vital and alive in that moment. I had missed that entirely because I was focused on comparing his conclusion to mine, thinking that the goal was to establish the truth of the situation.

Seeing my brother's story as about him, and not as the truth about the war, changed my entire perspective. I could understand him and feel connected to him again. This did not change my passionate opposition to the war, but it altered my focus. I was no longer determined to establish which of us was right and which was wrong.

I had gained more information about my brother and how to support and connect with him. This focus felt much better to me inside, as my heart could remain open to him, even as I disagreed with his perspective. I also saw that if I truly wanted to influence his opinion, it would be helpful to first connect with him by validating his experience and empathizing with his feelings of terror and anger toward the perpetrators of the tragedy in New York.

Agreeing to Disagree

A more effective way to approach a conflict of values is to use Supportive Listening to have a constructive exchange of ideas. The intention would be to understand the other person, learn more about what he thinks and feels, and agree to disagree. When we can allow someone else to think differently than we do, and honor his opinions and beliefs, our relationship becomes less stressful and the connection between us grows stronger.

In the previous example, a more effective response to my brother's concerns might have sounded like this:

> *"It sounds like you felt scared and angry when the buildings in New York were attacked on September 11th because you did not know if your family was safe. And now you believe it is a positive step for our country to try to deal with possible threats to our safety by attacking a country that could be the source of more harm to us."*

This response recognizes his emotions, the situation that stimulated them, and the impact on him. It also recognizes his conclusion about the most effective way to respond to his concerns. Notice that my response is not an agreement with his perspective. I am simply acknowledging how he feels about the situation and his opinions about it, without agreeing or disagreeing.

If my brother was willing and able to recognize my concerns, he might respond like this:

"So you feel very upset that our country is initiating a war with another country that has not openly attacked us because you think this will increase the level of fear and hatred toward us and encourage more violence against us?"

This kind of dialogue would allow both of us to maintain our values and create a true meeting of two individuals, each with a different perspective. Using these skills can help you recognize each other's concerns and opinions, allow them to be different, and not lose the natural caring you feel toward each other. Allowing for different values, while maintaining your connection as fellow human beings, represents a high level of maturity and self-confidence. It enables each of us to be different, yet still be connected.

Letting Go of Wanting to Be Right

Letting go of being right is difficult for many of us. We have learned that being right is the prize that gives us validity and power in the world. When you are caught up in a conflict of values, asking yourself these questions can help put things in perspective:

"Would I rather be right or get my needs met?"

or, "Do I want to be right or happy?"

Oddly, we tend to place such emphasis on being right that we may disregard our well-being and neglect our basic needs. We often mistake winning for happiness. When we win, however, this usually means someone else loses, and frequently this competitive approach damages the relationship. This is why so often the experience of winning feels hollow and incomplete once the initial excitement is over.

When you win an argument over values, it seems to strengthen your sense of self and reinforce *your* belief as real. You may experience an instant feeling of power and security. Yet because beliefs are *not* reality, your security is usually short-lived and easily threatened by someone else. Also, if you win a values conflict, it means that someone else has lost, and that person is likely to rise up and challenge you again before too long. In this way, you can end up in constant conflict, having to defend your beliefs as they are being continuously attacked.

A bigger problem with conflicts over values is that they do not address your real needs because they are focused on being right and making someone else wrong. In order to dislodge yourself from this common habit of competing with others to be right, it may help to ask yourself this question:

"What will I win if I get to be right?"

This question can help you distinguish between ideas or beliefs, and tangible needs. The usual answer is that you get a feeling of security or a stronger sense of self. However, being right does little for your sense of sustained happiness. Winning an argument tends to give you a short-lived sense of power, yet it does not nourish your long term well-being. It also tends to weaken your relationships with other people and further your sense of isolation.

When it appears as though another person's values threaten our own, it is important to notice that *nothing tangible is at stake*. Our values are merely ideas we hold on to because they seem to offer us certainty and security in the world. However, the sense of identity we get from our beliefs is fragile and easily shaken because they are really only thoughts or ideas.

A key to developing sustainable and nourishing relationships is being able to distinguish between thoughts and ideas, which are *not* tangible or real, and your basic needs, which *are* real. Values and beliefs are ideas, and as such, cannot provide the nourishment needed to sustain life. Needs are those things we require for our long-term nourishment, growth, and sense of fulfillment. In the next chapter, we will turn our attention to conflicts of needs.

Chapter 18

Collaborative Negotiation

As stated in the last chapter, conflict occurs when our values or needs seem to be at odds with those of other people. It appears that if their opinion is right, then ours is wrong, or if they get their way, we will not get ours, and this tension usually generates strong emotions. When we fight over whose value is right, we end up in a destructive kind of conflict that rarely reaches a conclusion. The only way to effectively resolve a conflict of beliefs is to agree to disagree. Needs, however, are a different matter.

A conflict of needs is when it looks like we are in competition with another person for something basic that we require for our well-being. Typically, this ends with someone winning and someone losing. While this may be the most familiar outcome, it often does not resolve the conflict. When one of us wins and one of us loses, there are still unmet needs, and the tension between us usually grows stronger. Far from reaching peace, competitive conflict like this only generates more struggle. In this chapter we will look at a new approach where the aim is to meet *both* people's needs.

Separating Values from Needs

Often a conflict will involve both values and needs, and it is necessary to be able to separate these so that the needs can be addressed effectively. A student in one of my classes shared a conflict that went something like this:

She was a nonsmoker and her partner was a smoker. She was uncomfortable with his smoking and had tried for years to get him to stop. She had been pressuring him to quit, telling him that smoking was bad for his health and not a good thing to do. In doing this, she had been focusing on the values part of their conflict. She believed smoking was wrong and bad, and he thought it was right and good. She had been trying to get him to change his value.

I asked if what she was doing was working. She said it was not, and every time she tried to get him to quit smoking, he seemed to smoke even more! This is a predictable result of trying to change another person's value. Pressuring other people to change the way they believe usually makes them cling even more tightly to that belief.

I suggested that she focus instead on her needs, and I asked her why she wanted him to quit smoking, or *what she would get if he did not smoke*. She told me she wanted clean air to breathe, a house that didn't smell of cigarette smoke, and not to have to clean up ashtrays full of cigarette butts. I suggested she approach him with an Assertion Message that included the tangible impact on her, and left out her judgments or opinions about his smoking.

When she brought up the issue of smoking with her partner the next time, she was not focused on cigarettes being good or bad, and did not have an agenda that he quit. She wanted to get her basic needs met and was willing to help him meet his basic needs at the same time. This took the conversation out of the competitive realm and shifted the focus away from who was right and who was wrong. As a result, the conversation was much more civil and did not turn into an argument or power struggle.

In order to get her needs met, I encouraged her to listen to his concerns and give them equal value to hers, remembering that the process would not be complete until both of them were satisfied with the results. Once this basic ground rule is established, both people in a conflict can relax a bit more into the process, knowing that their individual needs will be addressed. It meant, however, that she could not simply hammer away at what she wanted. She also had to listen to him and consider what he wanted.

She tried the process of Collaborative Negotiation that is described below, kept the focus on both of their needs, and came back to class in two weeks very pleased with the results. They were able to work out an arrangement where he set up a smoking room in their garage with a couch, television, and beer refrigerator. This met his need to smoke in a comfortable place and her need to not have cigarettes or smoke in the house. By this time, she had let go of trying to get him to quit and accepted that he valued smoking as a good thing to do. She also reported that since they had worked out this resolution, he was actually smoking a lot less!

Discovering Your Real Needs

We learned about basic needs in Chapter 9 (see list in the Appendix), and have discussed how unmet needs fuel our emotions and generate conflict with other people. We have practiced using listening and assertion skills to help us recognize these needs and find ways to meet them. Now, let's take a closer look at needs and why they often seem so elusive.

Once we accept that we do have needs and take responsibility for meeting them, it can still be challenging to discover what they are. One reason for this is that we tend to focus our attention on *strategies* for meeting our needs instead of the *needs* themselves. Our habit is to emphasize the *means* instead of the *end* that we want to accomplish, and this mistake undermines our problem-solving capacities.

Beyond physical needs like water, air, and food, the *things* we want in life are only a means to meet a need, not the need itself. A car, for example, is a means to meet a need for transportation, and a house meets our need for shelter from the weather. In our society, we meet many of our needs with money, such as food, clothing, shelter, recreation, and even self-esteem. We may say we need money, a house, or a car; however, these are only useful in order to meet more basic needs.

In developed societies today, a wide array of choices is available in everything from the kind of toothpaste we use to where we live and work. And the reason many of us want to accumulate wealth is to increase our personal choices. We equate more choice with happiness, thinking that if we can get exactly what we want all the time, we will be fulfilled.

Yet more choice does not always lead to happiness, because *we often don't know what our real needs are.* In the last chapter we discussed how we often mistake being right for being happy, or winning for getting what we want. We make this same mistake when we think a car, relationship, vacation, or simply getting more of something, will make us content. There is nothing wrong with wanting or having any of these things. It is just that if we do not know what needs we are trying to fill with them, there is little chance that they can actually serve to make us happy. This is why living with so many choices can be quite challenging in the end.

In our unconscious habit of mistaking the means for the end, we tend to accumulate things and are always trying to get something bigger and better. We forget that a house is simply for shelter, a car is for transportation, and money is to buy things that we need. We often think the solution to our unhappiness lies in getting a bigger house, a better car, or more money. We make getting these *things* the goal, instead of our happiness. This never really works, however, because we don't realize that these things can only *assist* us in finding completion, and do not complete us in themselves.

Growing wiser is mostly about learning what we really need. And, the abundance of goods and services available to many people in affluent countries today provide us with endless opportunities to discover what makes us genuinely happy. However, if we don't realize that our job is to *learn* what we need to be satisfied, this degree of individual choice can lead to confusion and frustration. It is also the source of a lot of conflict.

If we think that the aim of life is simply getting more of everything, we naturally are going to see ourselves in competition with everyone else. While there is still an abundance of everything that we really need for our physical and emotional well-being, the material resources of earth *are* limited. If we see our happiness as dependent on simply getting more, we focus on the limits, rather than the abundance, of what we want. And, it is this perceived lack that causes many of our conflicts, as we pit ourselves against each other for these limited resources.

While it is common to compete with each other to see who can get more of everything, it is not so common to fight over our actual needs, because they are so basic and have no obvious limits. We normally do not fight over air, water, shelter, or food as long as there is a reasonable supply of these around us. And it makes no sense to compete with each other for love, understanding, solitude, companionship, or any other emotional need, because we can all have these at the same time. In fact, recognizing the similarity of our basic needs makes us more alike and can provide the sense of connection we long for with each other.

Fighting over the Means

In most conflicts we fight over the *way* we want to meet our needs, and not the needs themselves. This is a tragic consequence of not knowing what our basic needs are, and mistaking them for the things that we *use* to meet our needs. When we focus on strategies instead of needs, we generate conflict, because our ways of getting what we want often *do* interfere with those of another person.

Remember the previous example of the couple who had a conflict around smoking? They were deadlocked in a heated contest over who would get their way. She wanted him not to smoke, and he wanted to smoke. It looked like what each of them wanted was in direct opposition to what the other wanted, and that only one of them could get their way. Most conflicts begin this way, with two opposing solutions.

When conflicts play out this way, they usually become destructive to the relationship and the people involved. We forget about what need we are trying to meet and instead put all of our effort into winning. It is almost impossible *not* to get caught up in a competitive struggle if we approach our differences from this angle. For many of us, conflict has become an involuntary habit that directly undermines our own well-being because we end up neglecting our own happiness in the process of trying to win or be right. In this light, it seems reasonable to consider conflict as an addiction.

When faced with the prospect of not getting our way, most of us automatically put up a fight. We cannot see the difference between our basic needs and the means we want to use to meet them. So when our strategies for meeting our needs interfere with someone else's, it appears that the other side is blocking us from meeting our need, and our basic survival instinct tells us we cannot allow this to happen or we will perish.

If we do not meet our basic needs, indeed we will suffer physically or emotionally. So our instinct to meet our needs at all cost is well founded. However, by mistaking our *strategy* for our *need*, we set ourselves up for competitive conflicts that are destructive to families, communities, nations, and our whole world.

In the end this kind of conflict actually undermines many of our basic needs. By pitting ourselves against each other we eliminate the possibility of receiving emotional needs like encouragement, understanding, appreciation, and love from other people. And by fighting over our basic physical requirements, such as food, water, or energy, we often end up destroying or using up the very resource we are trying to acquire.

The Limits of Compromise

Once we accept that a conflict exists, and choose to deal with it directly, we often assume that compromise is the best solution. While taking turns or splitting things in half may work as an immediate solution, it does not resolve conflict in the long run. This is because we are still focused on competing solutions and have not taken time to learn about the underlying needs.

A classic story used to illustrate this involves two children who both want the same orange:

A parent comes into the kitchen and sees two children fighting over the last orange, so he does what most of us would do, and simply cuts the orange in half. One child then peels his half, throws away the peel, and eats the orange. The other child grates the peel from her half to use for a cake she wants to bake and throws away the orange.

This story demonstrates the difference between the solutions that we tend to fight over, and the underlying needs that we are trying to meet with those solutions. The parent in this example assumed that he knew *why* each child wanted the orange. Since both of them could not eat the same orange, he came to the natural conclusion to cut it in half. Yet he never asked the children what they wanted to do with the orange. Had the parent asked this simple question, a complete solution to the conflict would have become obvious.

I share a sauna in the community where I live, and one day a community member and I were using it together. The sauna was not as hot as I like it, so I turned up the heat. Several moments later, I noticed that she had turned it down. I asked her about this, and discovered that she liked a gentler heat and preferred to stay in the sauna for longer periods of time. In contrast, I realized, I prefer stronger heat and staying in for shorter periods of time. The possibility of these different ways of using the sauna had never occurred to me before, as I assumed that everyone liked a sauna the way I did.

Once I discovered that we had a different preference, I asked her if we could find a way to work this out so both of us could get our needs met. Her response was that when I initiated the sauna, we would do it my way, and when she initiated, we would do it her way. This kind of compromise is common when people are trying to cooperate with each other, because it seems to be the fairest way to respond to competition. If we both want the same thing, we each get half.

This approach may work in the short term and offer us a way to deal with the immediate conflict. Yet it does not build closer relationships, nor is it satisfying in the long term. One of us always feels left out, bending ourselves to the other's preference for the sake of harmony.

Compromise may be useful to manage conflict when time or resources are limited or when a lack of ability to communicate exists. However, it does not resolve the sense of opposition because we still see the problem in terms of incompatible solutions. That is why compromise does not create a lasting peace.

To find a more satisfying resolution for everyone, we have to take our focus off the solutions that are being presented and look instead at the basic needs they are trying to address. Focusing on our needs enables us to generate new and creative solutions that meet all of what we want *without a sense of loss or sacrifice.*

My way of doing saunas is to have them short and hot. However, this is not my need; it is *the way I have tried to meet my need.* I realized that my needs in this situation were to get my body hot enough to sweat and to be able to jump into the cold pond without feeling chilled. I also wanted to conserve firewood and share the companionship of other members of the community. When I asked about her needs, I discovered that she did not sweat quickly and needed more time at lower heat for her body to begin to perspire. She also shared my needs to conserve fuel and to enjoy companionship with others.

I suggested that her proposal of taking turns doing the sauna our own ways could be one solution, and I wanted to consider some others. I thought about how we could meet all of our needs, and it occurred to me that she could start the sauna and stay by herself for a while at a cooler temperature, and I could come in a bit later when she was ready for more heat. We tried this a few times, and it appeared to resolve our conflict with both of us getting all of what we wanted.

Conflict As a Contest

The main problem we tend to have with resolving a conflict of needs is that we approach it as a contest. Most conflicts appear to be a competition between mutually exclusive outcomes. Either you get your way, or I get mine, and one of us wins while the other one loses. When other people do not do what we want, it can easily seem to us that they are *blocking* us from meeting our needs. This is the nature of conflict as we know it, and this thinking leads us to approach it as a struggle for power and control.

In the previous example about the sauna, it looked like only one of us could get our way, because we both had strategies for meeting our needs that excluded the other person's. We could easily have made this into a contest to see who would win, and probably we would have damaged our relationship in the process. Instead, she proposed to compromise and take turns having our way. While this solution could work and might avoid further conflict, it was a quick fix that did not acknowledge *why* we each wanted our way.

Compromise can still leave us resentful, seeing the other person as a continued threat because their way is so different from ours and we do not understand it. Without knowing why she liked the sauna cooler, I may have thought she was strange and that there was something wrong with her. I would have focused on our differences and felt a bit separate and distant from her. However, once I understood that her body responds to heat very differently than mine, I could see why she wanted the sauna that way. Once I understood her basic needs and saw that they were similar to my own, I felt more connected to her and willing to support her in getting what she wanted.

In this next section we will learn how to shift our focus from the initial opposing solutions in a conflict, to the needs that underlie them. Once we make this simple yet radical shift in perspective, the nature of the conflict changes. Instead of a competition, it can become a collaboration, with both of us helping each other find a way to meet our basic needs. Once we are clear about what we really want, often there is an obvious solution that will make everyone happy.

Initial Solutions

Suppose I am in conflict with my son about playing loud music on his stereo in the house. I don't want him to play loud music in the house, and he wants to play his music at a volume he enjoys. We could outline the conflict like this:

My Way	Son's Way
Don't play your music loudly in the house	Play my music the way I want in the house.

We have defined our problem, as most of us do, as two different outcomes that are mutually exclusive. Either he gets his way or I get mine. In this approach, we set up a power struggle between us, where each of us is competing against the other to get our way. Quickly, this kind of dynamic can turn into a contest to see who wins. We then may lose sight of what we really want and focus instead on winning this fight. Once the focus shifts to winning, the struggle for power and control can dominate and damage a relationship. Meanwhile, the basic needs that triggered the conflict are ignored.

Translating Solutions to Needs

A more effective approach is to redefine the conflict in terms of basic needs rather than solutions. To do this, we have to slow the process down and step backwards for a moment. We began this conflict by stating the outcome each one of us wanted. This is a *solution* or strategy for meeting a particular need. The solution is not the need; it is a *way to meet that need*.

In most conflicts, we fight over competing solutions because one person's strategy interferes with the others. In this case, my son's strategy of playing his music loudly directly interferes with my strategy of him *not* playing his music loudly. Our solutions are in direct opposition, and, if we stay focused on our preferred outcomes, we enter a win or lose struggle against each other.

To understand a conflict better, you can ask yourself and the other person what basic needs you are trying to meet by your proposed solution. You might ask:

"Why do you want (your way)*?"*

And you can ask yourself:

"What will I get if I get (my way)*?"*

In this example, I might ask my son:

"What will you get if you get to play your music loudly in the house?"

And I can ask myself:

"Why do I want my son not to play his music loudly in the house?"

When you ask this question with a sincere interest in learning about the other person, you find out what is motivating him to want the outcome he is fighting for. The question expresses care and concern for the other person and a desire simply to understand him better. If there is a tone of judgment or an attempt to get the other person to agree with *your* way, that person is likely to feel unsafe and not want to participate.

You can keep asking this question until each of you comes up with your basic needs. You will recognize the basic needs when you find common requirements for well-being that do not pose a threat to the other person. Needs, like emotions, are immediate and personal, and other people can easily understand them. They do not point to specific outcomes, contain no judgments or strategies, and do not interfere with anyone else's needs. Basic needs alone are not controversial. They include things like air, water, food, respect, safety and security. You can remind yourself about needs by referring to the longer list in the appendix.

Identifying your basic needs changes the entire feeling of a conflict. You can usually relate to the other person's need as something you also might want, and often you discover that you share similar needs. When you look beneath the conflicting demands to the needs that underlie them, you can relate to the other person as someone with needs like your own, not as someone who is trying to hurt you. You then can see that it is the demands or requested outcomes that are in competition with each other, not your basic needs.

By asking these questions, I might recognize that I can rest and relax and focus better on a project if the house is quiet. And, I might learn that loud music energizes and motivates my son to do his work.

We can then write them down like this:

My needs	Son's needs
peace and quiet	stimulation
to focus on a project	to focus on a project

Redefining the Problem in Terms of Needs

The next step is to put both people's needs into one sentence that defines the problem:

> *"So we need to find a way for you to get stimulation to focus on a project and for me to get peace and quiet to focus on a project."*

This sentence demonstrates how to redefine a problem in terms of each other's needs instead of the initial solutions that began this conflict. It changes the focus of the conflict from opposing outcomes to basic needs, and enables cooperation instead of competition. The format for redefining a problem in terms of needs is:

"So we need to find a way for you to get (your stated needs)

and for me to get (my stated needs). **"**

Now we have a definition of the conflict that allows us to work together toward a mutually beneficial solution, instead of pushing against each other to see who will get his way. Changing the framework for the conflict takes away the motivation to make it a contest and keeps the focus on getting our real needs met.

Talking about my need for peace and quiet helps him to understand where I am coming from in my request. This invites a willingness to help me out with my need instead of fighting against me. And, hearing about his need for energy and stimulation can help me understand where he is coming from. I see that he is simply trying to get his needs met, not interfering with mine. Both of us can relate to each other better now, because we can recognize each other's basic needs as things we also want at times.

Generating Creative Solutions

Now that we have identified the source of the conflict, we can generate possible strategies for getting *both* of our needs met. The next step is to think of new solutions together that could meet each of our stated needs. This process is sometimes called brainstorming, and it invites us to expand our options by thinking of as many creative solutions as we can.

Some guidelines for effective brainstorming are:

- Make a list of as many ideas as you can.
- Encourage both people to get involved.
- Do not evaluate or comment on any idea at this point.
- Write all ideas down on paper or a board.

This process allows a free flow of ideas without fear of criticism or censure. And, it may include crazy or funny ideas that lighten up the discussion and make each other laugh. Once the process has started, generate as many ideas out as you can think of together without any commentary or evaluation. Here is a brainstorming list for the current example:

Dad buys son a car he can sit in and listen to loud music	Son wears headphones
Dad buys son nice headphones for birthday	Dad builds a new house for himself
Son makes a soundproof room in the basement	Dad plays his own music loudly
Son plays music loudly only when dad is not home	Dad wears earplugs

When the idea-generating phase winds down, it is time for evaluation. We both get a chance to go over each idea, and if that idea *could* be part of a solution for us, we put our initials beside it. This does not indicate an agreement, as we are still just formulating proposals. It is only if an idea is totally out of the question for one of us, and we are sure we could not accept it in any form, that we do not put our initials next to it.

After we both have gone through the list, we keep only the ideas that have both of our initials on them, and we make a new list.

In this example, the new list might look like this:

Son wears headphones
Son plays music loudly when Dad is not home
Dad buys son a nice pair of headphones for his birthday

In reviewing each idea for practicality and appeal, the others were eliminated by one or both of us. Most of them involved too much time and money.

Proposing a Solution

Either one of us can take these remaining creative ideas and try to generate a proposal. I might propose that I buy my son a pair of headphones, he wears them to listen to music when I am home, and he plays his music as loud as he wants when I am not home. If the proposal meets both of our needs, it is likely that we both can accept it. If either one of us does not accept the proposal, we look at our list again and come up with a new one. If this still does not work, we can go back to the brainstorming process and generate more ideas.

Reaching Agreement and Detailing the Solution

Now we put the solution into a detailed agreement. I agree to buy my son a nice pair of headphones. My son agrees to put on headphones to listen to music when I am home, but play his music as he wants when I am away. It is helpful at this stage to be clear about any details that could be a source of controversy. In this case, it would be important to define a "nice pair of headphones." We could look at models and cost and decide on ones I can afford that will meet his needs for clear sound.

If the solution involves times and places, be sure to name them specifically and write down the basic details. Instead of "I will buy the headphones," it is better to say something like:

Dad agrees: To sit down with Son to get input on quality headphones tomorrow evening, and to buy them within two weeks from today.

Son agrees: Until I get the headphones, I will play my music so it cannot be heard in the rest of the house when Dad is home.

This helps everyone to understand what they are agreeing to do and makes solutions clearer and more likely to happen.

Follow-through

Some of you may be afraid of a process like this because the solutions can seem cast in stone, and you may not want to agree to something without knowing how it will really work for you. The beauty of this conflict resolution process is that it is totally in your hands the whole time. No one is making decisions for you or telling you what to do, and nothing happens until you both agree. If the proposed solution is not working for either of you, you can bring your concerns to the other person, try the process again, and come up with some new ideas.

To help this process feel flexible, it can be useful to set a time and place to check in with each other about how it is working. You might end the conversation by suggesting that you meet in a month to evaluate how you each are feeling about the solution you agreed upon. This kind of follow-through reinforces that the intention of the process is to find a sustainable way to meet everyone's needs. If it is not working, you both can try again until you find a way.

Reframing a Conflict

Put yourself into the role of the person in the situation below. Consider who the other person is and how the conflict is being expressed. What are each of you asking for or demanding from the other person that is generating the tension between you?

> You share a desk with someone at work, and each of you has a designated time when you can use it. Often when it is your turn to use the desk, the other person has left her papers and personal items scattered over it and you have to pick them up and put them somewhere before you can work. You have mentioned to her that this is a problem for you, and asked her not to leave her things on the desk when she leaves. She has responded that she does not know where else to put her things. Both of you are frustrated with this situation and don't know what to do about it.

Now try outlining this conflict and steps toward resolution using the format you have just learned. Here are the steps:

Step 1. Identify the two people involved, and describe the way each of you is presenting your side of the issue. Usually these will be solution statements that define a certain outcome each of you wants. You will know when you have described this accurately because the statements will oppose each other, and only one of them can happen. If I get my way, you cannot get your way; and if you get your way, I cannot get my way.

<u>My way</u>   <u>Your way</u>

Step 2. Then identify the needs that underlie these presenting outcomes, beginning with your own. You can find the needs by asking:

"What will I get if I get (<u>my way</u>)*?" or*
"What do I want (<u>my way</u>) *for?"*

For the example you are writing here, you have to imagine what the other person's needs are. This will help you to listen for another person's needs if you do try this process in a real situation. Of course, the only way to be sure about other people's needs is to ask them directly.

<u>My needs</u>   <u>Your needs</u>

Now, reframe the problem in terms of needs:

"So, we need to find a way for you to get _____

_____

and for me to get _____

_____."

In the above example, this is as far as the process can go. If you use this in a real situation, you can follow the rest of the process outlined above and go on to generate creative solutions, make proposals, and define the agreement.

Collaborative Negotiation

Collaborative Negotiation is a process of directly addressing your needs and trying to get them met while also including the other person's needs. It enables you to help yourself, and to help the other person at the same time. It offers room for individual needs that may change moment to moment, and it gives you a way to work together so decision making does not become a contest of wills.

Most of us do not know how to negotiate. We think of it as something you might do when you buy a car or a house. The concept is usually associated with labor unions, teacher's contracts, and business deals. We don't tend to think of ourselves negotiating in our daily relationships. However, in this new era of relationships based on equality we all need to learn how to negotiate with each other. This is how we maintain our individual sovereignty *and* stay connected with other people.

The common alternatives to Collaborative Negotiation include avoidance, competing to see who will win, and compromise. These approaches often do not work in the long run because they do not recognize the natural laws of conflict. Conflict is not an arbitrary obstacle to your happiness, as it so often appears to be. It is a predictable result of people's basic needs not being met. And, the only way to finally resolve conflict is to find a way to meet those needs.

In the earlier example, my son and I might eventually have worked out a solution similar to the one presented here without using this process. We probably would have tried fighting with each other, ignoring the problem, or making a compromise. At some point after we had exhausted all other means, we may have faced each other and talked about what was bothering us the most and how we could address our real concerns.

Many of us eventually recognize that our approach to a conflict is not working, and over time we find solutions that meet both people's needs in a way similar to the process outlined here. Collaborative Negotiation is not magic, but rather a natural and inevitable way to resolve conflicts so they don't keep returning. Sooner or later, many conflicts will resolve in this way, because one or both people recognize that collaborating to meet each others needs is what works. By learning this skill, we simply enable ourselves to spend less time struggling against each other and find a long-term resolution more quickly.

Mediation or Facilitated Negotiation

Some of us are better at negotiation than others. We know what we need, and are able to make direct requests and set effective boundaries. Yet this process can seem overwhelming or threatening to the rest of us, especially if we are not used to negotiating for our own needs. Collaborative Negotiation does not work unless both people fully participate, request what they want, and get what they need in the end. Sometimes this process just seems too overwhelming and we don't know how to begin.

If one or both people are feeling strong discomfort with the thought of entering into a negotiation process, it may be useful to involve a neutral third party. This is a natural role for a trained professional mediator. Such a person understands the conflict resolution process and can guide people through it. They will help each person express their emotions, values, and needs and be heard by the other. And they can facilitate the process of reframing the conflict in terms of needs and generating creative solutions.

A mediator or facilitator can make negotiation safer for both people by interrupting hostile communication and translating blame and accusation into basic emotions and needs. They can help both people take responsibility for their emotions and look beneath them to find the needs that are not being met. They also can slow the process down and keep it focused on one issue until it is resolved.

A mediator does not solve problems for you and rarely will suggest solutions. This person is not a judge and will not make decisions or tell you what to do. It is still up to each person in the process to say what their emotions and needs are, and work with the other person to get what they want. The process still remains in the hands of the people with the conflict. The mediator simply facilitates and allows this process to work more effectively. Going through a negotiation process with a mediator may also enable you to do it on your own later.

Collaborative Negotiation

The typical starting place for conflict:

My Way   **Your Way**

(my solution to the problem) ⟶ **VS.** ⟵ *(your solution to the problem)*

If the conflict remains defined in terms of opposing solutions, a power struggle is likely to follow where one side wins and the other side loses. To shift this, we can ask each other:

> ***"What will you get if you get your way?"*** or
> ***" What do you want it for?"***

1. <u>Redefining the problem in terms of needs, not conflicting solutions:</u>

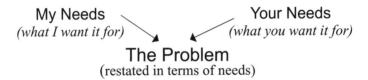

My Needs   **Your Needs**
(what I want it for)   *(what you want it for)*

The Problem
(restated in terms of needs)

> ***"So we need to find a way for you to get*** (<u>your stated needs</u>)
> ***and for me to get*** (<u>my stated needs</u>)***"***

If the conflict is redefined in terms of basic needs, there is an opportunity to work together so that both people get what they want, and both sides win.

2. <u>Brainstorm possible solutions.</u>
   Generate as many ideas as possible without *any* evaluation or criticism.

3. <u>Propose a complete solution.</u>
   From the list generated, make a proposal that addresses both people's needs.

4. <u>Plan who will do what, where, and by when.</u>
   Be specific – include all relevant details.

5. <u>Do it.</u>

6. <u>Evaluate the solution at a later date.</u>
   How did it turn out?
   How is it working for each of us?
   Do we need to make adjustments or renegotiate anything?

Conscious Communication
for Couples

Chapter 19

A New Map for a New Territory

Probably the most intense relationship we have is with a primary intimate partner. We usually feel more vulnerable with our partners and have more expectations that they will meet our needs than we do with any other person in our lives. The recent erosion of extended family and community networks puts a lot more weight on a primary relationship to serve many different functions. And, being part of a couple can be very confusing these days because our ideas about it have changed so dramatically in recent times. We have a whole new concept of what we want from a committed relationship, but little sense of how to get it.

Traditional Models of Marriage

For most of human history, the needs of society have controlled and regulated intimate partnerships. Marriages were arranged for the stability of the community and to meet the needs of extended family networks. The dynamics within a couple followed standard scripts, with each partner playing a predetermined role, and little room for individual variation. This rather rigid template for marriage, which many of us today would consider simplistic and antiquated, only began to change sometime in the last eight hundred years.

In *The Power of Myth,* well known mythologist Joseph Campbell suggests that while humans in all societies may have felt powerful sexual attractions to each other, they rarely stepped out of their traditional roles to act upon these. He traces the promotion of the concept of romantic love that we take for granted today to the bards of twelfth-century France. It seems that these musical poets were the first ones to openly encourage the formation of couples based on mutual feelings of attraction.

Psychologist Robert Johnson, in his book *We,* takes this idea further and suggests that no society before ours has ever based the formation of families entirely on sexual attraction. He concludes that the idea is in its infancy and we are still learning how to make it work. He points out that this way of partnering challenges us to work with the powerful and often overwhelming emotional energy unleashed by falling in love. And he suggests that when we do not have adequate means for containing this energy, it can be very destructive.

~~~~~~

I was raised in a modern Western society where marriage partners choose each other based on individual attraction rather than on social expectations. That was how my parents did it, and I never imagined it could be any other way until I lived for half a year in Sri Lanka. In this small island country off the coast of India, marriages are still often arranged by parents and extended family, with the partners themselves having little say in the matter.

One day I was visiting a family with a teenage daughter who spoke English. She was telling me that her parents had recently arranged a marriage for her with a boy she had never met. I expressed shock and astonishment and asked her how she could live with such a setup. She replied that she was quite happy to have her parents arrange this major life decision for her. She was relieved not to have to make such a decision by herself, and could not imagine how she could possibly know who would make a good partner for her.

She pointed out that our Western way of finding love through romantic attraction did not seem to be working very well. She knew something of the anxiety involved in dating, as well as the emotional traumas of being a couple when two people are left to figure it out on their own. She mentioned our fifty-percent divorce rate and said she was grateful not to have to go through all this. In contrast, she thought the traditional system practiced in India and Sri Lanka worked quite well, and she trusted her parents to make the right decision for her in this matter.

I came away from the conversation with an entirely new point of view on the subject of romantic relationships. I had already experienced my first love affair, and all the emotional drama that went along with it. I knew I had a lot to learn about loving another person and how to make a relationship work. As surprised as I was to admit this, her perspective made a lot of sense to me.

A Time of Change

While the idea of arranged marriages was long gone by my

parent's generation, there were still many rules governing primary relationships, and most people followed them. It was taboo to have sexual relations or live with someone before being legally married. Divorce was socially unacceptable, involved a complex legal process, and was forbidden by some major religious institutions. Having children outside of a marriage was something to be ashamed about. And, dating or marriage was limited to opposite sex people of the same race, religion, and social class.

I remember as a young boy that there was a huge brick institutional building across the street from my elementary school. Occasionally, I would see the faces of young women who were leaning out the windows as I walked by. My mother explained to me one day that it was a home for unwed mothers, and I could hear in her voice a hushed tone of disapproval. I remember, too, a time when my older sister had arranged a date with a boy who was of a different race, and my father forbade her to go.

These rules and expectations may seem trite and archaic today, because we have undergone such a radical shift in social norms since my parent's youth. In many Western societies now, partnerships are no longer defined as a man and a woman making a legal commitment for life that is sanctioned by a religious institution. While this form of traditional marriage still exists, many people are finding that partnership looks quite different.

Couples today cross all lines of social class, race, and gender, and there is no longer an expectation of legal marriage before being sexual, or the assumption that coupling is for life. More than half of us who legally marry eventually divorce, and many of us live together and have children without any state or religious sanctions. Many homes today include mixed families, single people, or couples that would have been seen as odd only a generation ago.

Social Upheaval

These dramatic changes have been disorienting for many of us. In my ten-year career as a divorce mediator, I saw firsthand the deep scars left behind as the hopes of a secure life-time marriage were shattered. I heard countless stories of the traumatic effects on children of having their parents separate. And, I went through my own bitter divorce and felt emotional pain that shook me to my core.

While the cultural shift away from arranged marriages to romantic love partnerships took centuries of time to complete, the radical change we are experiencing now is happening in one generation. Because of the lightning speed of this social upheaval, many of us are left scratching our heads and nursing our broken hearts. This is a challenging time when the old form is falling away rapidly, and a new one has not been established. It seems natural that many of us are confused and discouraged about how to proceed.

I can well understand why there is a movement to return back to the way it was before the rules and social expectations for marriage began to collapse. It appears that our society is falling apart and we are losing the most fundamental social unit we have. Yet, we have already come too far to turn back. Just as my parents would not have accepted a socially arranged marriage, most of us today cannot live by the traditional rules that defined marriage a generation ago. The only option for us now is to go forward through uncharted waters and find a way out the other side.

Traveling in New Territory, Without a Map

The old model of primary relationship suggested a static condition where change was considered threatening, and security and stability were achieved through obedience and conformity. The father went to work, the mother took care of the home and children, and the emphasis was on fitting in and playing your role. This often meant sacrificing individuality for the sake of harmony.

These traditional forms of marriage emphasized a specific outward appearance and offered a common format for everyone to follow. The individual people within a couple were encouraged to give up personal growth in exchange for a sense of security and stability. Yet this approach was bound to fail, as we are seeing now, because the human soul has an undeniable urge for its own independence and completion.

> A static situation, however comfortable,
> is ultimately deadening
> to a living human being.

Something is happening in our society today that is allowing us to move beyond our fear of growth. Enough of us have been willing to step away from the old form and take a risk that change would be for the better. However, now we seem to be caught in this chaotic place where there *are* no rules or formulas to follow, and many of us feel lost and confused. We are like young lambs who spent our first months of life in a secure pen and have just found our way out to the open pasture. We feel the excitement of freedom and the fear of vulnerability, at the same time.

We have moved beyond acceptance of a superficial working partnership where personal needs and individual freedoms are ignored for the sake of social cohesion and stability. Many of us no longer accept socially defined roles and lines of authority for marriage partners. Instead, we want relationships based on equality that value individual needs and personal fulfillment over social conformity. We want a partnership where both people are empowered to get their needs met. The problem is that we have no idea *how* to do this.

We begin relationships today with an expectation of a partnership of equals, yet as soon as we encounter conflict, we fall back into familiar patterns based on the rules we have rejected. Then we begin to feel suffocated and rebel against the tyranny of these traditional rules. The result can be tumultuous relationships that crash back and forth between the new ideals and the old familiar ways, and often end with one or both people deciding that the problem is the other person.

> In the span of one generation
> all the rules for being in a couple have changed,
> and we find ourselves in the precarious position
> of having few guidelines for navigating
> the most challenging of all our relationships.

Falling In and Out of Love

Most of us are drawn to romantic partnership out of a desire to be intimately connected with another person. We see these essential relationships as a way to complete ourselves and overcome the pain of isolation. When we fall in love with someone who is also falling in love with us, the sense of safety, security, and comfort is overwhelming. Suddenly it seems as if we are invincible and on top of the world. We naturally then look to our love partner to meet many of our needs for acceptance, love, and appreciation.

An awesome power is unleashed when two people fall in love with each other. Our struggle to care for ourselves is forgotten, and all we want to do is take care of our beloved, and to be taken care of in return. In this fog of infatuation, we can easily lose sight of our own growth and well-being. It appears as though the comfort and security we have found in the other person's love will solve all of our difficulties. We believe we have discovered something certain in this world of constant change, and we want to hold on tightly, fearing that if we let go it will disappear.

After some time, however, the other person's capacity to meet our needs begins to diminish. We often become disillusioned at that point and begin to question the relationship. We don't understand why our partner is not taking care of us as they once did, and why the relationship is not solving the problems it once fixed so easily. Soon we begin to experience the other person as a *cause* of our problems, and the relationship seems to be making life *more* difficult.

After the bubble of infatuation bursts and we are faced with the realities of daily life together, the relationship that once promised to save us may begin to feel like a threatening encounter with a stranger who does not care about us at all. At this point many partnerships either fall apart or become superficial. Once our illusions that the other person will complete us are shattered, most of us become quite disheartened and don't know what to do. We tend to blame our partner for this failure, and the relationship often turns into a tangled web of resentment and hostility, completely obscuring the love that was so powerfully present in the beginning.

When the relationship appears to be creating more stress than it soothes, we may naturally assume that the person we have chosen is the wrong one for us and that we have to get out of this relationship and find a new partner. Or we may choose to maintain a safe distance from each other, resigning ourselves to a superficial, functional relationship without much intimacy or genuine love. Some of us may conclude that partnership cannot work and give up on the whole idea, seeking to meet our needs for intimacy and connection in other ways.

Many of us have been buffeted about by romantic heartaches and traumatic heartbreaks enough to realize that falling in love is not an end in itself. The incredible lift we get from romance does not last, and it cannot save us as we once believed it would. We naturally feel disillusioned, depressed, or hopeless when a relationship does not ultimately resolve our loneliness or sense of insecurity. Perhaps the one thing most of us can agree on, is that being in a couple is not what we thought it was going to be.

These common responses assume that an intimate relationship is *primarily for our safety, security, and comfort.* Because the relationship sheltered us from our pain and hardship so well in the beginning, we assume that this is its function. The mistake we are making is not the person we chose to be with, or the idea of partnership itself. Rather, we are not seeing clearly the *purpose* of the relationship. We don't yet understand what it is for.

> If we think our partner is there to make us happy,
> we are likely to be badly shaken.
> Yet, if we are willing to consider
> a whole new purpose for intimate relationships,
> the struggles begin to make sense.

The Myth of "Happily Ever After"

Falling in love feels so good in the beginning because suddenly we are complete and all our missing pieces are in place, with little effort or struggle. It is as if someone waved a magic wand and instantly made us whole, without us having to do any work. Our stories about romantic love are primarily about the search for a partner and the glory of finding one. They have a fairytale quality, and tend to focus on the magic surrounding two people falling in love.

These enduring myths of romantic love present the challenge of relationship as finding the "right" mate and getting that person to fall in love with us. The love stories that get us teary-eyed all focus on the chase and the catch, climaxing as the couple has their first romantic moment together in each other's arms. We are taught that this is the primary effort required to make a relationship work, and after the wedding, things are smooth sailing. Once they have found each other, the couple simply lives "happily ever after," "until death do us part."

These stories about romantic love form the basis for our thinking about partnership. So it is no wonder that when a relationship begins to become difficult, we immediately question our choice of partner. We simply have no other context to explain why things can change so suddenly from the ease and comfort of a honeymoon, to the struggles of daily life together.

The fantasy of finding our prince or princess and living out our days together in marital bliss may have worked to explain marriage to previous generations whose priority was merely conforming to social expectations. However, this simplistic portrait of romantic love is woefully inadequate to deal with relationships today. The rigid social rules that allowed couples to function without dealing with their personal feelings or needs are falling away, and many of us are left facing a mountain of emotional charges and unmet needs that we don't know how to respond to.

We simply have not been here before, and what we have been taught has given us few means to make it work. The preparation we get for being in a couple is a childlike myth that does not help us address the real emotions and needs that arise in partnership. The familiar methods of denial and avoidance no longer work now that the props of social morality and traditional customs have fallen away. We have to face directly our own raw feelings, and those of our partner, and we often feel helpless and unsure about how to proceed.

> We need a new story now
> about forming a primary intimate relationship
> that offers us a clear map of the territory
> and gives us the means to navigate it.

We have been lulled into a dreamy stupor by our myth of romantic love, and many of us find it difficult to let go of the fantasy of finding the perfect mate who will instantly complete our lives. Often the only thing that will shake us out of this compelling dream is when the pain of being disillusioned again and again becomes too much to bear. If we can resist the temptation at these times to numb or distract ourselves, and simply stay present with our own feelings, the deep heartache we feel inside can teach us a valuable lesson.

A Rude Awakening

I once met a woman and fell instantly in love. We began living together within days of first meeting each other. She was convinced that we were soul mates and had been waiting during this lifetime to finally meet. She wanted to spend every moment with me and do everything I did. I was deeply attracted to her and had been single for some time, so her desire to be close to me seemed like an answer to a prayer.

For the first months of our time together I felt ecstatic, and all of my loneliness disappeared. It seemed that my life's struggles and pain were resolved just by being in her presence. Slowly, however, I began to feel suffocated by the relationship, and I noticed myself getting irritated and angry with her. I did not know how to get the space I needed for my own nourishment apart from her. And sometimes I unconsciously acted in hurtful ways to put distance between us, just so I could breathe.

I did not feel good about my reactions to her, and gradually I realized that I was not getting enough personal space for my own well-being. When I tried in a fumbling way to create a bit of breathing room between us, she often interpreted my actions as a rejection of her. She suggested that my need for alone time meant that there was something wrong with me. I began to doubt my own integrity and became confused about how to care for my own needs.

The situation became more constricted until it seemed that neither of us could care for ourselves or be our own person without threatening the relationship. As you might imagine, this relationship ended painfully several years later. She left as suddenly as she had come into my life, accusing me of being selfish, shutting her out, and treating her badly. And I was left in a state of shock, bewildered, hurt, and deeply confused about what had happened.

What began as the most exhilarating time of my life ended as one of my most tragic and painful experiences. I was emotionally devastated and shaken to the point where I considered suicide as a way out of my pain. Without realizing it, I had fallen into the belief that her love would save me from having to care for myself. I thought if we could merge our lives, my problem of feeling incomplete and separate from the world would be over. In the euphoria of falling in love, I had abandoned myself, mistaking this codependent kind of relationship for real love and connection.

With the collapse of our romance, my whole world crumbled. I had invested everything in that relationship, believing that her love was as certain as the sun. And, when the adoration she held for me suddenly appeared to turn into a raging attack, I felt an unbearable pain drive its way deep into the marrow of my bones.

The attraction of romantic love is that it can instantly lift us up and fill us with an intoxicating sense of power. It is easy then to become dependent on the other person's love and require our partner's approval to feel good about ourselves. And, if our partner's love suddenly turns into hatred, as sometimes happens, the effect is devastating.

When she left suddenly in a storm of anger, it seemed as if my whole insides were being ripped out and the ground underneath my feet was giving way. In the end I experienced myself as more separate, alone, and uncertain than ever before. There was no escaping the constant pain that was with me when I went to sleep and again when I woke up. I realized the seriousness of my situation, and knew that if I did not care for myself in the most basic ways I was at risk of hurting myself further or sinking into depression beyond recovery.

Learning from Pain

I considered myself a conscious and self-aware person. Still, it took me a while to recognize just how deeply I had been entranced by the myth of romantic love. Even though I knew better, a part of me still clung to the idea that I had found the one true love that would finally complete my life. I had tied my whole identity to my relationship with her, and when she left, there seemed to be nothing left of me. She had become the center of my world, and I didn't know who I was anymore without her.

I took time for healing every day and was careful not to numb or distract myself with addictive behaviors. I reached out for support to friends and family, looked for teachers and healers who I thought could help me, and tried to find gentle and nourishing things to do for myself. And gradually, through the pain of this experience, I began to let go of the idea that a romantic partner could magically lift my burdens from me.

The merit of unbearable pain is that it can move mountains. Rather, we allow mountains to move when we are faced with suffering beyond our capacity to resolve. This hurt was so deep and constant that it stripped me of all the illusions of romantic love that were hidden away in my subconscious. I woke up one day and realized that I no longer believed in the story of finding the perfect mate.

Soaring to the heights of romance had lost its appeal, because I had fallen all the way to the bottom and tasted the bitterness of this kind of love when it suddenly and unexpectedly turns into a volcano of resentment, fear, and anger. Whenever my mind would turn to the hope of another lover who would sweep me off my feet and make my world right again, my heart would begin to ache, and I would remember the pain I had suffered. I knew the problem was not her, or what she did, or even the idea of intimate relationship itself. The problem was the deeply abiding myth that someone else would complete me.

A New Beginning

For some years after this traumatic heartbreak, I would notice myself again lunging after an instant romance that promised to lift my burdens and fill my life with love. Yet each time I would come back to the painful truth that I had realized earlier, and was quicker to wake myself up from the dreamy fantasy. After one particularly absurd and humiliating episode, I finally made a clear determination within myself to establish a partnership that was not based primarily on romantic attraction.

I was done with the fairytale and finally ready for a truer experience of love. I wanted a sustainable relationship that would not easily come apart. I drew a firm boundary around my compulsive habit of choosing a partner based on the force of passion, and decided to focus instead on the potential for a deeply caring life-long intimacy.

Within months of making this vow, I met a woman whose heart shined as bright as the sun. I recognized her capacity for compassion and willingness to take responsibility for her own healing. I knew that these were the qualities I was seeking in a mate, and this was a chance to begin a relationship from a new direction. Instead of looking for instant love, I finally broke out of my old habit and chose a partner who I thought could help me *learn* how to love.

Our marriage is not without conflict, and sometimes I am not able to keep my heart open to her. However, we seem to have a more stable base from which to approach these times of turmoil. While this relationship is central to my life, it is not the center of my life. I have my own center, separate from hers. When things become difficult, it is easier to take a step back, gain perspective, and respond from a calmer and more caring place. The tension then passes more quickly, giving me a chance to return to the love I feel for her sooner.

Our relationship is not based entirely on the ebbs and flows of romance. While there are times of passion, we are not counting on these to give our marriage meaning. We both want to find the deeper love that will sustain and nourish us over time. We are willing to pass through struggles with each other, knowing these difficult times are showing us where we are in need of healing. And, the love that is growing between us feels more real and powerful than any of the passionate encounters I experienced before.

Chapter 20

Relationships are for Healing

Most of us have a nagging sense of being incomplete. We think there is something we still need to do or have before we can be content. We have not learned much about our basic needs or how to tell them apart from things that help us meet those needs. So we accumulate things, thinking that if we have more means we will naturally have more happiness. And one of the primary things we try to get is romantic love.

We tend to place a lot of weight on intimate relationships and expect them to make us happy. This seems to make sense because when someone we are attracted to falls in love with us, our self-doubt, fear, and insecurity magically disappears. Many of our needs are suddenly met, and the struggles and hardships of going through life alone instantly dissolve. Yet, this state of romantic bliss cannot last because it is based on a fundamental misunderstanding about the purpose of a primary partnership.

A relationship can provide a sense of joy, love, or completion, however, it is important to realize that it is not romantic love that we ultimately want, but happiness and peace. This sounds so simple and obvious, yet over and over we mistake the means for the ends they help us achieve. Happiness, peace, security, and love are what we want. And, when we attach these to a romantic relationship, we burden our partner with expectations that cannot be realistically fulfilled.

Taking Responsibility for Our Own Completion

When we look to another person to be our other half, and they look to us for the same, this is codependency. It is based on the assumption that neither of us is complete without another person, and that this other person can somehow fill in the missing pieces and make us whole. This appears to be an easy way out of the challenge of personal growth. Yet if you expect a partner to complete you, you will be tragically disillusioned – because *no one can do this for you.* Your task in life is to learn to complete yourself. The familiar idea of being two halves of a whole does not work in the long run, because each of us is our *own* person, longing for our own wholeness as an individual.

There is no magic wand that can make you whole and complete, and romantic relationships cannot fulfill the need for inner peace and certainty. This is work each of us has to do for ourselves. It can seem like an impossible burden at times, and many of us try to avoid it because it feels so overwhelming. We may try to escape the responsibility for our own self-completion through forming codependent relationships. Yet, these will fail us in the end, because nothing outside ourselves can meet this need for self-fulfillment.

In my late teenage years, I anxiously realized that I had to take care of myself for the first time in my life. My parents and schools were no longer providing most of my needs, and I had to learn how to meet them on my own. I was not prepared to accept responsibility for my own happiness and well-being, and I did not have a clue what that would look like. No one taught me to ask myself what I really wanted or how to find out what nourished me.

I fell in love for the first time around then, and I felt this great sense of relief that I no longer had to take care of myself. However, when my partner did not live up to my expectations of taking care of me I became disillusioned and tended to blame her. I had no other way to see the situation at the time, and sadly this frustration I felt toward her eventually led to the end of our relationship.

By being disillusioned often in this way, I have gradually learned that a committed romantic relationship is not a place to land and rest in permanent safety and comfort, but is primarily a vehicle for personal growth.

> While a healthy relationship
> can be a place of great love and support,
> its main purpose is to challenge us
> to grow and become whole individuals.

Uncovering Hidden Wounds

As each of us has basic needs for our well-being, we each also carry wounds from times when our basic needs were not met and we did not know how to help ourselves. These wounds tend to harden into tight places that we hide and protect so that we won't experience the trauma of our unmet needs again. We commonly try to ignore them, thinking if we cannot see them, they will go away.

These hidden wounded places then become blind spots in our consciousness. We accumulate painful memories that we have to avoid in order to maintain our sense of well-being, and believe that our safety depends on not looking too closely at them. In the process of trying to protect our wounds, we become more and more constricted and divided internally. The result is that we limit our own freedom and creativity because there are so many old hurt feelings that we have to step around so as not to arouse them.

One of the dilemmas of intimacy is that we long for a close connection to another person, yet we are reluctant to give up our personal privacy because we think our strength and safety depends on hiding our wounds. This makes it difficult for us to be emotionally close with another person. And, while romantic relationships seem to relieve us of our pain initially, they often make our lives more painful over time because they inevitably expose these hidden wounds.

Intimacy offers a level of safety that we do not commonly share with others, and whatever we have been hiding naturally begins to surface *because it can*. It is the abundance of love in the beginning of a romantic relationship that brings up the wounds, because finally it feels safe enough to let them out. It is also impossible to continue to hide parts of ourselves once we become emotionally bonded. Our secrets naturally get exposed when we open ourselves to another person in this way.

When Relationships Hurt

When you spend time with another person and are emotionally intimate with them, your behavior will eventually trigger some of their hidden wounds. Many of our traditional social rules and moral codes are aimed at preventing these painful interactions. Yet, no amount of rules about being nice and polite can keep you from hurting each other's feelings. These formalities that we often place so much emphasis on serve only to put distance between us. We end up protecting ourselves from having our wounds stimulated by staying emotionally distant from the people we love the most. This can leave us feeling isolated even in our most intimate relationships.

Our emotions are triggered so easily with our primary life partner because we spend so much time with them, are more vulnerable with them, and have high expectations that our partner will take care of us and meet our needs. We tend to unconsciously assign to them the role of providing our safety, security, and comfort. So we are more sensitive to what they say or do and can easily interpret any careless behavior on their part as an attack against us.

Instead of creating a wall of social etiquette to keep you from hurting your partner or to avoid being hurt, you can become more aware of what is happening in times of emotional turmoil. It is the nature of human beings that we hurt each other, or more accurately, *we irritate each other's wounds*. We do not mean to do this, and most of the time we are completely unaware that our words or actions are hurtful.

Most of us don't have much skill or experience in dealing with these old hurt places. So in the confusion and conflict that often results when wounds surface, we easily end up hurting ourselves and each other more. That is why it is so important to learn ways of approaching these sensitive places consciously. Then, instead of avoiding our wounds, we can heal them, and through that process realize a sense of completion and contentment that comes from being whole again within ourselves.

Blaming Your Partner

When a wound you have been trying to hide gets irritated by your intimate partner, things usually become difficult. One moment, there is nothing but warm fuzzy love and appreciation, and in the next moment, there is an ugly bleeding wound. This happens when your partner says or does something that triggers a strong emotional charge. You may feel afraid, hurt, angry, or resentful, and think the other person was intentionally trying to hurt you. It is easy then to interpret their behavior as a personal attack.

It is common to become defensive and hostile toward your partner when you think they have violated the trust you invested in them, and see *them* as responsible for *your* hurt feelings. In the name of justice or self-defense, you may then lash out and try to hurt them. This often triggers their old wounds, and soon you are both caught in a vicious cycle of blame and attack. In intimate partnerships, this kind of downward spiral is common. It often erodes the love and respect between you, and leads you to see each other as enemies, rather than allies.

When we believe our partner is causing our emotional charge, we often feel compelled to get them to change. This requires a lot of effort, creates power struggles in the relationship, and can result in more unconscious hurting of each other.

No one likes to be controlled, so your partner will inevitably react to your efforts by defending themselves, or attacking you. This may only reinforce your belief that your partner is causing your wounds, and convince you to further your attempts to change their behavior. If this cycle goes unchecked, it can deeply undermine the trust, stability, and intimacy in the relationship.

> Pitting ourselves against our partner
> is like boxing with our own reflection in the mirror.
> We blindly continue to punch away,
> not realizing that it is our own hand
> that is getting bruised and battered.

The main problem with this strategy of changing your partner so your wounds do not surface is that it does not work. No matter how hard you try, you cannot succeed in controlling the other person's actions so that your emotions do not get stirred up. And, often, the more you want them to be different, the more resistance and resentment builds, and the worse the situation becomes. This is because your efforts to get them to be different tend to violate their sovereignty. None of us can base our behavior entirely on avoiding another person's wounds because it does not allow us to be free.

Tending to Your Own Wounds

It may seem obvious that your partner is hurting you because you feel these intense emotional charges only in response to specific things they say or do. Remember, however, that the hurt you experience comes from the activation of one of your old wounds. It is like the pain you feel when someone bumps against a cut or bruise. The other person does not usually mean to bump you, and often has no idea they are hitting you in a sensitive place. The impact is certainly not enough to cause serious harm, yet the pain can be enormous, because *you already have a deep wound there.*

These deep emotional wounds come from your past, and you have been carrying them around unconsciously, assuming they are gone because you cannot see them. When they suddenly get bumped in your relationship, it seems natural to blame your partner for the pain you feel. Yet, if you step back a moment, you can see that the level of emotional charge is often way out of proportion to what your partner said or did.

You may explode in anger, cringe in terror, or collapse in hurt when your partner says or does something quite ordinary. In spite of how it may appear, those words or actions did not cause your intense reaction. The other person simply unknowingly bumped into an old wound.

The way out of such relationship conflicts begins with investigating your own pain and finding its source. If you can stop blaming your partner for a moment and ask yourself why you are feeling so much emotion, you may be able to see where you are wounded and in need of healing. Once you are aware of your wound and take responsibility for it, you can begin the process of taking care of yourself by simply having empathy for your own discomfort. Then you can discover your needs in that moment, and a way to meet them often becomes clear.

A Chance to Heal an Unresolved Trauma

One afternoon I was in the kitchen with my wife and three daughters, and I was upset because it was near dinnertime and it was not clear where everyone was going to eat. Two of the children wanted to go next door for dinner, and it was the third child's day to help cook. Before I came in, my wife had been discussing the situation with the children. When I asked her what was happening, she did not seem to know who was eating dinner with us and who was not.

I got emotionally charged by this situation because I had a need for clarity so that I could plan my evening time. I did not express myself very well as I tried to make some order out of the seeming chaos. I asked the children to stay in the kitchen until we could sort this out, and when one of them asked why, my response was something like: "Because your mother is not clear." My intention was merely that we collect ourselves as a family and be sure we were all in agreement about the evening plan before anyone went anywhere.

A moment later, my wife became upset with me. The situation began to feel very uncomfortable as my wife and I slid into a conflict in front of the children. We managed to get through the conversation and make a plan for the evening, and then I asked my wife if we could talk privately. We listened to each other's feelings, validating them as best as we could, and began to regain the sense of trust and intimacy that had been temporarily lost in the tension of the conflict.

After a while, my wife began to sob deeply. I asked her if she wanted to talk about what she was feeling, and she responded that she did not know, but something was coming up from deep inside her. A moment later, a flash of recognition came across her face, and she began to cry even more intensely. I stayed with her, concerned about her feelings, yet not assuming responsibility for her tears. I simply became curious about what was bringing up all these emotions and was aware that I wanted to help her if I could.

She told me then that when I had said, "Your mother is not clear," she remembered her father using words like that when she was a child. She was instantly brought back to painful memories of her father criticizing her mother in front of the children. This had been a traumatic experience for her, and the buried pain became suddenly fresh and alive in that moment.

My wife then moved close to me and indicated she wanted to be held. I held her in my arms for a while as she continued to cry deeply. It was then clear what had driven the tension between us in the kitchen. A deep and long-forgotten wound from her early childhood had been re-stimulated by my words. Although my intention was not to criticize or blame her, the situation was close enough to what had happened in her family so long ago that she could not tell the difference.

If we had not taken the time or had the skills to listen to each other with empathy, none of this would have been revealed. We could have spent hours or even days upset with each other over a misunderstood comment. We would have assumed that the other person was trying to hurt or blame us, and most likely we would have closed ourselves off so we could not be hurt more. Neither of us would have known how my words impacted her, or why she was upset.

After she had cried deeply and received my love and support, her whole energy softened and became brighter. She looked as though a great weight had been lifted from her, and she seemed lighter and filled with joy. That old wound had begun to heal because it was finally exposed, and love had been allowed in to take the place of fear. Instead of feeling alienated and shut off from each other, we felt much closer and more connected. I learned something about a sensitive place in her, and she was able to relieve some of the burden of a traumatic event she had been carrying unconsciously from her childhood.

Learning How to Love

If you are under the illusion that a relationship has already completed you and is solely for your comfort and security, the appearance of your wounds and the wounds of your partner can be a shock. The glitter of first love tends to dissolve rapidly when your partner bumps into one of your old hurt places. Suddenly the bliss of union can turn into a tangled web of hostility, and defensiveness.

You may be surprised by an outbreak of anger or watch in confusion as a deep well of tears pour forth in response to something seemingly insignificant that was said. Most of us don't know why this happens or what to do about it, and we watch helplessly as the love that was once so powerful gradually becomes obscured behind resentment and anger.

If your love for the other person is based on your initial romantic attraction, it often becomes buried at this point and may never surface again. However, if you view relationships with the understanding that they teach us *how* to love, you have a chance to respond differently to each other's emotional charges. You may be able to resist the urge to hide or run from these wounded places in yourself and your partner, and instead learn to work with them. This approach allows you to realize a much deeper more sustained kind of love in the end.

One of the most certain aspects of intimate relationships is that they bring up strong emotions. Instead of simply blaming our partner when this happens, we can try seeing the situation from a new point of view.

> ## Conflicts in relationship show us where we already have an unhealed wound that needs attention.

Without these emotionally charged situations, it is difficult to know where our old wounds are. And, if we don't know where we are wounded, we cannot heal.

As we heal our own wounds with the support of our partner, the love between us naturally grows stronger. Emotional healing removes the obstacles which have built up inside us that block the flow of love in our lives. As these blocks are dissolved, we become free of the fear that kept us tightly bound up and isolated inside our fortress of defenses. And, when the fear no longer controls us, we naturally and effortlessly care for other people, as we care for ourselves.

Sustaining Relationships

In many traditional models of marriage, the glue that holds couples together has been social pressure or the hooks of codependency. We did not consider leaving a relationship because of the risk of legal, social, or religious consequences. And, we had unspoken agreements to take care of each other's needs that made us dependent on one another and unable to function well on our own.

While these dynamics worked to keep marriages intact, they did not foster a deeper love or sense of connection in the relationship. Social obligation as a motivation for staying together does not lead to increased intimacy, and this old model is collapsing because it does not fulfill our deeper needs. Our priorities have changed from obedience and conformity, to personal growth, individual creativity, and greater intimacy. These changes give us space to connect more genuinely, without the limiting rules that kept us safely distant from each other. Our job now is to learn how.

We begin by giving up our expectations that the other person will fill our needs for us, or that conforming to social rules can provide security. A better glue than fear and insecurity to hold relationships together is an investment in understanding each other's healing process. This kind of involvement would likely have sounded absurd to people in our society a generation ago. And, even now, some of us may be baffled at this suggestion and have no idea what it means. Yet, it is vital that we take a closer look at what a relationship can and cannot do for us if we are to move forward out of this confusing time.

Many of us now place a higher priority on finding our own personal happiness than we do on fulfilling social obligations. So, for a relationship to be significant and sustainable, it has to support our own growth and completion. Many of us have outgrown the notion of conforming to our society's expectations as a means to find fulfillment in our lives, and are searching for what really makes us happy. We are gradually realizing that there is no formula anymore, and we have to learn how to do this for ourselves.

It no longer works to expect your primary partner to *make* you happy. Yet, that does not mean that you cannot find the happiness you seek *within* an intimate relationship. In fact it may be that a committed relationship is one of the best vehicles you can have for learning how to find love and fulfillment. You know that your hidden wounds will surface in such a relationship, which gives you a chance to see and heal them. And, a relationship based on mutual respect, trust, and caring provides a nourishing environment for you to do this work of self-completion.

In this new era of relationships, you strengthen your union most by encouraging each other's growth and completion as individuals. If you learn how to support your partner's healing process, you become more valuable to that person and increase the incentive to stay together. The effort you put into understanding where your partner is hurt, and learning how to help them heal those hurts, becomes a foundation over time. And, that foundation is more solid and secure than anything based on social rules or moral obligation.

> The most sustainable relationship is one where both partners keep getting healthier.

Our Longing for True Love

As old wounds heal, the fear and contraction that went into protecting those hurt places can release, which creates a fuller capacity for love and joy. When you practice Conscious Communication skills in your relationship, both of you become more whole and happy people, and over time you have more to give to each other.

Real love begins to arise when you learn to feel the other person's suffering without taking responsibility for fixing it. Your inherent capacity for compassion is a deep caring that is not tainted by your own unconscious wounds or unmet needs. This kind of love does not suddenly turn into resentment or hostility, because it is not dependent on the other person deserving it. It originates within you and flows out naturally to your partner when you recognize their vulnerability, asking nothing in return.

It may seem as though this kind of love is beyond our capacity and that we are stuck in the selfish patterns that humanity has repeated forever. Yet, this outlook can lead to feeling hopeless and depressed. We cannot forget our longing for true love, yet we do not seem to have the means to ever achieve it. Instead of resigning ourselves to crumbs of love used as tokens of exchange, we can use our most potent relationships to learn where real love originates.

True love is nothing like the airy romantic version most of us learned to believe in. It is a solid and steady force that reveals itself as soon as we release our fear. This kind of love *can* be found within an intimate relationship, but we must first release our expectations that our partner will provide it for us. Once we recognize that it is our responsibility, there is no limit to the depth of genuine love that can grow between two people.

Chapter 21

Becoming Allies Instead of Adversaries

Imagine going out in your yard and digging a vegetable garden in the grass with only your bare hands. You *could* do this, but it would take a lot of time and effort, your hands would be bruised and battered, and the garden would be mediocre at best. Now, imagine that someone offered you a shovel, rake, and hoe and showed you how to use them. Preparing the garden still would require hard work, and you would have to learn to use the tools and stay focused on the task. However, with the tools and some basic training, it is possible to have a much better garden without hurting yourself.

Trying to sort out the challenges of being in a couple today is like digging a garden with your bare hands. It takes an enormous amount of work, it is often discouraging, we frequently hurt ourselves, and the relationship is not as good as it could be. One reason is that *we do not have any tools*. Learning skills for being in a couple is like learning to use a shovel, rake, and hoe for planting a garden. It still involves hard work, yet with tools the chance of success is much greater.

Creating a Relationship That Works for You

Learning Conscious Communication skills will help you work constructively with your emotions and address your needs openly. They allow for both of you to nourish and support yourselves while also nourishing and supporting the relationship. With practice you can contribute to each person's individual well-being and growth, while strengthening the friendship, intimacy, and capacity for love in the partnership.

This approach is not about creating a mold to fit the relationship into, as was the norm with traditional marriage. Rather than establishing a new model for what a partnership should *look* like, this approach focuses on what the relationship *feels* like from the inside. Beginning with that point of reference, you will use different skills to achieve different results that apply to the specific dynamics you have as a couple.

Our traditional model of marriage is like a prefabricated house.

You may get to choose the color and rearrange the furniture inside to suit your needs, yet your choices are limited by the basic structure of the building. This one-size-fits-all approach to creating a new family is easy in some ways because you don't have to make a lot of decisions, and you do not have to pay attention to your deeper emotions or needs. The prefabricated format does not leave room for individuality or personal growth, however, and thus it tends to constrict your freedom in a way that diminishes the love and intimacy between you over time.

This new model for intimate relationships is like a custom-made house that you can shape any way you like. In order to build a house yourselves, however, you need to know how to use basic carpentry tools and understand something about building construction. Each one of us has to learn some skills and how to apply them because there is no set recipe to follow, and no one else can do this work for you.

It is up to each individual within each couple to shape a relationship that works for both you and your partner. It takes more effort, but the benefit is that you will have the capacity to create relationships that uniquely fit your own individual needs, and can be modified as your needs change.

> Today, we might define a healthy relationship as one in which both people are included and get their basic needs met.

Establishing Clear Boundaries

Setting firm boundaries and keeping a healthy space between you is one of the most important skills for couples to learn. This appears to contradict our natural impulses because romantic relationships are the one place we usually let go of our personal boundaries. The very nature of falling in love is that we want to lose ourselves in the other person. Romance has such a powerful draw because we get an expanded sense of ourselves and experience belonging to something larger. The idea of merging with someone else looks so appealing because we can transcend our personal limitations for a moment. Yet, sooner or later, your wounds get mixed up with the wounds of your partner, and the relationship becomes impossibly entangled.

Understanding the idea of healthy boundaries and learning how to maintain them can be one of the most difficult challenges in a primary intimate relationship. We tend to assume that *any* sort of distance is bad and means that something is wrong. Yet one of the most common scenarios in long-term relationships is that each partner gradually feels less connected and more distant from the other. In reality, the wish to merge with another person does *not* lead to increased intimacy, but instead creates confusion, hurt, and blame, which only furthers the distance between you.

No matter how much we might wish it were otherwise, we all are separate individuals with our own unique emotions, values, and needs. While these may match our partner's some of the time, at other times they seem to be in opposition. Most of us have a habit of seeing differences within a couple as a sign of incompatibility, so we usually try to ignore them. This inevitably leads to a denial of our personal emotions and needs, however, and cripples our capacity to take care of ourselves individually.

We usually think that dissolving the boundaries between us brings us closer together, yet it often ends up undermining the vitality of the relationship in the long run. When you think your partner's emotional process is about you and confuse your emotional process with theirs, you cannot help each other and often end up re-wounding one another. This is the common habit of codependency, where your personal boundaries and needs are obscured by the demands of the relationship.

In earlier chapters we learned how to take responsibility for our own emotions by using Assertion Messages, and how to encourage other people to take responsibility for their own emotions through the use of Supportive Listening. We discussed how to allow other people to have their own emotions, values, and needs, and focus on both of us getting our needs met in a conflict. These skills are essential for creating a healthy intimate relationship because they maintain a clear boundary between you. This boundary enables you to separate your wounds from those of your partner, and allows you to support each other's healing rather than compete with each other to see who is right.

Hooked by Each Other's Wounds

The closer you are to another person, the more your wounds hook each other. When your wound is exposed, it often irritates the other person's wound, and vice versa. One reason for this predictable yet unsettling phenomenon in primary relationships is that we identify with and project ourselves onto our intimate partner so much. More than any other person in our lives, we often have trouble differentiating from our mate. So, when they go into emotional distress, it naturally brings our emotions to the surface.

After enough of these difficult emotional struggles, it can easily appear that we have made a big mistake and chosen a partner who keeps hurting us. However, another perspective is that, below our normal level of awareness, we choose a partner who will perfectly expose the hidden wounds in us – *so those wounds can be healed.*

> We choose partners *consciously*
> because they offer us unconditional love and
> acceptance, and *unconsciously*
> because they perfectly expose our hurt places
> that are in need of healing

Our Undeniable Urge to Grow

We usually think of growth as a physical process that our bodies go through. It is obvious that the body starts out small and gradually gets bigger, until it stops when we are full-grown adults. We know about supporting the growth of the body by creating conditions for healthy physical development. We feed our children the best food we can so that they get the nutrition they need, and we try to keep them warm, safe, and well rested. Once this process is over and the child's body has matured into an adult body, we think of them as finished with the growing process.

Yet, the culmination of our physical growth merely marks the beginning of our emotional maturation. Having the capacity to care for our physical needs, we can now begin to learn about our emotional needs. For the rest of our lives, we are faced with emotionally challenging situations that are opportunities to grow in a way that is entirely different. Instead of the body getting larger, our minds and hearts expand, which is a more subtle internal process.

Each of us has an urge to grow and complete ourselves mentally and emotionally. Just as the seed of an oak wants to grow into a fully mature tree, each of us has a seed within us that is trying to grow into a whole, mature version of ourselves. We can resist this longing for completion or place responsibility for it onto someone else, but we can never destroy it. Our need to grow and learn from life will always surface again. The only way to satisfy this innate desire is to recognize it, and learn to create the best conditions for that unique seed of yourself to mature into a whole being.

In the old models of primary relationship, the urge for individual completion was buried beneath a mountain of social rules and expectations. The new model we have been discussing here is based on recognizing this individual growth urge *as our primary purpose in life*. Instead of stifling it for the sake of social order and conformity, we can use this longing for fulfillment to create strong and durable relationships that serve each individual's deepest needs. This new approach to intimate relationships suggests that as each individual partner becomes more complete, the relationship also becomes more complete.

> A relationship grows weaker
> when you abandon your individual growth
> for the sake of unity or harmony.
>
> A relationship grows stronger
> when it supports and encourages each partner
> to be more whole and complete in themselves.

Some of us think we can have the freedom to become ourselves only if we remain outside of a committed relationship, because we have known only the limiting model of traditional marriage where individual growth was denied. While being independent can help to undo our habit of codependency by teaching us how to take care of ourselves, this is often *not* the optimal circumstance for individual growth. Living without an intimate partner is relatively easy once you find a way to deal with the loneliness. Your wounds do not get triggered so easily, and it can seem as though you have nothing left to heal.

A conscious relationship, on the other hand, is a perfect vehicle for personal growth. You can count on intimacy with another person to expose your wounds. And, if both partners are conscious and skillful, each can offer the other a supportive place for healing to happen. The challenge is to learn how to make a safe container within the relationship, where each person is encouraged to be responsible for their own feelings and needs, and knows how to support the other in their individual process of growth.

Power Struggles

An essential step in making the relationship a safe place for both partners to grow is learning how to make decisions together that include each person's needs. In traditional models of relationship, women often took care of the children and household while men went out to work and supported the family financially. These clear role definitions helped to minimize conflict by assigning areas of responsibility. Couples did not have to work out who was going to take care of what, because family life followed a predetermined formula. However, these strict divisions also limited the growth of each individual and often restricted intimacy and collaboration in the relationship.

Most of us now want a partnership of equals, where one partner does not hold more power than the other, and neither is excluded from some areas of decision making. It is common today for men to want a more active role in parenting and for women to want a career outside the home. Many of us expect this to be the case and are initially relieved when we don't have to be the only one responsible for parenting or supporting the family financially. Yet, as these old traditions fall away, we find ourselves in a vacuum, with no clear way to make everyday decisions *together.*

In trying to share areas of responsibility like parenting or finances, we often run into major conflicts. Because we have learned how to make decisions by one side taking control and leading the other, we can quickly get caught up in a contest to see who will dominate. Many conflicts result from the strong need *each* person has today for power and control over their own lives. Once we recognize this need and address it directly, we can learn to work together so that both of us share leadership, instead of opposing each other.

Working with Relationship Tools

I work with many couples who come to me stuck in power struggles and not able to find a way out. When a relationship is fraught with tension around who gets their way, the love and caring can become easily lost. I often begin by teaching them how to maintain a healthy boundary and allow each person to be responsible for their own feelings using the skill of Supportive Listening.

I may ask one partner to begin talking about an issue they are struggling with, and the other partner to listen for basic emotions and needs that are being expressed. I ask the partner who is listening to set aside their reactions, hear their partner's story as information about their partner and not as judgments about themselves, and reflect back the essence of what the other person is saying.

This act of reflecting the other person's emotions and needs is perhaps the most essential skill for being in a couple. It begins to create a healthy space between the two partners, and enables each person to focus on their own emotional charge and begin taking care of themselves. In these couple's work sessions, I have each partner practice this whenever the other partner is expressing strong emotions. I then encourage them to practice this skill on their own as often as they can.

As a couple's session continues, I show each partner how to present their concerns in a way that is more likely for them to be heard by the other, using Assertion Messages. I interrupt the familiar language of blame and redirect the person talking to their own immediate emotions and needs. I encourage them to set aside any judgments or conclusions and not to jump into immediate solutions.

The next step is often to facilitate a Collaborative Negotiation using the steps outlined in Chapter 18. I ask each partner what they want, and help translate their strategies into basic needs. I then invite them to work together to come up with solutions that may meet both of their needs.

Hearing Our Partner Instead of Defending Ourselves

In one situation, I worked with a couple who were in conflict over raising their two young children. She complained that he was not involved enough in taking care of the children and that she had to do most of the work herself. She began our session by making statements to him like: *"You never think about meals or getting the children ready for bed, and most of the time you don't seem to care about how they are doing."*

Because she began the session with her concern, I decided to focus on her for a moment and asked him to silently witness the process without responding. I could see that he was a bit agitated by her comments, and I guessed that he wanted to defend himself. I suggested that he be aware of the emotions he was feeling right in the moment, and that he try to listen to what she was saying as information about her, not about him.

I then suggested that she rephrase her feedback to him by talking about herself, and not about him. I asked her what emotions she felt when he did not help feed the children or put them to bed, and how these situations affected her. She said she felt frustrated and angry when he did not participate in helping with the children at mealtimes or bedtime because she was overwhelmed and felt lonely and isolated from him. She acknowledged that she also felt resentful toward him, and that this was keeping an emotional distance between them.

I then asked him to reflect back to her what he had heard, without adding any of his own judgments, interpretations, or responses. I suggested that he focus on her emotions, the situation that triggered them, and the impact on her. With some coaching from me, he was able to simply reflect her until she was satisfied that he heard her concerns. He said something like: *"You sound frustrated and angry when I do not get involved with feeding the children or putting them to bed, because it leaves you feeling alone and overwhelmed."* At this point, she seemed more relaxed and open, as if a weight had lifted from her.

I asked him to respond to her by talking about himself, using the format I had suggested earlier. He said that he had once been more involved with the direct care of the children, and that he stopped because she was so critical of him. At this point, I saw her become a bit more tense and asked her to simply listen, be aware of her emotions, and hear his words as information about him, and not about her. I asked him to describe what she said to him that he thought was critical, the emotions it brought up in him, and how the situation affected him.

He remembered her saying things like: *"You're not going to feed the children that, are you?"* or, *"Did you make sure they went to the bathroom before bed?"* and said that he felt annoyed and frustrated. I asked him how it affected him, and he responded that he felt like a small child being scolded by his mother. He said this situation made him very uncomfortable because he wanted space to do things his own way, but she seemed to want him to do them her way.

I then asked her to respond by reflecting what she had heard him say, focusing on his emotions, the situation that triggered them, and how the situation affected him. I suggested that she leave out her own interpretations and withhold her responses for a while. And she was then able to rephrase what she heard him say until he was satisfied that she understood him, by saying something like: *"So you feel frustrated and hurt when I question your parenting because you want to be able to do things your own way?"*

At this point, they both seemed more relaxed and open to each other, and it seemed that there was less tension and distance between them. As the discussion progressed, I became less involved and stepped in only to suggest rephrasing or to validate or clarify one of their concerns. I asked them to continue with Supportive Listening until the other person was complete before they responded with their own feelings and needs, and keep their listening and assertions within the guidelines I had given them.

Finding a Solution Together

They were able to slow down their interaction and hear information about each other that had been hidden under years of resentment and disconnection. They were also able to express some of their built-up emotions and take responsibility for them, instead of blaming them on the other person. At this point, I asked if each of them could state what they thought the other person's needs were.

He suggested that her needs were for support and connection. And, she guessed that his needs were for autonomy and encouragement. I then wondered out loud if there was a way they could work together to meet both of their needs. He said that he wanted to be more involved with the children but did not want to be criticized for the way he did it. And, she admitted that her way of giving him feedback may have discouraged him from being involved in parenting altogether. She added that she still wanted to have some say in how he took care of the children, but that she was willing to learn a new way to do it that could work for him as well.

I asked him how she might give him feedback if she had a concern about his parenting. He said he would be more open to her feedback if she asked him to discuss the situation privately and then talked about herself without making judgments about him. He also asked that she not comment on everything he did, and let him learn sometimes from his own mistakes.

She agreed to his requests, and made a request of her own that he not simply withdraw when he felt frustrated or upset with her. She talked about how difficult it was for her when he disappeared and how lonely she felt without his participation and support. He agreed that if he was upset by something she said or did, he would ask her to discuss it privately, and he would talk about himself and not make judgments about her.

We ended the session by reviewing what each of their needs were, and recapping the plan they had created together to address these needs. They understood that having productive discussions like this would likely take some time and practice, and that their old patterns of reaction to each other would not dissolve overnight. However, they left feeling more hopeful about their situation because they could see a way out that had not been visible to either one of them before.

Creating a Container

Imagine you are at a primitive campsite and need to build a fire to cook food, keep warm, and be safe from predatory animals. If you don't give it much thought, you might make your fire on the forest floor or in an open field, where it could easily spread out of control. But if you build a simple ring of stones around the fire, it can serve your basic needs without being destructive. In this setting, fire is essential for your survival, but if it gets out of control, it could destroy you and everything around you.

An intimate romantic relationship is like a fire. It can meet many of your needs for love, nourishment, safety, and acceptance, and it can provide an excellent vehicle for your personal growth. At the same time, it generates a lot of heat and can easily get out of control.

Traditional ways of approaching intimate relationships involved strict social rules so that the fire of romantic attraction would be tightly contained. People recognized the hazards of falling in love and trying to sustain relationships while dealing with intense emotions. This is one reason for formalizing marriage as an institution with defined limits and predetermined boundaries.

Today many of these old methods of containing relationships through moral obligation and societal expectations are collapsing because they were so rigid that they smothered the fire of romantic love. And, we are now experiencing firsthand the destructive nature of intimate partnerships without any containment. It is clear that we cannot go back to the old rules, yet we desperately need some new way to handle the heat now, so that it does not burn us.

Containing a relationship, like a fire, does not mean clamping a lid on it. That would only put the fire out. An effective container allows the fire to burn hot, yet stay within a confined area. You simply need to learn how to build a ring of stones around your fire so that it does not spread out of control. Then you can learn to work with it, so the fire provides the nourishment you need without hurting you in the process.

Practicing the skills of Conscious Communication together can create a container for your relationship that allows each of you to go deeper into your own personal healing process, without hurting each other. The stronger the container, the deeper you can go, and the more alive and satisfying your relationship becomes. Like the ring of stones around a camp fire, the container for your relationship allows the energy generated between romantic partners to be strong and serve the needs of each person, without becoming destructive.

It is essential to understand the difference between this kind of nourishing container, and the old model of containment which simply diminished the fire of intimate relationships. Many of us recognize now that dowsing the fire of passion through the force of social obligation or morality kills the essence of it. So we have discarded many of the traditional boundaries surrounding intimate relationships and allowed the fire to burn hot again.

We now have to learn how to use this fire for its intended purpose – so that each individual can become more whole and complete. This is what finally satisfies us, and this is what a relationship can help us achieve. However, to make the power of romantic love available to help us, we must have a structure able to contain such a force. Once we understand that the function of intimate relationships is to further our healing, the need for the supportive structure provided by basic relationship skills becomes obvious.

The kind of containment provided by using Conscious Communication skills is a nourishing self-discipline that enables us to separate our judgments from our feelings, and our conclusions from our basic needs. The practices presented in this book give us a means to sort out what is real in our experience from what we imagine to be real. This allows us to discover what we really want and learn ways of meeting our needs that do not threaten our partner.

Using the Tools

We tend to develop routines and patterns of communication with our primary partners and then stick to them. Even if they don't work very well, at least they offer some sense of familiarity and security. Trying to change these habits can feel threatening, and often one or both of us resist learning a new way. So, it is wise to approach changing the way you communicate with your partner gently and carefully.

Reading together about Conscious Communication skills, and talking about them with each other, is a start. You may find it easier at first to practice them outside of your primary relationship, with a friend, co-worker, or family member. It can also be helpful to attend a class or workshop together. A teacher can translate information from a book to your specific situation and help you apply communication skills to issues you are dealing with now.

Remember, these new tools are not a formula or standard of behavior. They are meant to refocus your attention on how you feel, what actually happened, what you want, and how you can effectively communicate that to your partner. It is important to see them as new options, rather than rules, and not to judge each other in your use of them. Instead, look at it as experimenting with some new choices to find out what works for both of you.

Getting Support

Many of us find ourselves working out the struggles of our primary relationship in isolation, where no one else knows what goes on between us. This adds greatly to the challenge of making a partnership work, as it can be difficult to get perspective or to see things from a different angle. And, when someone *is* paying attention to the struggles in our relationship, they often respond with advice, evaluations, or reassurances that do not help.

Conscious Communication skills are not difficult to understand, yet they can seem impossible to apply on our own. If this process feels too challenging for you, or is not working well, it may be wise to involve a third person who understands the skills and can help you utilize them. The patterns of how your unconscious wounds trigger each other can be difficult to see from inside the relationship, and a third person can often help you recognize them. This professional can also help establish the boundaries necessary to sort out whose emotions and needs belong to whom.

People often leave a relationship just at the height of stress, when it seems that our partner is trying to hurt us and we can't take it anymore. Yet, it is just at this point that real change can happen. When you become disillusioned and the way forward seems impossible, you are forced to try something completely different. If you abandon the relationship then, you lose all the work you have done to get to that place and will have to start all over with a new partner.

Seeking help for strengthening a relationship is not a tragedy. It does not mean you are unhealthy or that something is wrong with you. These days, given that more relationships come apart than stay together, and many of us quickly go from one partner to another, finding support is a smart thing to do. The tragedy is when one partner leaves a relationship before seeking help. I have seen firsthand how devastating these sudden separations can be in my work as a divorce mediator, and in my own relationships. To anyone who has witnessed or been part of an emotionally charged separation, it is clear how much chaos and confusion they leave behind.

Finding Real Love

We have inherited a simplistic view of romantic relationship in which the challenge is merely to find the perfect mate and fall in love, and then we live happily ever after. This story implies that the love that swells up in the beginning will automatically sustain itself throughout our lives together, and there is nothing more we need to do about it. Yet for those of us who have tried this approach and watched the love erode into bitterness, resentment, and hostility, it is clear that something is missing.

Few of us really know how to love. We may recognize it when it is there, and seek it endlessly throughout our lives. Yet, we know little about where love comes from. We have been taught to go searching for love and to cling to it when we find it. We believe it is rare and that, once we find it, our only hope is to bind it up tightly so it cannot go away. However, when we treat love in this way, as a commodity we need to accumulate, we end up killing it. Love dies and withers when we see it as something we need to possess.

Real love is not something we fall into or happen to stumble upon. It is not a rare substance like gold or diamonds that we can only hope to find if we are lucky. It is not a magical occurrence, an arbitrary benefit, or something we exchange with another person. And, it is not something we can accumulate and store in a vault for later.

> Love is a daily requirement for each of us,
> and perhaps the most essential
> of our basic needs.

Love is what most of us are really after. And, it only appears rare, mysterious, and elusive to us because we have forgotten how to find the source of love within ourselves. As we do with most of our basic needs, we often confuse love itself with the means of getting it. We mistake money, property, achievement, popularity, drugs, alcohol, and sex for love. And, most of all, we mistake a romantic relationship for the source of love. This seems quite natural since we usually experience the greatest amount of love when someone we are in love with is also in love with us.

Yet, these things that we try to accumulate and possess because they bring love into our lives are not the source of love, as we often assume. They only awaken the love that lies dormant within our own hearts. They open the channels we have blocked within ourselves out of fear, because we have been hurt. And, it is the healing and release of these old wounds that enables us to feel again the natural flow of love which has been there all along.

The intention of a conscious partnership is to *learn* to love. This means gradually increasing our capacity for compassion based on learning about the other person's hidden wounds, while also learning about our own. Romantic relationships present a perfect opportunity for this because they give us a taste of how wonderful love can be, and then provide endless opportunities to learn to find it again within ourselves. The skills presented here simply help us refocus our attention on our own heart, where the source of genuine love has always been, waiting for us to uncover it.

Developing a Technology
for Peace

Chapter 22

Skills for Democracy

Sometimes a great notion will take hold of us and we orient our lives around it without making the changes necessary for it to be realized. While our capacity to conceive of high ideals can motivate us toward growth, it can also paralyze us. We often mistake the idea with reality, and are not able to see the practical steps we need to take to get there. We then end up thinking we have accomplished our goal, while nothing has really changed.

A Bold Experiment

Democracy is such an ideal. It is a beautiful vision of a society where each individual is respected and included as an integral part of the whole. We may take democracy for granted because it is an idea that has woven itself into the fabric of our society. Yet this notion was considered radical only a few centuries ago. The prevailing idea then was that common people were too ignorant and selfish to govern themselves and were incapable of making wise decisions collectively. It took the rebellious and independent-minded settlers of the New World to attempt an experiment as bold as founding a new country on the basis of this improbable ideal.

For most of the history of Western civilization, nations were organized by monarchs who held absolute authority. This was considered necessary to maintain order and stability, and most people accepted it as the way things were. Many people in the time of the American Revolution believed the idea of democracy could never work on such a scale, and that the United States was bound to fail. Yet somehow this dream took hold and began to work, and to this day, the early years and founding documents of this young country continue to inspire other nations of the world.

The ideal of democracy has now become the foundation for many societies across the globe, and it is difficult to imagine the attraction of authoritarian leadership anymore. As a result of this success many of us assume we have already achieved the goals of equality and personal freedom. We tend to forget that democracy is in its infancy and is still evolving. We think that because we all believe in the ideal of democracy we have realized it.

Yet, we have only to consider the struggles of implementing democratic principles in a society like the United States over the past two centuries to see that this is a work in progress. While democracy is based upon each individual having equal rights and responsibilities, this was far from true in the beginning. People of color, women, and anyone who did not own property were all excluded. It has taken a civil war and intense popular movements and political battles to get as far as we have in learning how to include everyone, and we still have a long way to go.

Learning How to Include Each Other

The premise of democracy is that society is made up of independent individuals who are inherently connected to each other. As the strength of a chain depends on the integrity of each link, a community is only as strong as its weakest individual. This idea makes enough sense to build nations upon it, yet we are still learning how to apply it in our daily lives.

> The idea of democracy
> is that if each one of us develops
> to our full potential,
> our community as a whole will be
> stronger and more sustainable.

The new expectations we have for equality in our relationships with other people represent the next steps in our process of learning to live by the ideals of democracy. We've realized that ignoring our individual feelings and needs for the sake of social conformity does not work well in the long run, and investing authority outside of ourselves weakens us as individuals and as a community. In a similar way, the founders of our modern democratic movement realized that monarchs controlling people for the good of all was not the best way to set up a society.

Despite our democratic ideal, however, we are still more familiar with a hierarchy of power where one person has clear authority over another. This top-down decision making structure makes for less conflict and more stability, because one person can make decisions more quickly than many. Yet, it is ultimately a weak and ineffective model for sustaining long-term relationships and strong communities. Those who are not in positions of power are not motivated to become strong individuals, and they easily become dependent. Decisions made by a few individuals also tend to be less effective in the long run than those that include everyone's wisdom.

Many of us are no longer satisfied with obedience to authority for the sake of unity. We want our own voice to be heard, and we expect all of our relationships to be based on equality. Our society as a whole is making a radical shift away from a traditional model of top-down authority, to one of shared power. In relationships between parents and children, employers and employees, teachers and students, and governments and people, we tend to expect a level of cooperative decision making that was not normal just half a century ago.

The notion of resolving conflict with both sides winning, or relationships where both people get their needs met, is the most recent development in the evolution of the ideal of democracy. To the past generation, these ideas were unheard of, and even today many of us consider them too idealistic to be practical. Yet, we are undergoing a major shift in the way our relationships are structured, and it is essential that we learn how to interact with each other now in a way that recognizes both our individual sovereignty *and* our interdependence.

The problem is that we have not had a way to do this. Our ideals can only set the stage for such a radical evolution in human society, and then we need tools that enable us to make this shift a reality.

> If we want to realize the "self-evident truth"
> that "all men are created equal", we have to
> develop tools that enable us to include each other,
> and make room for our differences, at the same time.

Developing Tools for Cooperative Relationships

One of the things that distinguishes us as humans from most other species here on earth is our use of tools. As far back as we can see, people have made devices to help them meet their daily needs. Our use of technologies began very simply with sharpened stones or sticks and has steadily evolved into the complex and powerful tools we have today.

We now live in an age of astonishing technology that allows us to do things that were unimaginable to people who lived just a generation ago. We can push a button on the computer and find almost any information in minutes. We can travel around the earth in a day, talk directly to someone on a different continent, and send images through wires instantly. Yet most of us do not know how to communicate honestly without blame, or hear another person's experience without judgment.

Our use of tools has focused almost exclusively on expanding our physical capacities. We think of technology as providing a means to get a task done using less effort or time. And while our amazing new mechanisms empower each of us to take care of our physical needs more effectively by ourselves, they have *not* helped us take care of our emotional needs or build stronger relationships with each other. In fact they tend to isolate us further, because we need each other less and less for our own survival.

Our successes with technology and widespread use of the earth's fossil fuels have enabled a level of independence from each other that is unprecedented in human history. In many developed countries each person can have a car, maintain a home, move where we want, and find food, clothing, and shelter by ourselves. This has truly been the Golden Age of individual freedom and mobility. Yet the price we are paying for this personal autonomy is irreversible damage to our natural environment, and a dramatic erosion of our ability to live and work together cooperatively.

It appears that this is all changing now, as we experience the results of valuing individuality above relationship and community. It is dawning on us through revelations like global climate change and the pollution of our air and water, that we live on a small planet with limited resources, and the actions of each person affect every other person. We are recognizing that human activity can cause destruction to our environment on a scale that threatens all of us. And the creation and inevitable spread of nuclear weapons means that the consequences of unchecked global conflict would be devastating for our entire world.

Evidence of our lack of skills in personal and international relationships is all around us, and it is becoming increasingly apparent that competing with each other is undermining our own chances of survival. From divorce and the breakup of families to war between nations, our world is being torn apart by our own incapacity to resolve our differences peacefully. We may still find competition compelling and seek the familiar sense of purpose that comes from struggling against an enemy. Yet if we allow our habit of opposition to go unchecked, we will surely destroy everything we are living for.

As we face any number of looming global catastrophes, our continued existence on earth will likely hinge on our ability to get along with each other. In the era ahead, cooperation will be the most important skill, and building community will become essential to support life. It is time now for us to recognize that our impulse to compete with each other is a fatal attraction, and then to channel our amazing capacity for technology into creating a means to live in peace.

We have to expand our definition of tools to include ways of staying connected with each other through conflict, and making decisions that include everyone's needs. It is no longer sustainable to manage relationships by force or withdrawal. It is necessary now to develop ways of dealing with our differences that recognize our inherent connection with each other, while at the same time honoring our individuality.

Making Peace

We have long tried to find a solution to the problem of war. After enough exposure to human violence, even the most calloused among us end up disillusioned with the idea of a righteous conflict where good triumphs over evil. It is apparent to anyone who has seen the real impact of war that it is a bad idea. Everyone is hurt by so much violence, and in the end there are no winners. Yet if we look around us, we have to admit that we still don't know how to live together here on earth in peace.

Many of us talk of peace when we are in opposition to a war, and we tend to think of it as a value. We say that *we* are in favor of peace, and *they* are in favor of war. Yet this is not a helpful or accurate use of the idea of peace. Few people would say they like war, and no one speaks of valuing violent conflict. People who support war usually see it as the *only way* to establish peace. In that sense, they value peace just as much as we do.

The only way we know to have a world without conflict is to have a dominant power that maintains control by threatening harm to any opposition. Our strategy for achieving peace has been to threaten those who appear to oppose us with so much force that they submit to our authority. Despite our democratic ideals, we still tend to revert to authoritarian leadership in times of conflict when we need a sense of security. We have not yet learned to allow each other to be sovereign individuals and get along together as equals. We don't know how to make room for our differences in a way that increases our integrity and stability as a community. So we have war after war, each with the aim of achieving a lasting peace.

When we make peace a value, it remains a perfect ideal with no real means to achieve it. An ideal does not get us very far in reality because it tends to remain a fixed point of perfection that we never attain. Instead of learning how to make peace, we merely believe in peace and talk about how right and good it is. It becomes solidified as an abstract concept that we can identify with, but has no real impact on us.

People have tried to approach peace this way forever, and it does not work. Peace cannot be legislated or achieved through making war a crime. It cannot be attained by constricting our human impulse for personal expression, or by frightening people into surrendering their opposition. Peace is not a concept or an ideal, but rather the outcome of an intelligent process that addresses conflict directly and deals with its root cause.

> Real peace is something we *do*,
> not something we believe in.

The Value of Conflict

To understand what real peace is, we have to recognize the motivation for conflict. Focusing on our differences is the way we distinguish ourselves from each other and establish our individuality. And, conflict is a natural consequence of this process of differentiation.

There is going to be some friction involved until we all have the space within ourselves to allow other people to be different, and still remain connected.

We have to go through conflict for each of us to be our own person and make room for other people to be their own persons. Instead of treating conflict as a problem, we can learn how to use it as a means to expand our self-definition, so that each of us can have our own values and needs, while at the same time recognizing that we are connected. Conscious Communication skills enable us to recognize our differences without being threatened by them. These tools give us a way to maintain our individuality, while also belonging to a larger family or community.

Being independent has become so important to us in recent times because this is a fundamental urge we all share. Democracy is a system that recognizes and supports this basic human desire for personal freedom, and that is why it is so popular. However we are seeing the consequences of focusing exclusively on our independence in the myriad problems we face today in our world. Now is the time to recognize that...

> however independent we may become,
> our fate is intrinsically tied
> to that of every other person on earth.

Democracy is not just about individual freedom. It is about each of us taking responsibility for our own lives, and finding a way to live together that includes each other as sovereign individuals. This is very different from each person doing exactly as they please. With all of us living on the same planet sharing the same limited resources, we have to find a way to work this out together so that each one of us is able to acquire our basic needs without hurting or limiting anyone else. We have to recognize that personal freedom only happens within a larger context that includes everyone else's freedom.

The Source of Love

Expanding our sense of self to include other people, while maintaining our individuality, is how we cultivate real love. Love is something we search for endlessly here, yet few of us know how to find, because we carry feelings of hurt and resentment that keep us from feeling it. We want to care about other people, yet we also feel a need to shut ourselves off so we won't be hurt anymore. Often we seek for love with a hidden desperation, while deep down we no longer believe in it at all.

It is easy to think about love as a virtue and hold it at a distance as something to strive for. Yet it is our daily interactions with family and friends that *teach* us how to love, especially when strong emotions arise. So we need a way to respond to these everyday situations that brings us closer to our ideals.

> Instead of pretending to love,
> we can learn to find the love that is genuinely there,
> buried beneath our fear.

Love is more than an ideal. It is perhaps the most essential ingredient to life, and closing ourselves down to love fragments and weakens us internally. Beyond believing that it is good or right, we have to actively participate in the process of recognizing where love comes from and allow it to grow inside us. This will challenge us to grow beyond our limitations, and become something larger and more complete than we are now.

Conscious Communication skills are intended to help us reconnect to the source of love within ourselves. These tools are simple, but not easy to practice, because we have made such a habit of self-defense. We think our survival depends on being tough and cut off from our own feelings. However, denying our emotions only isolates us from each other and makes it impossible to realize the love we want in our lives, because it gets buried so deeply underneath layers of hurt feelings.

We *can* learn to respond to our own hurt and the pain of other people in a way that opens us to love instead of shutting it out. Setting aside our story in order to hear and validate another person's experience helps us to move beyond the draining habit of constantly worrying about our own welfare. And, learning to recognize and make room for our own feelings allows a natural compassion to develop for ourselves that is quite different from self-pity. Once we regain this connection with our own immediate experience and that of the people around us, we have the means to know what is real by sensing the flow of love within our hearts. This sensitivity can then become a true rudder, steadying our course and showing us how to be helpful to other people, while also taking care of ourselves.

Peace and Love

Almost a half century ago, a revolution occurred within an entire generation of young adults. It quickly spread across Western-influenced countries and is still spreading today throughout the world. The theme of this movement for social change was peace and love. It was a passionate and beautiful expression of our highest human ideals. And it planted seeds that are only now beginning to bear fruit.

In the decades that followed this popular uprising, it appeared as though the revolution died and the ideals it stood for were buried beneath business as usual. It seemed that all our idealism was powerless to change the way things were. Peace gave way to other wars, and love was overshadowed by greed, hatred, and fear. Many people gave up on these ideals, thinking that real change could never happen.

If we imagine something, however, we can realize it, and an ideal is simply the place to start. Beliefs are powerful because they show us what is possible, and our dreams tell us what we most want in life. Peace and love are not only possible; they are basic *requirements* for our health and happiness. Yet they are not something we can achieve or accumulate. They are like the air we breathe and water we drink, and we constantly need a fresh supply.

The task in front of us now is to learn how to generate peace and love in our daily interactions with the people around us. If we want these in our world, this is where they need to take root. A book like this one can demonstrate some skills and suggest a different way to think of ourselves in relation to other people. Yet, we are only at the beginning of learning how to make these work, and it will require all of us to evolve this technology of peace and love into a new template for humanity.

We seem to require opposition now as a way to distinguish ourselves from each other. By focusing on our individual preferences, we define who we are as unique individuals. Separating ourselves in this way may be a necessary step in the process of realizing that we are all connected. So there is a great benefit to us in learning how to go all the way through conflict to a final resolution. Resolving conflict constructively allows us to experience ourselves as part of a greater humanity connected to all of life, instead of isolated from each other in our own separate worlds.

Peace happens when we finally realize that we are each a unique expression of the same source. Before we can have real peace, however, we have to acknowledge the ways in which we are different. And, it is conflict that makes us aware of our differences. When we experience for ourselves that we are individual stems of the same plant *and* share a common root, the need for conflict simply fades away.

> When we recognize that our similarities
> outweigh our differences,
> conflict will disappear
> because we will have no use for it.
>
> This is true peace.

Chapter 23

A Language of Connection

Conscious Communication skills present a new kind of technology that enables us to strengthen our relationships with each other, while maintaining our independence. Any new technology stretches us to learn new abilities and adapt to new structures. Imagine driving one of the first cars along rough dirt roads made primarily for horse or foot travel. Think about making a call on the first telephone, flying the first airplane, recording the first television program, or using the first personal computer.

All of these experiences must have felt strange and seemed out of place with their surroundings. These new inventions were likely dismissed as irrelevant or too strange to be of any real importance. And, the first pioneers who developed them were probably seen as misfits and treated with suspicion because they were stepping out of the boundaries that defined what was normal in their time.

Yet, look at how each of these major new technologies has dramatically reshaped our world. Today we take it for granted that we can fly anywhere on earth in a day, see moving pictures sent by air waves on a television screen, or find information in minutes on our computer. We tend to forget that these things are possible because some courageous visionaries took a chance and tried something that seemed impossible and unrealistic at the time.

Expanding Our Use of Tools

Skills that enable us to feel empathy for other people, while also taking care of ourselves, are not only a new technology - they expand the whole concept of tools into an entirely new realm. Instead of giving us more capacity to organize and control our material world, this technology increases our ability to relate to each other. Conscious Communication skills allow us to spend more time cooperating than competing, and offer a means to build relationships that are nourishing and supportive, rather than stressful and depleting.

Some of us will naturally resist taking such a structured approach to something as personal and private as our feelings and needs. It is understandable that this notion might feel uncomfortable and awkward. It requires self- awareness and sensitivity, and deals with an inner world in which many of us have little experience.

It also may not be possible to express what is most alive in our heart with mere words. Feelings and needs are not as tangible as judgments or opinions, and often there is no language that is adequate for expressing our deeper truth. This new way of approaching relationships does not pretend to join us with other people or assume that we really know what they are going through. Rather, it recognizes that every one of us is having a unique experience, and the best way to connect may be simply to witness each other without judgment.

As you consider using these techniques, remember that this is a whole new way of relating to other people and will not make much sense when compared with our familiar ways. Of course it is going to sound strange to say, *"You seem upset that I forgot your piano lesson"*, just as it will sound strange to hear such language. You may think of a "worst case scenario", such as hitting someone with your car, and realize how absurd it would sound to say: *"So you are angry that I ran into you with my car?"*.

Keep in mind that these skills are not suited for all people in all situations. The formulas are primarily for shifting your focus away from concepts and ideas, and toward feelings and needs. Many of us need clear and concise phrases, such as, *"You sound... when... because..."*, in order to interrupt our habit of responding with our head instead of our heart. Naturally they will sound mechanical and fake while we are getting used to them and learning how they work.

No technology works perfectly at first, and it usually takes trial and error to improve a new system. Conscious Communication is an evolving set of skills that will develop and become more effective the more we use them. This is not for people who simply want to play it safe, fit in, or appear normal. Trying this new language involves taking a risk and experimenting with tools designed to help us live together in peace and address our deep needs for acceptance, belonging, and independence.

This approach does not pretend to be a perfect vehicle for understanding each other. It simply points us in a new direction and brings us closer to being able to share our direct experience with another person. Just as with other technologies, once a significant number of us get comfortable using these skills, it will change the way all of our communication works. Someday it will seem quite natural to talk about our deeper feelings and needs and work out our differences cooperatively, rather than competing with each other to see who is right.

Engaging on a Different Level

I remember once meeting an acquaintance in the grocery store. I had some extra time, and he seemed to want to talk, so I listened to him for a while. He was a teacher like myself and wanted to talk about some of the frustrating experiences he was having trying to set up workshops in our area. I listened supportively, nodding my head and occasionally reflecting back to him some of what he said, without adding any of my own ideas to the conversation.

He was expressing strong opinions about aspects of the community we lived in, and I could sense that he wanted me to agree with him and take his side in some of the controversial issues he was talking about. I felt a bit uncomfortable with this, and made an extra effort to simply acknowledge his experience with neutrality. When he finished discussing the issues that were upsetting him, he made a statement indicating that he thought I agreed with his point of view.

I responded by telling him simply that I had a different experience of the situation he was describing, and my opinions about it were not the same as his. He was surprised to hear this and said he was shocked to find out that I was not in agreement with him. I did not want to get into a competitive exchange of ideas, so I acknowledged his response without adding anything else and the conversation ended there.

In this conversation he had assumed that I was in agreement with his judgments because I did not disagree or assert my own point of view. We are so used to conversations where the focus is to align our perceptions that many of us do not know any other way to communicate. Our usual way of connecting with each other is through comparing ideas like this and trying to find agreement on what is good and what is bad. And, if other people don't offer an opposing view point, we tend to assume that they agree with us.

My approach of listening to his feelings and thoughts without adding my comments was new to him, and I could tell it made him a bit uncomfortable. Yet, I was not interested in comparing ideas or trying to find areas of agreement. I was interested in learning about him and his experience, and I didn't need to talk about my own experiences in order to feel a connection with his.

Getting Beyond Opinions

The kinds of conversations we are most familiar with focus on comparing opinions, as the man in the previous story was trying to do. Our language consists largely of evaluations and judgments, with an emphasis on figuring out what is right, as if there was one truth that was the same for all of us. The ultimate goal of this way of thinking is to create a uniformity of beliefs and ideals that we can all agree on.

Our usual interactions with other people involve sorting experiences and people into categories of good and bad. We tend to be afraid of those who act or think differently from ourselves. So, we either try to get other people to be like us, or we try to be like them. While this approach of comparing and aligning judgments may seem necessary to establish a sense of order and cohesion in our world, the unfortunate result is that there is little room for individuality. It tends to create a deadening rigidity where each of us is blindly trying to be like everyone else.

This is because

> each one of us is a unique person
> with our own set of ideas,
> and our opinions never fully match those of
> another person.

By placing so much weight on what we think, we actually end up separating ourselves from each other, and unknowingly increase our sense of isolation. This common way of communicating inevitably causes conflict in our relationships because there are always areas of disagreement that cannot be resolved.

If we want to have the freedom to be ourselves in our relationships with other people, we need a decisive way to break out of our habit of comparing ideas. Communicating consciously disrupts the impulse to compare and align our judgments, and stops us from reducing immediate feelings and needs to rational conclusions. The structured responses suggested in this book are specifically designed to interrupt our familiar habits and bring them to our attention so that we can see their effect.

These skills simply get us onto a new track and direct our awareness away from thoughts *about* our experience to the *immediate experience itself*. Otherwise, we spend our lives viewing the world through the same preconceived ideas without ever realizing that we are trapped inside a conceptual world that has little to do with what is really happening in this moment.

> In the absence of a language that enables us
> to constructively express our true feelings and needs,
> we automatically fall back upon
> familiar ways of thinking
> that confine us to our judgments and conclusions.

If we let go of our story of what is right and what is wrong, we become free of the limitations of these narrow reference points. This creates the space for each of us to have a different experience, and shows us that our relationships do not depend on sharing the same opinions. In this way, the techniques presented in this book enable us to communicate more directly and honestly. Instead of referring to evaluations and judgments, we learn to reference to what we are feeling and needing right now. This helps us to connect more easily with other people, because we don't usually compete over feelings and basic needs the way we do over ideas and solutions.

Changing Old Habits

The process of changing familiar communication patterns is similar to giving up any habit or addictive behavior. It takes a certain amount of discipline and determination to break through the resistance to change. Even when we know it is for our own good, most of us don't want to let go of things that feel familiar.

Breaking the momentum of the habit is the hardest part. When something new interferes with your comfortable routines, the first reaction is usually to resist it and get back to familiar territory. Yet, if you allow yourself to be stretched beyond your comfort zone, you may find that your whole attitude changes because you see things with fresh eyes.

Practicing these skills is an effective way to free you from your ideas of what is right and wrong, without simply replacing these with new ideas. Instead of encouraging the formation of a new set of values, the tools of Conscious Communication are designed to interrupt the basic mental process you use to *create* your beliefs, and direct your attention instead to what is actually going on in the present moment.

As we have discussed before, while our ideas of what is good and bad may add a sense of certainty to our lives, they confine us to a very limited range of experience and inevitably generate conflict within our relationships. We end up making these absolute judgments without having enough experience or knowledge to know what we are talking about. And, our conclusions often block us from seeing what is really happening.

On the other hand, tuning in to your feelings and needs keeps you present with yourself and able to track what is going on around you. Instead of relying on your rational mind to pass judgments and draw conclusions, you can learn to measure your experience by your emotions. If you are emotionally charged, it is clear that one of your basic needs is not being met. You can then focus on what that need is, and find a way to meet it.

Focusing on rational judgments and conclusions, as most of us do now, keeps a distance between us. Whereas, paying attention to your feelings and needs enables you to relate to others in a more genuine and satisfying way. If you keep this process simple, and do not feed your emotions with stories, your feelings can give you an accurate way to navigate your life. You can learn to trust your emotions, knowing that they are your responsibility and are merely pointing to basic needs that require your attention.

Remodeling Our Relationships

The real difficulty of using this new language of connection is not that it is too mechanical or rehearsed, but that it challenges our familiar point of view. These skills are designed to stretch our normal perceptions, and to apply them we have to suspend our most fundamental habit of trying to sort out right from wrong. Like any process that results in true growth and change, this can feel uncomfortable.

Learning a new language in order to communicate more effectively is like remodeling our home. It disrupts our familiar routines and makes ordinary tasks more difficult. We resist the process before it begins and cannot wait until it is over. Yet, the result of remodeling is usually a wonderful new space that looks and feels better, and functions more effectively.

Questioning our daily interactions with other people is likely to be challenging in a similar way. We may resist looking too deeply at our own habits of thought and ways of expressing ourselves, just as we resist tearing up an old carpet or prying loose rotten floor boards in an old house. We don't know what is underneath and are afraid we will find a mess that will take more time and effort to clean up.

Indeed, we often *do* find more than we bargained for when we begin to repair an old building. A rotten floor board can reveal a collapsed foundation and lead to expensive or time-consuming repairs. It may seem like a better idea not to look too closely and leave things the way they are. But if we ignore rotting wood or a moldy carpet, soon we will have much larger problems to deal with. When you maintain a house you learn over time that it is easier to deal with leaks and holes as soon as you notice them, before they grow bigger.

Most of us can understand the wisdom of looking in the basement to check whether the structure of the house is sound. And, we readily accept that some tools and skill are necessary for maintaining a building. Yet, we have trouble with the idea of looking at our deeper feelings or needs and developing skills to help us maintain a relationship. Instead, we too often prefer to leave a conflict alone, hoping it will go away by itself. Or, we convince ourselves it is the other person's problem and make them responsible for fixing it.

Usually the last thing we want to do is look at ourselves and uncover our own feelings and needs. We are afraid our feelings will overwhelm us, or our needs will be too great to manage. So, we don't even want to look, thinking it is better not to know what is going on inside us on a deeper level.

If we are not willing to look at our own patterns, however, our relationships deteriorate into decaying old houses with rotten boards that we tiptoe around so as not to crash through the floor. Instead of offering us intimacy and connection, they can start to seem dangerous and threatening. Stuck, with no effective way to address this difficult situation, most of us either abandon the relationship or distance ourselves from each other so as not to stir up strong emotions.

Experimenting with New Skills

Establishing cooperative relationships where your feelings and needs are recognized may seem like a good idea at this point. Yet, putting these theories into practice is a different story. Many of us find the skills of Conscious Communication difficult to use because they require such a radical shift in our basic orientation. This new language often sounds too strange, and even if we believe in it, we can't see ourselves using it.

If we learn the theory, but do not practice it, Conscious Communication is just another good idea. And, if we practice the language without changing our perspective, it is just another formula we try to fit ourselves into in order to be correct. Actually opening our minds and expanding the way we *think* about ourselves and other people takes real effort. It is easy to become discouraged and give up, thinking these tools do not really work.

In the past nineteen years I have taught over a thousand people in college classes and private workshops how to use these skills effectively. In each class someone usually complains that the skills sound too phony and could never work in real life. I ask them to set aside their doubts and simply try using Supportive Listening or Assertion in a live conversation when emotions are running high. In almost every case, when people who were certain this approach would not work actually tried it out in an appropriate situation, they came back astonished at what happened. Usually the other person responded by opening up and talking about what was really going on for them, and the relationship ended up feeling closer and more connected.

The most important part of changing your communication habits is to just try out these skills with an open mind and see what happens. This requires a leap of faith, as you cannot know the result of your experiment ahead of time. Try the formats suggested here as closely as you can, while making room for the way you think about your relationships to change. It does not matter if you believe in them or not. You only have to be willing to be clear about your intentions and notice what is happening.

Finding Support

Many of us will need help to be able to effectively use these skills, and it is a good idea to find a teacher who can offer support and guidance. Someone who understands these skills, and knows *why* they work, can show you how to apply them. Each situation we face requires a slightly different approach, and a skilled instructor can demonstrate how to adapt the awkward sounding phrases presented in this book to specific people and conversations in your life. A teacher with experience can help you discover the spirit of honesty and compassion that is behind this new phrasing and find a more natural language to express what is true for you.

The best way to develop this new language is often in a workshop or class with a facilitator and other participants. The teacher can describe a skill like Supportive Listening or Assertion, demonstrate it, and guide you through hands-on role plays where you practice the skill yourself with direct coaching. We usually have to use these new phrases several times in a safe and contained environment before they start to feel normal.

A series of such workshops gives you a chance to learn some new skills, try them out in your life, and report back on what happened. Practicing in real situations, reviewing the results, and getting feedback from a teacher will help you develop fluency in the new language of Conscious Communication. An ongoing class or training session can provide the motivation and support to use these skills on a regular basis. As the skills become familiar, they will sound more natural and you will get a feeling for how they work. And, with practice they will come alive for you, becoming less stiff and formal as you develop your own style.

Afterward

A Personal Journey

As a young man facing adulthood, I found myself struggling to find a way to be genuine in the world. I was uncomfortable with a witty and cynical approach to life, yet being polite and understated did not suit me either. I wanted to be honest *and* compassionate, and I found few examples of how to manifest this kind of personal integrity in life.

My experiences relating to other people left me discouraged about how to be a part of society, and still be myself. I was not willing to settle for a life of lonely desperation, distancing myself from other people for fear of being hurt. Neither was I satisfied with superficial social relationships that offered a momentary sense of belonging but did not meet my need for real connection.

The Quest

I desperately needed to find a meaningful way to connect with the world around me, and as this need became increasingly urgent I decided to set off on my own search. My journey eventually led me to undertake a silent meditation retreat for a month in a Buddhist monastery in a remote corner of Asia. And, there I found an answer to my dilemma in an ancient spiritual practice.

This practice did not involve believing in new ideas, but presented instead a means to find truth directly for myself, through my own awareness. By paying close attention to the workings of my own mind, I was able to witness the abstract nature of my thoughts. I saw how absolute my judgments and opinions appeared to be and realized they were actually quite arbitrary, shifting like sand in the desert. I began to understand that the truth I was seeking was not an intellectual conclusion, but an immediate experience. It dawned on me then that I had been trusting my rational mind to guide me in life, instead of my heart.

I discovered that when opinions were set aside, what remained was awareness of a present experience. I became aware of body sensations, feelings, and thoughts, and I experienced them with a simple clarity that finally made sense. I realized that this simple knowing of the present moment led to a natural and effortless response of acceptance and compassion to the world around me.

This realization changed everything. I no longer looked so desperately for validation for my ideas or concerned myself with what other people thought. I knew that the truth lay in my own heart and that the way I felt inside was the most important indicator of what was real. My frustrated quest for honesty in the world was finally satisfied as I gradually learned to let go of my treasured judgments and reveal the raw emotions and needs that lay beneath them.

A Utopian Community

After my experience in the monastery, I wanted to be part of a peaceful, cooperative community in which I could live close to the earth with people who cared for each other and all of life. And so I went to live on a remote piece of land in the northwest of the United States in an experimental community. We shared ideals such as equality, nonviolence, cooperation, and respect for nature, and we assumed that these common beliefs would bond us in a new kind of cooperative society.

Most of us shared a mistrust of authority and wanted to live without rules or government, free to follow our own impulses. What had drawn me to the group were these ideals of open membership and no leaders. All of us had seen how power could be concentrated by governments and corporations to weaken and control people. We believed this was not good for any of us, and we were determined to find a new way.

It did not take long, however, before tension and conflict built up among us and began to undermine what we had set out to do. People who had been friends no longer spoke to each other, and families began to move to home sites in remote areas of the land to avoid dealing with other people. It became clear that we had no way to resolve conflicts or make decisions together. People could express their concerns and frustrations, but there was no forum for constructive dialogue and individuals were left to work out difficult situations on their own. Often, the result was that small issues became larger and people grew increasingly hostile and distant from one another.

The only ways we knew to make decisions or handle conflict were the old ways we had learned from our society. Simply rejecting these had not changed anything, and we automatically turned to aggression or withdrawal when relationships became challenging. Our capacity for denial was so powerful that we blindly resorted to these old dysfunctional habits, even as we believed we were doing something new.

In the absence of any decision-making process, a few men made decisions about money and land use behind the scenes. Without a way to resolve every day tensions, people armored themselves emotionally, and the community divided into opposing factions. Our ideals of harmony and cooperation were not enough to actualize the dream we shared. We had unconsciously brought with us all of our society's evils – the very ones from which we were trying to escape. And we had no way of dealing with these patterns beyond pretending they did not exist in our community.

When Ideals Fail

Thus began the great disillusionment. What started as a bold attempt to live in a radically different way from our parents' generation was turning into a nightmare of chaos and confusion. Some of us gave up on the dream and left. Others became resigned to a new kind of suburbia, living our lives in protected isolation from each other. I felt disheartened and desperate to find some way to resurrect our vision of a harmonious new society.

I realized that, while all of us who lived in that community believed in cooperation and equality, we had no *way* to achieve this. We had launched this great vessel to carry us across the sea, yet we had no motor, sail, or oars to propel us, and no keel or rudder to keep us on course. We had thrown all these structures overboard because they had been used in our past in such harmful ways. We assumed we could make this journey on the strength of our beliefs alone, yet it became clear that we needed more than good intentions or fresh ideas. What we needed were skills.

This realization began my lifelong quest for practical tools for living and working with other people. Remembering someone from college who lived in a community that practiced cooperative decision making, I wrote to him and began to gather books that offered methods for meeting facilitation, consensus decision making, interpersonal communication skills, and conflict resolution. I devoured these resources and found inspiration and practical skills in them that I could put to use immediately.

I spent the next few years trying these skills out within our community, and eventually some of us were able to organize a decision-making body that worked by consensus. We worked out an agreement on a land payment system that equalized our financial responsibilities, provided a structure for shared leadership, and gave the community a more stable foundation. After some time I moved on. Yet, this experience took root as an abiding passion in my life for fostering community while maintaining individuality.

Training and Experience

I first began to learn about communication skills at The Evergreen State College in Olympia, Washington, where students helped shape the content and structure of courses through a collective meeting process. During these years, I also became involved with training people in nonviolence and consensus decision making to prepare for civil disobedience protests aimed at bringing public awareness to the dangers of nuclear power and nuclear weapons.

After college I undertook intensive self-study to learn meeting facilitation, conflict resolution, and shared decision making for use in the experimental community mentioned earlier. I went on to live in other communities and attend workshops in communication skills, and was later certified as a professional mediator after a year-long training program at Woodbury College in Montpelier, Vermont. I spent the next ten years practicing divorce and family mediation in collaboration with the Vermont Family Court. During this time I also began working intensively with couples and teaching interpersonal communication skills at the Community College of Vermont, and a variety of other institutions and organizations.

The first books I read that described tools for facilitating meetings, making decisions by consensus, and resolving conflicts cooperatively, came from the Movement for a New Society, a Quaker group based in Philadelphia. I then read *Parent Effectiveness Training,* by Dr. Thomas Gordon, which detailed a system of interpersonal communication skills for family relationships. When I began teaching communication, I used *People Skills*, by Robert Bolton PhD. as my primary text. And more recently, I discovered *NonViolent Communication* by Marshall B. Rosenberg, Ph.D., and attended trainings presented by him.

These latter three authors refer to Carl Rogers, a well known American psychologist who originated a nondirective or client-centered approach to psychotherapy, as a pioneer in developing interpersonal communication skills. I am deeply indebted to the work of these teachers for helping to inspire and inform the theories and practices presented in *Conscious Communication*. Their books and others that have influenced my work are noted in the bibliography.

Inspiration

The inspiration and ideas for this book come as much from my life-long spiritual search as they do from my training and teaching in the field of conflict resolution and interpersonal communication. After some years of practicing meditation I realized that being calm and nonjudgmental is not easy in daily life situations. I could quiet my mind and achieve some level of internal peace through a solitary spiritual practice, yet as soon as I engaged with other people I found myself in turmoil again.

In learning how to communicate more consciously, I began to recognize that the shift in perspective these skills facilitated was the same kind of transformation that happened through meditation. In both practices, I was letting go of familiar beliefs and patterns of thought and allowing a profoundly new perspective to reveal itself. Both ways involved releasing judgments and opinions and focusing on a present-moment experience, instead of a mental thought or conclusion *about* that experience.

These realizations ignited a desire in me to find and teach the essence of this new approach. I knew that changing the way I communicated with other people resulted in a fundamental change *within myself.* There was a power in this new language that broke loose old patterns of thought and freed me to realize the kind of honesty and intimacy I longed for with other people. And I wanted to illustrate this internal shift in order to reveal the hidden mechanism that transforms relationship struggles into opportunities for deeper understanding and connection.

Relationships as a Spiritual Practice

Conscious Communication has become a way for me to discover truths that open my mind and heart just as much as deep inner experiences with meditation. The beauty of this practice is that it uses our ordinary interactions with other people as the primary focus, and can help each of us with something we do every day. In the process of using these skills to work on our relationships, we also grow and expand ourselves so that our lives have a sense of genuine direction and progress.

Conscious communication skills offer me a way to practice the ideals of generosity, compassion, honesty, presence, and selflessness on a daily basis. I teach them because sharing these practices with other people keeps them alive for me, and I gain a continually deeper understanding of how they work. The aim of being truthful *and* compassionate gives my life a meaning and purpose that sustains me day after day.

Instead of seeing other people as strangers who are entirely different from me, I realize that we all share similar struggles, and most of us want the same things out of life. I see that other people, in all their vexing complexity, are more like me than I could have imagined. And gradually, my fear of isolation dissolves in the recognition that we are all different, yet all connected, at the same time.

Appendix

Definitions of Key Terms

Below is a summary of the most significant terms used in Conscious Communication. These are not dictionary definitions, but rather a further explanation of how these words are being used in this book to convey key concepts. These words are each defined in contrast to another word or words opposite them, in order to clarify their relevance.

Self-care
Our capacity to care about ourselves
and take responsibility for our own basic needs

vs

Self-absorption
Our habit of continuously referring to ourselves based on our anxiety about meeting our needs

Needs
Basic requirements for our physical or emotional well-being

vs

Values
What we believe is right and wrong

Solutions
Strategies or ways of going about meeting our needs

Feelings
Direct raw emotional experience

vs

Judgments
Our thoughts about our emotional experience

Perception
Our interpretations or thoughts about our experience

vs

Experience
Our basic emotions without thought or interpretation

Codependency
Basing our self worth on the judgments of other people

vs

Connection
A sense of belonging with other people based on a mutual understanding and acceptance of each others feelings, needs, and values

Disconnects

Referring to Yourself:	Focusing on your own story rather than on the other person's experience.
Digging for Facts:	Asking questions that do not relate directly to the other person's experience.
Being Logical:	Thinking you can solve the other person's dilemma by using logic.
Analyzing:	Trying to solve the other person's problem by sharing your perspective on it.
Taking Sides or Blaming:	Trying to make other people feel better by taking their side or blaming someone else for their situation.
Using Shame or Guilt:	Trying to get other people to change by pointing out their mistakes.
Imposing Your Own Values:	Thinking the solution to another person's dilemma lies in simply pointing out right from wrong.
Disguising Judgments as Questions:	Trying to get other people to see their mistakes by asking leading questions.

Advising:	Thinking you have the solution to another person's dilemma, and that solving the problem is just a matter of them following your suggestion.
Reassuring:	Trying to solve another person's problem by making things look better than they are.
Praising:	Thinking you can help other people by judging them in a positive way.
Hinting:	Trying to get other people to do what you want without asking directly.
Demanding:	Trying to get other people to do what you want by ordering them to do it.
Threatening:	Trying to get other people to do what you want by making them fear your punishment if they do not comply with your demands.
Being Sarcastic:	Using witty or biting comments that indirectly criticize another person in an attempt to get your needs met, or change that person.

Miles Sherts   *Conscious Communication*   www.LanguageOfConnection.com   www.SkyMeadow.org

Model of Emotional Responsibility

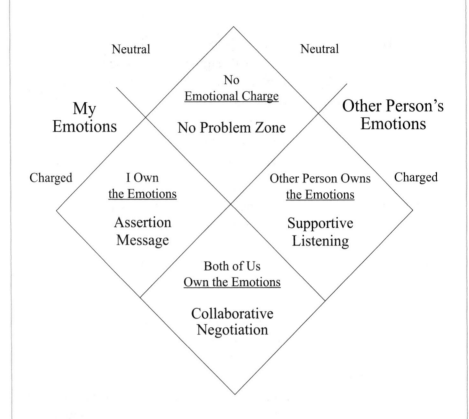

Once you can determine who has the emotional charge, this chart will help you determine which skills would be most effective. When the other person has an emotional charge, an effective response is Supportive Listening. When you are the one emotionally charged, Assertion may be useful. And when both of you are emotionally charged, a combination of Assertion, Supportive Listening, and Collaborative Negotiation may work to maintain the relationship, while you simultaneously take care of yourself.

Miles Sherts   *Conscious Communication*   www.LanguageOfConnection.com   www.SkyMeadow.org

Emotions

Angry   Sad   Hurt   Afraid Upset Confused Annoyed Frustrated

Mad   Overwhelmed   Anxious   Concerned   Worried   Tense   Stressed

Alarmed   Shocked   Ashamed   Guilty   Embarrassed   Humiliated

Exhausted   Excited   Happy   Satisfied   Proud Content   Elated

Depressed   Discouraged   Depleted   Hopeful   Inspired   Lost

Jealous   Threatened   Resentful   Relaxed   Relieved   Vulnerable

Basic Needs:

Food   Water Air Clothing Shelter Warmth Sleep Recreation Exercise

Appreciation   Connection with other people   Recognition   Support   Love

Money   Transportation   Work   To feel useful   To help other people

Safety Security   Stability   Respect   Solitude   Peace   Health Comfort

Connection with higher self - source - God   Self-esteem Sense of belonging

Independence   To feel powerful To contribute to another person's well-being

Intimacy   Personal space   Inspiration   Rest   Purpose   Meaning Joy   Energy

Miles Sherts   *Conscious Communication*   www.LanguageOfConnection.com   www.SkyMeadow.org

Supportive Listening

Creating a safe place for other people to discover their own feelings
and needs, and begin solving their own problem

Opening Questions:

"You look upset, want to talk about it?"

"Looks like something's bothering you; I've got time if you want to talk."

"What was that like for you?" or *"How do you feel about that?"*

Attentive Silence: Eye contact, full attention, open posture.

Simple Encouragements: *"Oh." "Uh-huh." "I see." "Then?" "Wow!"*

Three-part Supportive Listening (connecting feelings, facts, and impacts):

It sounds like you feel... (<u>feelings</u>) *"It sounds like you feel upset*

when... (<u>facts</u>) *when he makes decisions without talking with you first*

because you... (<u>impacts</u>) *because you don't feel included"*

Open Problem-Solving Questions:

1. **What do you want?** (possibly followed by)
  a. **What would you get if you get** (<u>your solution</u>)?
  b. **What would that look like?**
2. **What have you tried?** (possibly followed by) **How did that work?**
3. **What could you try?**
4. **How do you think that would work?**
5. **What else could you try?**
6. **How can I help you?** or **What kind of support do you need?**
7. **Do you want some ideas?**

Reflecting Proposed Solutions:

"So, you are going to try (<u>specific solution the other person described</u>)"

Assertion

Expressing your feelings and needs honestly without blame or attack

<u>Informal Assertion</u>:

"Would you wash the dishes tonight?"

"I'm afraid I will be late for work, can you help me?"

"I don't feel comfortable with that."

"I feel scared when you talk to me in a loud voice."

<u>Three-part Assertion Message</u> (connecting feelings, facts, and impacts):

I feel…	(<u>feelings</u>)	*"I feel hurt and lonely*
when you…	(<u>facts</u>)	*when you go away on your day off,*
because I…	(<u>impacts</u>)	*because I miss spending time with you."*

<u>Delivering an Assertion Message</u>

"There is something I need to talk with you about. Is this a good time for you?"

You	Other Person
Assertion Message	
	Defensive Response
Supportive Listening	
	Defensive Response
Supportive Listening	
	Less Defensive
Assertion Message	
(repeat until…)	Hears the message and responds to your concerns

<u>Possible Conclusion Statements</u>

"Would you be willing to…(<u>direct request</u>)?"

"So, you are going to… (<u>what the other has offered</u>), and I am going to… (<u>what I have offered</u>)."

Miles Sherts   *Conscious Communication*   www.LanguageOfConnection.com   www.SkyMeadow.org

Collaborative Negotiation

The typical starting place for conflict:

My Way   Your Way

(*my solution to the problem*) ⟶ **VS.** ⟵ (*your solution to the problem*)

If the conflict remains defined in terms of opposing solutions, a power struggle is likely to follow where one side wins and the other side loses. To shift this, we can ask each other:

***"What will you get if you get your way?"* or
*" What do you want it for?"***

1. <u>Redefining the problem in terms of needs, not conflicting solutions:</u>

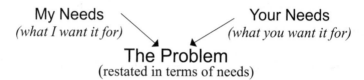

My Needs   Your Needs
(what I want it for)   *(what you want it for)*

The Problem
(restated in terms of needs)

"So we need to find a way for you to get (<u>your stated needs</u>) ***and for me to get*** (<u>my stated needs</u>)***"***

If the conflict is redefined in terms of basic needs, there is an opportunity to work together so that both people get what they want, and both sides win.

2. <u>Brainstorm possible solutions.</u>
   Generate as many ideas as possible without *any* evaluation or criticism.

3. <u>Propose a complete solution.</u>
   From the list generated, make a proposal that addresses both people's needs.

4. <u>Plan who will do what, where, and by when.</u>
   Be specific – include all relevant details.

5. <u>Do it.</u>

6. <u>Evaluate the solution at a later date.</u>
   How did it turn out?
   How is it working for each of us?
   Do we need to make adjustments or renegotiate anything?

Miles Sherts   *Conscious Communication*   www.LanguageOfConnection.com   www.SkyMeadow.org

Bibliography

A Course in Miracles. Foundation for Inner Peace, 1975

Bolton, Robert Ph.D. *People Skills.* Simon and Schuster, 1979 and 1986

Campbell, Joseph. *The Power of Myth.* New York Doubleday,1988

Gordon, Thomas Ph.D. *Parent Effectiveness Training.* Random House, Inc., 1970 and 2000   www.gordontraining.com

Johnson, Robert A. *We.* HarperCollins, 1983

Rosenberg, Marshall Ph.D. *NonViolent Communication.* Puddle Dancer Press. 2003 www.cnvc.org

Rogers, Carl R. *A Way of Being.* Houghton Mifflin Company, 1980

About the Author

Miles began learning communication skills in 1981 in order to facilitate meetings and help resolve conflicts in an experimental community. He trained as a professional mediator in 1988 and practiced family mediation for the next ten years, assisting communication and decision making between teenagers and parents, and divorcing couples with children. He has taught interpersonal communication and conflict resolution skills as an adjunct faculty at the Community College of Vermont and in schools, organizations, and private classes since 1990.

Miles founded Sky Meadow Retreat in 1999 as a holistic learning center, organic homestead, and conscious community. He lives in Vermont with his wife and three daughters, where he leads workshops and retreats in Conscious Communication, Insight Meditation, and other forms of personal transformation. He also works with couples, offering group and private retreats that focus on using these skills in a primary intimate relationship. And, he offers private trainings in Supportive Listening, Assertion, Collaborative Negotiation, Meeting Facilitation, and Shared Leadership.

Miles Sherts

For more information: www.SkyMeadowRetreat.com

To purchase this book at discount from the author:
www.LanguageofConnection.com